After Stories

AFTER STORIES
Transnational Intimacies of Postwar El Salvador

Irina Carlota Silber

Stanford University Press
Stanford, California

STANFORD UNIVERSITY PRESS
Stanford, California

© 2022 by the Board of Trustees of the Leland Stanford Junior University.
All rights reserved.

No part of this book may be reproduced or transmitted in any form or by any means, electronic or mechanical, including photocopying and recording, or in any information storage or retrieval system without the prior written permission of Stanford University Press.

Printed in the United States of America on acid-free, archival-quality paper

ISBN 9781503609099 (cloth)
ISBN 9781503632172 (paper)
ISBN 9781503632189 (electronic)
Library of Congress Control Number: 2021052422

Library of Congress Cataloging-in-Publication Data available upon request.

Cover photo: Reclaiming the fields, Chalatenango. Early 1990s. Ralph Sprenkels
Cover design: Rob Ehle
Typeset by Motto Publishing Services in 10.5/15 Adobe Garamond Pro

For Antonio, Cenzo, and Inés

CONTENTS

List of Figures ix
Preface xi

1 Before — 1

2 Numbers — 42

3 Bodies — 72

4 Objects — 102

5 After — 132

Acknowledgments 167
Notes 173
References 219
Index 249

FIGURES

Figure 1: Family, Chalatenango. Early 1990s. — 6

Figure 2: Author in El Rancho, Chalatenango, 1997. — 15

Figure 3: Repopulation, Chalatenango. Early 1990s. — 22

Figure 4: Reclaiming the fields, Chalatenango. Early 1990s. — 25

Figure 5: Children in the afternoon, El Rancho, Chalatenango, 1997. — 36

Figure 6: Children waiting in the Grupo Escolar, El Rancho, Chalatenango, 1997. — 37

Figure 7: Infants of postwar, Chalatenango. Early 1990s. — 40

Figure 8: Travel in Chalatenango, 1997. — 51

Figure 9: Tweeting official numbers. — 61

Figure 10: Community festival and postwar play, Chalatenango. Early 1990s. — 137

Figure 11: Commemoration of child martyrs, Chalatenango. Early 1990s. — 158

PREFACE

Breathe in and imagine the soft sway to the left and to the right. Breathe out. We are packed in tightly, backpacks on our laps and two gallons of potable water between our feet. Our thighs, probably sticking to the vinyl upholstery, are pressed up against a neighbor—perhaps it is a young mother, like really young, fifteen years old, holding her infant daughter as she creates a little breeze by waving an embroidered handkerchief that she keeps ready on her left shoulder. She has a few colones in her brassiere.[1] We learn this because that is where we now keep our forty colones for the week's visit. Or perhaps we are seated next to an elderly man wearing a worn straw hat. The machete for the milpa tied to his hip, he moves out of our way. We say "con permiso" (with permission, or excuse me) as we scooch in. He is accompanied by his teen grandson, who is sporting jeans and a striped polo shirt. They are coming from doing a *mandado* (an errand) in the capital of Chalatenango. It is hot and the air sweet-sweat smelling. It is such a good smell. We'll come to miss it. Crave it. It is a bit fetid, for sure, but we will conjure it to remind us of Chalatenango's earth, the land erupting with corn, fresh beans, and flowers—deep red, fuchsia, violet, orange—all blooming. Such a beauty and bounty of commingled smells: homes with their wood-burning *comal* (griddle) and tortillas "toasting," the hand-washed laundry drying on a line and wafting its perfume left by the big blocks of soap that we learned to handle. And that whiff of bus diesel. We are in what is called a microbus, a small passenger van that has been ingeniously refurbished on the inside to seat at least twice its original capacity. There are no seatbelts, and we are happy to have a spot and make the 10:00 a.m. ride. Otherwise, we would have to wait for the 1:00 p.m. pickup truck, where we would have to hold onto the side, hoping not to fall off on that bumpy curve where we know a curly-topped, adored toddler tragically flew from his mother's grip. Some of the windows open, some do not. We start off on a cracked, sand-colored cement road, up an incline, through communities that line the way. There are new development-funded cinder-block homes—not yet painted, just the original standard gray—interspersed with others made of bahareque (often bamboo and adobe).[2] It is not yet the turn of the twenty-first century, which will be marked by massive emigration to the United States and the resulting majestic homes in Chalatenango, with enormous wrought-iron gates and four-wheel-drive vehicles parked out front. We are young back then. My hair is plaited. We try not to romanticize and fall in love with a country and its people.

This book is about El Salvador, about the aftermaths of war, and about how generations of Salvadorans create meaningful lives. It is also, as a result, an indictment of US foreign and domestic policy, past and present. This is important to me, as an Argentine-born and US-raised anthropologist. I've been steeped in this work for a long time, and so this book also tracks relationships and intimacies "in the field" over time. The terrain of everyday life has shifted locally, globally, professionally, and personally for me and for many of the people we'll meet in this book. In part, I offer my thoughts in an effort to engage with these shifts—small and large—speak truth to power, and step up and step aside with solidarity and a politics of recognition.[3] Anthropology as a discipline continues to wrestle with white supremacy, its colonial history, and its relationship to "public scholarship"—how anthropologists develop, pursue, and present their research, with whom, to whom, and for what purpose. You'll see, Reader, that I'll be presenting an always partial, positioned, and reflective account with the aim to contribute in some way to the arc of justice. I write to you all directly, inviting you to join me as readers, thinkers, listeners, critics, and coconspirators, as world-makers in the beauty of our diversity. I do so in the same way that was modeled for me during my first trips to El Salvador in the early and mid-1990s.[4] Back then, women and men in the Salvadoran countryside—in the Department of Chalatenango, the former war zone where I spent most of my time conducting doctoral research (in the summers of 1993 and 1994, and in 1996–1997) in a repopulated community comprised of recently transitioning insurgents and their community supporters—would instruct their listeners, including me, to really "imagine it." "Imagínese," people would often say to initiate their storytelling, asking me to imagine being a laborer like them on a cotton or coffee plantation in the 1970s, escaping in the 1980s through the mountains, in the dark, with just the stars for light, body walking behind body during a military bombardment or to imagine being a guerrillera in the FPL (Popular Liberation Forces), one of the five branches of the insurgent Farabundo Martí National Liberation Front (FMLN).[5] Chalatecas and Chalatecos, which is what residents of Chalatenango call themselves, pushed me to understand, to feel, in the richness of their narratives' sensorium, their lived experience and their theories of knowledge about macro- and microlevel social, political, and economic forces that contextualized the stories they shared.[6] These are stories that they continue to share, decades later. When I write to you, Reader, it is to honor this invocation of "imagining it" and to extend a politics of recognition that goes both ways.[7]

This book fits into an ever-expanding body of work, most recently by a new generation of interdisciplinary Salvadoran scholars.[8] To date, there are books and studies about El Salvador's literary culture and political history, about the armed conflict (1980–1992) and insurgent politics, and about the postwar period and people's wartime memories. Scholars, activists, and policy makers have written on the impact of transitional justice, on the power of electoral politics and gendered social movements, and of course, on the Salvadoran diaspora, couriers, coyotes, gangs, and unaccompanied minors from the Northern Triangle—just to mention a few topics.[9] This book moves us across geographic locations, from the rural countryside of Chalatenango to the United States, to places like northern Virginia, New Jersey, and Los Angeles. It also moves us across time as I weave together stories from my early anthropological fieldwork that started in 1993 in El Salvador and that continues, with a different pacing, ebbing, and flowing even as I edit these words in 2022.

I hadn't intended on writing this book, but I've been pulled to "imagine it" for more than twenty-five years because of the relationships born from fieldwork. As anthropologist Lila Abu-Lughod reminds us, it is important "not to underestimate the devotion to others that fieldwork entails."[10] Reflecting on her own experiences in the foundational text *Veiled Sentiments*, she emphasizes the "give and take" required and the ways that "fieldwork is a (rare) form of respect and care for other people."[11] Abu-Lughod's insights help me to share and to frame what I have come to think about as the intersection of insurgency and displacement and about my own anthropological responsibility with stories that started out as ethnographic and can now illuminate contemporary historical processes. Because this book moves back and forth in time and across locations, I offer some thoughts on intergenerational, diasporic Salvadoran lives in the making perhaps of a particular US-Salvadoran story.

I've been thinking a lot about the lives of young Salvadorans I first met in the early 1990s who were raised through a Chalateco everyday-radical politics and who many years later migrated to the United States after more than a decade of peace and democracy. They span age groups, from infants born in the early 1980s through those first years of postpeace in the early 1990s. Some children were born amid battle and flight in areas that would later become repatriated communities. Others were born in the Mesa Grande refugee camp in Honduras and recalled their early years of repopulation marked by the death of their kin. And still others were born in those very early days of peace. They constitute what I term the *1.5 insurgent generation*—the now young adult children of the forgotten former rank-and-file Salvadoran revolutionaries—who are remaking transnational families in expected and unexpected ways. While I'm intentionally borrowing or playing with the sociological literature on the 1.5 immigrant generation—understood as youth who migrate from their land of origin to a new country at a young age, are raised in this new context, and straddle a series of cultural, linguistic, legal, political, and economic fields between their often first-generation parents and their second-generation siblings born in a new land—my project is not a conventional case study or sociological examination of generation.[12] Reader, this is a book about the Salvadoran diaspora and about what Ralph Sprenkels theorizes as "postinsurgent" lives[13] in the *longue durée* of a postwar full of struggle, possibility, and a living through it all in the everyday as generations redefine the very meanings of "posts."[14]

Specifically, this is a book that tries to help us think through key themes that I argue are hegemonically leveraged in the "knowing" about "El Salvador." I've organized the book, chapter by chapter, around three key tropes. We'll explore assumptions around the following: (1) the alarming *numbers* of all things violent, (2) the traumatized, injured, *débil* (debilitated) and subversive criminal-migrant *bodies*, and (3) the *things or objects*, and their lack, of war and postwar. I'll be suggesting that numbers, bodies, and things have come to define and flatten much academic and popular imagining around war, displacement, the migrant, and the refugee for El Salvador and beyond. But I'll also be thinking about how these same three categories can illuminate other kinds of knowing and connections around El Salvador's postwar. And so, while these three themes form the central chapters in this book, they are threaded through my focus on *stories* that circulate across and between communities through diverse audiences and that also form part of my own ethnographic archive. In offering them, often including the original Spanish to theorize along with my interlocutors' words, I seek to underscore the long struggle of Chalatecas and Chalatecos for truth, justice, and accountability and expose the alternate narratives of postwar truth-telling that emerge in daily life and the kind of world-making these alternate narratives can inspire.[15]

In part, I've noticed how these stories create a *before* and an *after*, or rather, many befores and many unanticipated afters: before the war, before the influx of AK-47s when insurgents just had homemade bombs, before refugee camps, before the cease-fire, after the peace accords, after the 1994 "elections of the century," after the historic FMLN presidential victory of 2009, after the surge of migration, and after the birth of a first grandchild in a distant, unknown land. These befores and afters call for the recognition of an everyday wartime heroism *and* for rescuing histories of violence, memories of trauma, and an abundance of loss. These befores and afters negotiate the ups and downs and persistence of transmigrant life. These befores and afters, replete with bodies, numbers, and things, entangle with my own anthropologist and personal paths of inquiry, curiosity, solidarity, *acompañamiento*, hope, outrage, and love. As a result, they bookend our narrative path.

The five chapters build on each other—peopled, storied, and generational. In some we'll explore the ethnographic archive that we can now read as history, and in others we'll think about how migrants curate their own archives. We'll be attentive to the underbelly of things often exposed in the juxtaposition of the spectacular stories and the quieter ones, some told in a whisper and that reveal an affective radicality of making a life amid insurgency and the *longue durée* of dispossession.[16] Throughout, we'll see examples of what I'm calling an ethics of collective care, which responds to processes of debility that in the war and its after are key elements in the making of a Chalateca life. I'm careful of seeming too romantic, of eliding what we now know about the embodied experiences of intergenerational trauma, and of placing the burdens of utopic hope on youth amid the now established arc of disenchantment.[17] Yet I do hope there is a truth in underscoring quotidian moments of dignity, of beauty, and of the intimate practices of reckoning and even forgiveness that erupt despite or alongside the lack of reintegration, reconciliation, and justice in El Salvador's diasporic postwar. I'll argue that this is a paradox lived across generations, embodied anew by the 1.5 insurgent generation.

Reader, I'm not alone in asking questions about generation.[18] This has been a recent theme in the literature on Central America in particular, and I'm excited by what this focus can open up for us, what tensions and possibilities emerge across contexts and generations.[19] Some, for example, have explored the supposed apolitical stance of youth that is matched interestingly by their increased "tolerance" for gender and ethnic justice and belief in democracy.[20] Others are illuminating how new generations are questioning party politics' sacred dogma and historical hierarchies and the binaries of Left versus Right that these reproduce.[21] Work on migration, including Leisy Abrego's *Sacrificing Families*, has explored the pain and longing across families and generations in the diaspora.[22] Research has also highlighted the shifting subjectivities of returned youth and their "existential anguish."[23] This scholarship informs my own.

What I'll be arguing about generation is quite ordinary: it matters. On the one hand, I contend that the 1.5 insurgent generation's moral frameworks are born from their kin's revolutionary participation, the radical political project they were reared in, and that this socialization paradoxically produces entrepreneurial, law-abiding—although mostly unauthorized—migrants.[24] And on the other hand, the arguable moral clarity of those who remain in

Chalatenango sustains a hegemonically leveraged politicized identity in the region that continues to fight against impunity. As we travel across temporalities and geographies, we'll think about how these trajectories are entwined, about those who are absent, and about those who remain. We'll also think about how labor and ideology are tethered through remittances and in the persistent invocations for memory, truth, justice, and repair. As such, my interest in generation offers a study at the intersection of insurgency and migration, attentive to numbers and bodies and to injury and agency, a study on all that was lost (and sometimes gained) as we explore histories that negotiate a continuum of violence with narratives of survival, strength, and persistence.[25]

There are many ways we could step into this book. There are, as I have indicated, so many befores to honor. Chapter 1 will bring us through a few as we chart out a positioned and partial course. The first chapter also sets the tone for the book by asking us to break apart assumptions that we may have about El Salvador. That's why we'll start by meeting a revered elder from the community that I call El Rancho in the municipality of Las Vueltas in Chalatenango, El Salvador. She shared a few folktales with me in 1996, and I have carried them with me ever since. Chapter 1 will also explain my research method and provide a brief review of Salvadoran history, postwar ethnographic context, and the impact of migration. Subsequent chapters will focus specifically on the book's themes.

Chapter 2 offers my interpretation around the frenetic sense of numbers and analyzes, for example, the statistics of epidemic violence and waves of migration. Here we'll explore my theorizing on *violencia encifrada*—codified, encrypted violence made possible by numbers that are entangled with storytelling and memory.[26] Chapter 3 explores stories about the bodies of war and postwar to bring into the conversation theories of disability and what Julie Livingston and Jasbir Puar, among others, discuss as *debility*. Theorizing in Spanish, through the concept of *debilidad*, I'll forward what I'm terming an *ethics of collective care* as central to El Salvador's *longue durée*. Chapter 4 highlights both the act of carrying and the materiality of postwar. In part, it offers a reading of the things that Salvadoran *retornados*, those human beings who have been deported back to El Salvador, carry back with them. I term this an *archive of the returned* and ask us to hold in tension memories and futures.

Chapter 5 serves as the concluding chapter and plays with what I'm calling Salvadoran *after-stories*, about how El Salvador continues to be framed in that *longue durée* of postwar but how it shifts and shapes paths across generations. This too is the "afterlife" of revolution. I borrow from historian Saidiya Hartman's theorizing on the "afterlife of slavery" in which she shows us that slavery still "persists as an issue in the political life of black America . . . , because black lives are still imperiled and devalued by a racial calculus and a political arithmetic that were entrenched centuries ago."[27] And so, in this last chapter, I attempt to theorize "what comes after," so to speak, these after-stories and the afterlives of revolution by bringing it all together—the everyday unfolding of diasporic lives rich with acts of labor, love, and renewed calls for memory, truth, and accountability.

Reader, we'll be traveling back and forth in time and across borders, from that microbus ride in the mid-1990s to virtually accompanying the fortieth anniversary commemoration of the 1980 Río Sumpul Massacre in Chalatenango, during which approximately six hundred Salvadoran men, women, and children were killed. We'll be thinking through anthropological responsibilities and transnational intimacies, and we'll learn from generations of Chalatecas and Chalatecos who represent the raison d'être of the revolution and who were to be the fruits of struggle. We'll be exploring the many alternate ways of knowing and what they can conjure for us all.

For now, let's begin in November 1996, in Chalatenango, El Salvador, with an admired elder that I will call Nanita and her love of storytelling. *Imagínese*. Imagine it.

After Stories

CHAPTER ONE

BEFORE

IT WAS MY THIRD EXTENDED VISIT to a former war zone in El Salvador, to the municipality of Las Vueltas in the Department of Chalatenango. I was just starting fourteen months of doctoral research, which would culminate in my first book, *Everyday Revolutionaries: Gender, Violence, and Disillusionment in Postwar El Salvador*.[1] In that book, I explored what I call the entangled aftermaths of war and displacement in the lives of former rank-and-file revolutionaries. I unmasked a central paradox of El Salvador's neoliberal, deterritorialized democratization: the postwar inability to survive under a democracy that produced insecure, clandestine, precarious, obligated, violent, and yet at times productive possibilities in migration. Ultimately, I argued that gendered postwar disillusionment was a key characteristic of El Salvador's "transition to peace" and neoliberal democracy. I wanted to highlight the positioned and powerful critique of past insurgent sacrifices—the broken promises and bankrupt dreams of struggle—articulated by what I term the too often elided "everyday revolutionaries."

But back then, in November 1996, my research was still coming together. Change was in the air, and hope was in the air. Youth was in the air. Even the experienced were so young. The protagonists of war and their children were just that, children born in war, in refugee camps, or in repopulated communities in that moment of transition to peace—infants of postwar. In retrospect, this focus on the agents of insurgency and peace building eclipsed other research paths, including the experiences of Chalateco and Chalateca elders. Recently though, I came across one of my earliest field recordings with Nanita, a respected and much-loved community elder.[2] Nanita wasn't my grandmother, though she had told me to call her so as she welcomed me into her home. Young and enacting solidarity through ritual kinship, I did.[3] On most evenings Nanita would unwind her long silver hair and let it drape across her back while she smoked a cigarette. She would sit in the hammock, typically reserved for her husband upon his return from the fields, and swing gently with thin puffs of smoke around her. She was beautiful. The Chalateco nights were beautiful, expansive, and starry or, during the rainy season, heavy with powerful storms.

I picture Nanita in all her glow. Already, back then, much had changed since the earliest days of postwar—things that spoke of the importance of infrastructure.[4] Nanita's home had a tile roof over the *corredor* that had replaced the original *lámina*. We were talking by the light of a single hanging lightbulb and not a kerosene-lit candle. A cement-block sink, or *pila*, was erected in the passageway that held the community's recent potable water streaming from a new faucet. Nanita's daughter who I will call Elsy was putting the youngest of her children to bed, and I'm not quite sure why, but Nanita asked if I wanted to hear a story, from before. Having read a significant amount of testimonial literature from survivors of war in El Salvador about their militant or insurgent pasts, I was expecting to collect her lived experiences that included her gendered and generational wartime labor; she had prepared thousands of tortillas for the guerrilla insurgency—at the beginning of it all, when participants were called *milicias*—before heading for the Mesa Grande refugee camp in 1983. Instead, Nanita softly, her voice was always just above a whisper, offered a few *cuentos* (stories) that her father had told her when she was young. One was about a wandering king and a humble, poor yet generous woman who had given the king a drink of water from her broken pitcher and, as a result, months later received goblets of gold. The longest story was about a man and his wife, a pig, a pair of shoes, and a gender-bending thief.

BEFORE WAR STORIES: NANITA'S FOLKTALES

Nanita started her story this way: "Había una vez un anciano que le decían, el Abuelo. Entonces, llegó un joven y le dijo, 'Abuelo, enséñeme a trabajar como usted trabaja.'" (There once was an old man that they called the Grandfather. One day a youth arrived, and he said, "Grandfather, teach me how to work like you do.")[5] I have to admit that the story was quite difficult to follow. Somewhere along the way, the *joven* became a thief (*un mañoso*), a trickster character who fooled the old man and his wife in various ways. Reader, please bear with me; this may not be the opening story you were expecting.

The *mañoso* first stole the old man's coveted pig, only to then return it to be butchered. Did he not want to do the work? Was this a skill already being lost? With the old man's guard down, the thief traveled to the couple's home and befriended the Abuelo's wife. Indeed, he breached private gendered spaces by asking to borrow the old man's razor and mirror in order to shave. He did so to suss out where the elderly couple stored their meat. I wonder about all the intrigue, the intimacy of asking to borrow another man's razor, the bodily vulnerability, the act of grooming, a young man in front of an old woman. In chapter 4, we'll come back to wartime razors and bits of mirror, so hold on to this image. In any event, the old man learned about the young man's visit and subsequently moved the meat to a locked *cofre*, a chest.

But once again, the thief outmaneuvered the elderly couple by stealing the *cofre* keys and the old woman's *justán*—back in the day, women and girls wore slips as undergarments beneath their dresses or skirts.[6] The thief, dressed in the slip, "haciéndose que era la mujer" and posed (or performed) as the Grandfather's wife. Through various queer acts of gender-bending deception, the thief took off with all the meat, leaving the elderly couple outwitted. Taking on the voice of the old man, Nanita explained, "A pues, hoy sí nos dejaron sin la carne y sin tu justán" (Well now, today we are left without the meat and without your slip). The last soft words on the tape are Nanita's in her playful voice: "Hasta aquí llega" (That's it), indicating that the story was over.[7]

When I first collected this story, I didn't know what to make of it. I was supposed to be researching narratives about the armed conflict and people's gendered sacrifices. Soon I would learn, though, that the testimonial genre, so powerful in the war, was temporally (and temporarily, I would now add) exhausted, as I documented in *Everyday Revolutionaries*.[8] What I mean is that most of the people I spoke with in the 1990s in Chalatenango had stopped giving their testimony about the war. The *testimonio* serves as an act of witnessing, a personal yet collective and public call for human rights and social justice, co-constructed and aimed at a particular "international" audience. Indeed, in the past I have written about how one family used a book of testimonies as toilet paper when they ran out.[9] So, following the advice of one of my mentors, linguistic anthropologist Bambi Schieffelin, I focused on the talk of everyday life that was full of people's cogent theories on their sources of pain and hope. Many residents in the repopulated communities of Chalatenango, where I conducted my research and where Nanita lived, reflected on their mediated agency amid the arc of brutal wartime repression and postwar deception. Nanita's story didn't seem to fit, and in retrospect, I have a hunch that I set it aside out of anxiety, and in an attempt to heed the call by Black feminist scholars to decolonize anthropology.[10] I was supposed to be doing important anthropology of human rights and what would become a critical perspective in the field—public, engaged, or activist anthropology. I wasn't supposed to be "collecting" a reductionist or essentializing "folklore." At the time, very little had been written about El Salvador in the discipline of anthropology in the United States, and I was concerned about falling into a "salvage anthropology."[11] And so, like generations of anthropologists before me, I set the audio recording and its transcription aside, securely locked in my personal and professional archive. This archive is also part of the story.

Recently, in an effort to restore decomposing tapes, I began digitizing them. Some tapes consist of interviews with community leaders, popular education teachers, women and men on community councils, and leaders of various nongovernmental organizations (NGOs), but so many are of events, an attempt to capture the naturally occurring speech, those everyday conversations that happened at large gatherings, at workshops, at meetings, and in households. I digitized the tapes in real time, listening to the recordings as they transferred into sound files. That was when I heard Nanita's soft whisper, her storytelling performance that I missed back in 1996 and that I synopsized earlier. Am I wrong to imagine her coy smile? The original transcript is full of ellipses, words that I could never make out. Words that I desperately want us to understand. What key do they hold for us about Chalatenango and the arc of one woman's life?

And so, Reader, all these years later I asked Nanita's daughter Elsy to help me understand the story for this book, and she reconstructed it for me. As readers of *Everyday Revolutionaries* may recall, it is thanks to Elsy that I gained entrance to so many spheres across Chalatenango and the United States. Nanita's earlier story appears whole, neat, and tidy, but it came together in spurts—filed away over decades and then restored and reanimated across locations over a few days. I shared with Elsy the audio file that carried Nanita's voice, apologized for the poor-quality sound, and asked if she had understood the stories. Did she remember them? Could she explain them and help me fill in the blanks? Had her mother told her these stories as well? Were they folktales or parables? What was their cultural meaning? I had missed so much of the stories. I was hoping that Elsy's explanation would make it clearer as to why her mother had shared them with me. I created a barrage of questions. Too many questions.

Meanwhile, I was worried about my request. What emotions could get stirred up in hearing a mother's cadence twenty years after her death? The last time I had shared photos I'd taken in the 1990s, Elsy had wept. For better or worse, I shared the files and engaged in a virtual and often asynchronous temporal fieldwork exchange that I have come to rely on and to love. Within thirty minutes, a relatively fast turnaround, I received a cheerful voice memo from Elsy saying that she knew the stories and would tell them to me again. But then Elsy followed up with her own request. I could hear her cousin Lorena in the background. Right or wrong, truth or fiction or memory induced, I pictured them sitting in the large purple room in Elsy's home in the repopulated community that I call El Rancho, a *cantón* in the municipality of Las Vueltas where I have conducted most of my research.[12] The request: could I please send them the photograph of little Amelia when she was "tiernita" and lying on the bed? Could I send it to them now? I clarified, "You mean the pictures from the 1990s?" "Yes," was the response.[13]

Elsy and Lorena described a baby wrapped in a light blanket. But the only picture that I could recall was one of a chubby little baby glistening and puffy in a red wool-knit onesie with a white pom-pom hoodie. I took the

FIGURE 1. Family, Chalatenango. Early 1990s. Photograph courtesy of the Sprenkels Melara family, © Ralph Sprenkels.

photograph in 1997 and at the time was amazed by the Chalateco cultural practice of swaddling newborns in warm winter-like clothes to help them regulate their body temperature, to protect them during those early vulnerable months when they were most susceptible to "mal de ojo"—a belief in harm by the ill will of others. Babies in Chalatenango were often red-faced, dewy, and warm to the touch. During fieldwork I took a lot of pictures of kids on request, printed them out in San Salvador, and delivered them to families. People didn't have a lot of photographs back then and were keen to memorialize the family-building moments of life in the aftermath of war, as Ralph Sprenkels's portraits so poignantly highlight.

I remembered taking the baby pictures. I found the stored pictures and sent them off (recontextualizing photos of photos) and was thrilled to hear that they were the right ones. Twenty-three years later, Lorena, Elsy, and I shared what can be understood as an archive of memory that we affectively mobilized together. Elsy sent the picture to now twenty-three-year-old Amelia living in the United States. I wonder what prompted their request. Was it Amelia's birthday? What had Lorena and Elsy been reminiscing about? Had the sound file with Nanita's stories jogged some sort of temporal return? And in what my colleague and friend Ayala Fader and I have talked about as "ethnographic wanting," that always ethically compromised pull to know more and more, I wondered about Amelia and her sisters and their lives in the United States.[14] I wondered about this 1.5 insurgent generation born, raised, and defined by the experiences of transition, from refugee camp to repopulation community, from children of insurgents to FMLN (Farabundo Martí National Liberation Front) political-party supporters, from war to postwar, from adobe house to cinder block, from community chorro to running water in the home, from Chalatenango to New Jersey, and so on.[15] But I didn't ask. I set part of my ethnographic wanting to the side and responded with, "My pleasure! Don't forget to tell me the stories! ¡Mil gracias!"

And though it took a while, Elsy called me one morning to talk about her mother's stories that spanned generations, stories originally told by Nanita's own parents. Elsy reminded me how much her mother loved to tell her *cuentos*. When I asked her to think through their meaning and why she thought her mom had shared them with me, she said, "¿A saber?" (Who knows?) And that was that. No Geertzian deep, interpretive, thick description to follow.[16] We shared a story. We shared some laughter. As John L. Jackson Jr.'s work reminds us, we should be careful with the "hubris that has probably always imagined ethnographic thickness to be far thicker than it actually is."[17] Jackson suggests "thin description" instead, a critique of the assumptions around thickness, a critique of the alluring power of ethnography, a reminder that "seeing through another person's eyes is not the same thing as actually seeing that person."[18] I want to honor that call and have us "see" Nanita and Elsy, and Lorena, and Amelia.[19]

So, Reader, that was that. That is that? After going over the story about the old man, the old woman, a pig, and a thief, Elsy asked if I wanted to hear a few more old stories, about a duped king and the trickster character Pedro Urdemales. We talked for a long while. As we were wrapping up our conversation, Elsy asked if I wanted to hear one last story, one from her own before, from her *guerrillera* past. It's a good one, full of multispecies "oddkin" that Donna J. Haraway suggests marks our current moment.[20] That story will close this book. For now, I hope that Nanita's stories and my relationship to them, a relationship shared across generations and borders, opens up for us a way to think deeply about the "before" of war as we chart out the book's path.

The rest of this chapter is quite traditional, so to speak. First, we'll go over how I've come to think about my ethnographic methods—protracted, intimate, and in *solidaridad* (solidarity). Then I'll provide a brief review of Salvadoran history and ethnographic context. Subsequent sections of the chapter highlight war stories, including the perhaps expected (gendered-read male) ethnographic evidence of early insurgent and clandestine organizing. These are narratives, that in my first book, I had elided as I foregrounded women's memories of insurgency that came up in everyday spaces. The final part of the chapter takes us to the 1990s (my own before) and introduces the 1.5 insurgent generation when I first met them, when they were babies or tykes. These are ethnographic reflections that today we can read as contemporary history. We'll address the question of generation more fully in the last chapter of the book, but for now I want us to *feel* that hope, that utopic expectation for the future, the 1.5 insurgent generation as the fruits of the revolution.[21]

PURSUING A METHOD: PROTRACTED, INTIMATE, AND IN *SOLIDARIDAD*

Anthropology offers significant ethnographic research practices and interpretive tools that ground this project. Primarily, the book is based on various modes of participant observation and data collection memorialized through time in reflective fieldnotes, captured in audio recordings and transcripts, and engaged with through shifting material platforms from an archive of letters to an archive of digital messages. Fieldnotes in particular are interesting things and are understood as a key practice of ethnographic research. They are descriptions of places, events, and interactions, full of so many people, so many sounds, smells, yearnings, and worries. I've kept mine, printed out, from computers and software long gone. Pages and pages hole punched, in an electric-blue ring binder five inches deep with all sorts of Post-it notes sticking out, frayed and curled by time. Exploring this binder decades later takes me back to 1993, 1994, 1996, and 1997. This is a "before"

I had not predicted—ethnography made history. This knowledge production is of course positioned, partial, and interpreted by the anthropologist (me) in situ and then after—decades after. I want to emphasize that the doing of ethnography, rooted in participant observation, changes through time and contexts; it ages—both expanding and shrinking in unexpected ways—along with you. I find this temporality revealing and exciting for what it can offer, for the work it can do in asking new questions, in returning to "new-old stories"[22] differently, and for the work that recuperates, challenges, and resuscitates truths still to be told. I hope this will become clear in the chapters that follow.

Methodologically, this book integrates various sources of knowledge production, including statistics, material culture, and narratives recorded during many phases of fieldwork. It is based on research that spans more than twenty-five years and crosses multiple sites and moments of ethnographic analysis, from rural Chalatenango, El Salvador—a former war zone (1980–1992) and site of popular organizing and FMLN[23] peasant insurgency—to family reunions on the outskirts of Washington, DC. Specifically, I trace the intergenerational trajectories of rank-and-file families from a repopulated community that I first met in 1993 as well as many of their insurgent kin who have unexpectedly remade their lives in the United States.[24] Focusing on the lives of the protagonist and 1.5 insurgent generations, I integrate participant observation of community life in Chalatenango, extensive research on family histories, kinship networks, and experiences of displacement with research that began in the mid-2000s in the United States in sites across the Northeast (New Jersey, Virginia, and Maryland), and in Los Angeles, California, where many Chalatecas and Chalatecos now reside. I also include data gleaned from return trips to Chalatenango starting in the mid-2010s with recently returned migrants and with kin who never left. Additionally, new media technologies and ethnography of "virtual worlds"[25] center the text as I follow how different modes of communication (from homemade videos delivered through courier, to Facebook and WhatsApp) factor in people's lives and in my own intimate research practices. I am careful about using pseudonyms for people, for specific communities, and for *cantones* or their smaller *caseríos* due to the politicized nature of this material and ultimately because of issues of migration. Since the beginning of this project, new technologies have indeed made the transparency and mapping of research sites an important topic of ethical concern.

Protracted

I understand all of this research through what I'm calling *protracted, intimate ethnography in solidaridad*. In the past, I've discussed this work as longitudinal, and of course it is, as it has followed several families from the municipality of Las Vueltas in the Department of Chalatenango off and on since 1993, when I conducted my first research trip. While Chalatecos and Chalatecas have remained in the communities they repopulated during the war, many have also emigrated primarily to the United States.[26] This research has ebbed and flowed and has not always been consistent. I have been at this for a long time, unexpectedly so. As a result, I suggest the term *protracted* because it introduces an often-unspoken element of the longitudinal, its underbelly, at least for me. *Protracted* in its transitive verb form is about prolonging or extending time with the sense of wasting it, of causing a delay. Or it can mean "to prolong."[27] I want to point to how longitudinal research, despite the depth and richness that it can ultimately offer in terms of affective relationships and collaborative knowledge production, asks "research subjects" to keep at it, keep that space open, that time clear for a researcher's repeated return.

I am part of a generation of anthropologists that came of age in the 1990s, when the discipline was in the midst of critique, epistemic and reflexive. I "grew" into becoming an anthropologist by reading the surge of work that exposed the discipline's colonial roots[28] and addressed questions of power, representation, authority, and positionality.[29] The decolonial turn was presented to my cohort at New York University through the pedagogy of the late Caribbeanist anthropologist Constance Sutton as she filled her syllabi with subaltern feminist writers of color, the first scholars to push for decolonizing anthropology and to develop an antiracist pedagogy.[30]

An early focus on situated knowledge[31] and a positioned women-of-color critique[32] commingled with a then emergent field of activist anthropology often rooted in a Marxist political-economic approach that exposed regional processes of inequality.[33] Anthropologists such as Linda Green, Nancy Scheper-Hughes, Charlie Hale, Philippe Bourgois, Carolyn Nordstrom, and Carole Nagengast were creating new conversations about "activist" and "militant" anthropology that emerged from their work on continuums of violence and "fieldwork under fire."[34] Additionally, for scholars of Central America, the comprehensive two-part review by Carol Smith and her colleagues of the status of anthropological research in the region rooted what would become for many of us a commitment to stretch the boundaries of anthropology.[35] It is in this context that a generation pursued doctoral dissertations on topics such as the aftermaths of war,[36] the anthropology of human rights and genocide,[37] transitional justice and truth commissions,[38] transnational labor organizing and sweat shops,[39] urban discourses of violence,[40] the articulation of human rights and Indigenous rights discourses,[41] and the role of cultural politics in nation building.[42] We participated (though many of us were not yet published) in the shaping of these anthropological perspectives—activist, engaged, participatory, collaborative, intersectional, and positioned—and experimented through trial and error in their aligned ethnographic methods and theory building. This is also part of my protracted research positioning.

Intimate

Today, these methodological framings have entered squarely in the field and generate important debate through public anthropology's attention to witnessing and its commitment to what Robert Borofsky and Antonio De Lauri explain as "reframing the terms of public debates—transforming received, accepted understandings of social issues with new insights, new framings—and fostering social and political change that benefits others, especially those anthropologists work with."[43] This is a call beyond an "ethics of do no harm," which in part suggests "an aspiration for reciprocity, public engagement and kindness."[44] In my own work I have felt this as an intimate *compromiso* that has been long unwinding and has changed since I first walked into the NGO offices of CORDES (Fundación para la Cooperación y el Desarollo Comunal/Foundation for the Cooperation and Community Development of El Salvador) in Chalatenango City and into the community of El Rancho in 1993.[45]

This *compromiso* is situated in my connections to Chalateca community life, to various households across generations, and to the very arc of Salvadoran scholarship and the politics of citation. Sometimes it's fraught, sometimes it feels like not enough, and sometimes it's not directly related to Chalatenango. Let me explain with an aside of sorts.

The intimacy of *compromiso* has led to my work as expert witness for the historic El Mozote Massacre case. One could argue that this is my most evident form of public scholarship. It didn't take place in the Department of Chalatenango but rather in the Department of Morazán. In February 2019—along with the late Ralph (Rafa) Sprenkels, my dear friend and renowned scholar—I was sworn in by Judge Jorge Guzmán Urquilla as "Perito Antropóloga" (or Expert Witness) for "Proceso Penal 238/1990," known as "Masacre El Mozote y lugares aledaños," at the Juzgado Segundo de Primera Instancia de San Francisco Gotera. We would be asked to deploy our anthropological skills for a historic legal case. It was the biggest deal of my professional life. I was committed, honored, and simultaneously anxious about doing the job right, about the tremendous work ahead, and about holding up my small part that could contribute to ending impunity.

Briefly, the massacre in El Mozote and nearby communities took place December 9–17, 1981, and it is recognized worldwide as among the worst, most brutal, and largest massacre in contemporary Latin American history.[46] Rufina Amaya was the first survivor to give her testimony to the world and spent decades fighting for justice.[47] Despite years of Salvadoran and US government denials and cover-ups,[48] extensive human rights and legal work confirms that the US-trained elite, special forces of the Atlacatl Battalion massacred nearly a thousand unarmed civilians—the majority of whom were women, children, and the elderly.[49] Men, women, and young children were separated and killed en masse in the center of town in El Mozote and then indiscriminately killed across neighboring communities during the subsequent days of the massacre. This was wanton destruction. Homes, livestock, community stores—everything and everyone who had not managed to escape or had the good fortune to be away was burned and destroyed.[50] The average age of the murdered children was six.[51]

For many in the international human rights community, the trial of the massacre at El Mozote is seen as a precedent-setting case, an opportunity to finally hold those responsible for the horrific violence accountable and to stand with the victim-survivors of the massacre and their descendants in their extraordinary public and powerful struggle for justice—their testimony in the court historic. Rafa and I, along with the other key expert witnesses who were proposed on behalf of the victims, or "accusers," also recognized that we were helping to create a template for the pursuit of justice for the first time in the Salvadoran court of law.[52] "Que reto más bonito" (What a beautiful challenge—to work toward truth and justice), Rafa would remind me during the months of intense work ahead. Indeed.

I've told you about this work in Morazán because my time as *perito antropóloga* and my longitudinal, diasporic work (this book) are connected by who I am and how I've tried to do anthropology intimately and honestly, with solidarity and with love. This is not a romantic call for bearing witness through channels of expertise (in everyday fieldwork or for the courts). I've built my career eschewing the label of "expert" through my teaching, which tries to decenter professorial power, and through my research and writing, in which I foreground the lived experiences, intellectual capacities, and potent reflections of Salvadorans I've had the privilege to be in conversation with for nearly thirty years. There are affective moves, however, that root my understanding of anthropological responsibility and that inform the calls to witness. Because the genre of the dictamen or the expert report that I submitted in 2019 surely had its own framing. It needed to answer clearly and directly the questions posed by the presiding judge within the case's juridical frame.[53] And certainly this work negotiated what Elana Zilberg explains as the "double binds" inherent in negotiating the demands of scholarly production (anthropology) and the role of expert witness (activism).[54]

Of course, I'm not alone in thinking critically about the practices of witnessing—there is an abundant literature here, including studies on the power of the *testimonio* in Central America.[55] For feminist anthropologist Lynn Stephen, bearing witness is linked to testimony and is "a key epistemological tool for alternative knowledge production in the field of Latin American and Caribbean anthropology and in decentering the normative geopolitics of knowledge."[56] She reminds us that social movements deploy testifying as central to their pursuit of justice and how the *testimonio* can illuminate intersectional "transborder structural violence"[57] that an engaged, activist, public testimonial-inflected anthropology can contest. Scholars of El Salvador have been thinking through this for a while, and a new generation is developing significant participatory social memory projects, local museums, and visual culture exhibits that I think are really carving out new equitable and powerful paths that take on the very best of testimonial practices.[58]

Or take Deborah Thomas's *Political Life in the Wake of the Plantation*, where she suggests the term "Witnessing 2.0," which stretches clearly beyond the eyewitness accounting of human rights models to "embodied practice."[59] Thomas mobilizes an intimate, transformative, transgressive vision of change making in a world where we can all take part. This Witnessing 2.0 is "a practice of *recognition* and *love* that destabilizes the boundaries between self and other, knowing and feeling, complicity and accountability."[60] It aligns with Asale Angel-Ajani's critique that calls for bearing witness can be a "veiled attempt to (re)establish the authority of the ethnographer."[61] Instead, Angel-Ajani writes that we should "[open] up our ears to experiences that might not fit what we think we know. Critical reception might just lead to ethical engagement."[62] As I read it, Thomas's is a liberatory, reciprocal project. I borrow from it and from Angel-Ajani in thinking about my love for a country and its people and about the stories such as Nanita's that opened up this book. Because through protracted ethical listening, we can disrupt what we think we already know.

Finally, an element of this protracted ethnography has also over time developed similarly to what Alisse Waterston describes as "intimate ethnography,"[63] a type of biographical storytelling that places an "intimate other," in this case her father, within a dialectic study of larger processes of historical violence.[64] Here though, I am making no claims to familial intimacy—although I have entered into ritual kinship relationships over the decades. Rather, I want to disclose how intimate ethnography is embodied, felt, sensory work and is often biographical in its storytelling. It is also processual and not immediate. It takes time to become close and familiar, to develop

FIGURE 2.
Author in El Rancho,
Chalatenango, 1997.
Photograph by
Antonio Rossi.

and exchange knowledge, trust, affection, disappointment, despair, hope, worry—all of it. Positionings change. For example, I was seen at different points in my research as another young *chele* (white), an *internacional* in solidarity whose accent wasn't quite Argentine or gringa. I was seen as someone who had the privilege to eventually leave (and I did) and who had not experienced the brutalities of war. I also didn't have development money and thus often didn't meet the expectations in the 1990s of being an international volunteer in grassroots solidarity. But much later, in the migratory context, I've been seen as part of a heterogeneous Latinx community,[65] as a mother, as a teacher, and as someone who stayed in touch, as someone to share stories and meals with and reflect on experiences in Chalatenango and build new memories with. Many years later, during *reencuentros* with Chalatecos and Chalatecas, particularly with the 1.5 insurgent generation, I was asked repeatedly, "Were you the one with the braids?" I was. I wore braids every day in my bandanna-wearing youth. This mutual recognition, this intimacy does not erase hierarchy, my privilege, my South American whiteness, or the power of my naturalized US citizenship. That is why I end this section on method by bringing us to solidarity, to *solidaridad*. It is from this position that I started this project many years ago, as an undergraduate at George Washington University just learning about the Salvadoran diaspora in courses taught by Roger Rasnake—to whom I owe a great debt.

In Solidaridad

Solidaridad has a long history and call in Central America in countries such as Nicaragua and El Salvador.[66] Susan Bibler Coutin's classic work on the sanctuary movement[67] details the everyday actions by faith-based social movements that linked US activists, primarily in churches, with Central American migrants as they advocated for just US immigration and foreign policies.[68] In 1993, when the armed conflict had really just ended, being in *solidaridad* had its own particularity and currency, which I have written about in the past through my positioning as a South American gringa and through an analysis of a postwar wave of international-development volunteers with little experience in the country.[69] In El Salvador, *solidaridad* has been predicated on *acompañamiento*, on practices of accompaniment, on standing up and standing present—what today we may call ally-ship.[70] My protracted, intimate research takes place on shifting terrains of solidarity. Sociologist Serena Cosgrove suggests that we have entered a new phase, into academic Solidarity 3.0, which is "deeply interpersonal and powerfully political" and extends across institutions.[71]

Cosgrove, writing about Nicaragua's current militarized repression by the Ortega and Murillo regime, offers a vision of solidarity that is rooted in epistemic critique, strategic actions, mobilizing personal relationships, "collaborating across difference," and witnessing.[72] This is a call for solidarity that is predicated on protracted and intimate relationships, ethnographic and institutional.⁷³ It is similar to Roseann Liu and Savannah Shange's call for "thick solidarity . . . , a kind of solidarity that mobilizes empathy in ways that do not gloss over difference, but rather pushes into the specificity, irreducibility, and incommensurability of racialized experiences."⁷⁴

I place Cosgrove's call for a Solidarity 3.0 "that is affective, reciprocal, radical, strategic, and self-critical" and that bears witness in the service of becoming "accomplices in the struggle"⁷⁵ alongside the critiques of what a new generation of feminist theorists of color define as a "fugitive anthropology"— an activist approach that works within complicated and entangled liberatory projects in the always "contested space of the academy"⁷⁶ rooted in the "legacy of white heteropatriarchy."⁷⁷ This is a *solidaridad* that must do better and learn from the historical elisions (and problematic whiteness)⁷⁸ that characterized the US–Central American activism of the 1980s solidarity movement.⁷⁹ It must work against the ultimately racist performative "work of love" that constructed what Patricia Stuelke calls "sacrificial Central American victimhood."⁸⁰ Sociologist Ethel Brooks has long cautioned about the politics of "living proof," the "offering of life stories, subjectivities, bodily materialities, and practices by women as acts of courage and political claim staking."⁸¹ Because these are always unequal testimonial exchanges of living proof that are decontextualized and circulated, whether in solidarity movements or NGO circuits that claim to speak for and meet the needs of war-torn Salvadorans. Brooks pushes us to question what happens to "those whose lives become living proof," who by their very positioning speak for those who are absent.⁸²

Protracted intimate solidarity can lead us to different imaginings. In fact, many see hope in the future, in a broadly defined activist youth, and in a new generation of Central Americans and Central American Americans who refuse this past affective work of solidarity. For example, Stuelke explains that "they demand a new solidarity imaginary that escapes the reparative politics of the past" and reminds us that "solidarity needs suspicion too."⁸³ It is Solidarity 3.0 and, yes, a healthy suspicion that guides my protracted, intimate ethnographic research that I hope can contest some of the politics of our contemporary moment, with its shortsightedness, xenophobia, racism, and historical amnesia, or, alternatively, its logic of "humanitarian reason" that is ironically reductive.⁸⁴

In sum, my methods are long and unfolding, full of starts and stops, and full of changing ethnographic worries and commitments to anthropological and personal responsibility. They are guided by specific relationships with several extended families still rooted in El Rancho whose adult children live either in El Salvador or across the United States. As I've mentioned before, throughout the book I provide pseudonyms for people, except for leaders whose statements are publicly available. I have also masked identifying characteristics and sometimes created composite interlocutors. I have been careful with dates and with attributing stories to particular people and families. I believe this move was demanded by the long arc of this project; the unanticipated futures of after-stories and new-old stories; and a concern for how "security" gets deployed. This doesn't make it any less possible to honor the particular, to disrupt or dislodge the violences and hierarchies around generalizations that abound for "El Salvador."[85] We'll travel together through everyday sidelined and often forgotten stories that are of course partial and not mine but that bend toward a politics of recognition, of love, and, I hope, of justice.

CONTEXTS OF WAR AND POSTWAR

Reader, to move forward, we need a bit more history and context. There is, as I mentioned earlier, a tremendous literature on El Salvador and its diaspora that informs my work, and I provide citations throughout for where to dive deeper and read the surge of work by new generations of scholars. In what follows, I provide a brief overview of the contexts of war and postwar and introduce the Department of Chalatenango, the municipality of Las Vueltas, and one of its *cantones* (small communities), which I call El Rancho, where I have conducted most of my protracted, intimate ethnography in *solidaridad*. I also introduce the topic of Salvadoran migration.

The Salvadoran armed conflict (1980–1992) claimed the lives of seventy-five thousand people, disappeared another seven thousand Salvadorans, and displaced five hundred thousand civilians.[86] Research shows that the United States supported the counterinsurgency with $6 billion of military aid over a decade.[87] A key strategy of this counterinsurgency was scorched earth operations known as *tierra arrasada*, which targeted civil society in rural areas by killing people and destroying their homes, local buildings, churches, fields, animals—everything. These military operations were rooted in the Cold War ideology of *quitarle el agua al pez* (drain the water from the fish), where the water was understood as the civilian population and the fish as the guerrillas. According to reporting, 1980–1984 were the most brutal years in rural areas, with human rights organizations denouncing forced displacements, massacres, and the disappearances of children.[88] Thus, state terror was a defining aspect of the armed conflict, and today, scholars continue to unmask the shifting strategies and US involvement, including by military intelligence.[89]

The war officially ended on January 16, 1992, with the signing of the United Nations–brokered peace accords between FMLN insurgent forces and the conservative, right-wing ARENA (National Republican Alliance/Alianza Republicana Nacionalista) government. Much scholarship and policy has addressed this period. Soon El Salvador's "negotiated revolution"[90] became a key case study in the analysis of comparative peace processes,[91] and it continues to be heralded as a model of disarmament, demobilization, and reintegration (DDR).[92] The peace accords were extraordinary in many respects, from reforming the military and historically violent and repressive police forces to legalizing the insurgent FMLN into an official political party. Significantly, the peace process included the publication of the United Nations Truth Commission's report, *From Madness to Hope*, which found that the Salvadoran state, through its systematic institutionalization of violence, was the overwhelming agent of terror.[93] Of the twenty-two thousand investigated cases of human rights violations from 1980 to 1991, "those giving testimony attributed almost 85 percent of cases to agents of the State, paramilitary groups allied to them, and the death squads." The report found that the FMLN was responsible for 5 percent of cases of human rights abuse.[94] Soon after its publication in March 1993, a law was passed granting amnesty to all those involved in massacres and war crimes mentioned in the truth report (on both the Right and the Left). In forthcoming chapters we'll return to the legacies of this impunity and the long arc of activism that overturned the amnesty law.

Studies about El Salvador's armed conflict and its aftermath are expansive, moving across generations of scholars who each bring their positioned questions. For example, research has reframed our understanding of peace building as evidenced in what anthropologist Ellen Moodie discusses as the "aftermath of peace."[95] For Moodie, El Salvador after war is characterized by an anxious and depoliticized uncertainty that discursively resignifies violence into common crime, what she terms democratic disenchantment. Christine Wade also demonstrates how peace building must consider "local actors." She richly documents the key role of local elites—economic, political, and military—in the nation's "captured peace," and the ways that elite groups, such as the ARENA political party, consolidated power through peace building.[96] Much of this early research also focused on theorizing postwar reconstruction and local transitions to democracy through the role of peasant insurgent activism, agrarian processes from below,[97] and the binds of collective action.[98]

A key area of interest was women's participation in the insurgency and beyond. Researchers pointed to the critical and varied role of women in political-military structures as well as to the multiple gendered challenges women encountered during the postwar period in both urban and rural communities.[99] This gendered perspective is crucial because women accounted for approximately 30 percent of FMLN forces, yet reintegration programs often did not consider or meet their needs.[100] A significant focus of this work also concentrates on the ongoing violence decades into postwar and beyond the hyperrepresentation of gangs.[101] Anthropologist Ainhoa Montoya, for example, examines the sensemaking activities by ordinary Salvadorans as they live through the routine violence of democratization in what she calls a "context of a violent peace."[102] Hers is ultimately an exploration of the "gray zone of politics" that puts into relief the workings of "violent democracy."[103] Other scholars continue to explore the importance of rural spaces that have their own historical relationship to state power and extractivism.[104] And while early work tended toward the romantic or the disillusioned,[105] recent work by Salvadoran scholars intervenes on debates through an interdisciplinary excavation of the past, exploring the sequalae of trauma and new mappings on the role of silence, memory, and commemoration. The 2019 special volume of the journal *Realidad*, published in El Salvador, is a key example.

Ethnographic Context

My own research has focused on northern El Salvador, in the Department of Chalatenango, a rural, mountainous, poor region of the country where, historically, most people were small-scale peasant farmers who migrated seasonally for wage labor in order to survive. This was an area in which the 1970s teachings of the progressive Catholic Church, known as liberation theology, ran deep alongside other movements for social justice. By the late 1970s repression by paramilitary, military, and police forces was brutal, and Chalatenango became a key site of wartime oppositional organizing and an area that was destroyed by military conflict. The war was marked by a back and forth in people's degree of participation. Men, women, the young, and the old fled (some were carried on backs and in makeshift hammocks) through hills in what residents called *guindas*, leaving behind just about everything in their communities in order to escape state-sponsored violence.[106] Many joined the FMLN guerrilla forces for a time—voluntarily, obligated, or forced—or at great risk, crossed borders into refugee camps (primarily Mesa Grande in Honduras) and smuggled guns, medicine, and the injured. In 1987, many civilians mobilized a mass social movement, left Honduran refugee camps, and repopulated their destroyed communities, all the while supporting insurgent forces.[107] These became repopulated communities, or spaces that Ralph Sprenkels describes as "postinsurgent social fields," where former insurgent political and military organizations characterized by deep hierarchical relations and networks informed everyday life and ultimately, people's possible postwar trajectories.[108]

At the end of the armed conflict and early into the postwar transition, these repopulated communities were quite homogeneous politically (FMLN supporters) and from the early to mid-1990s found themselves targets of international and national development efforts to reincorporate excluded and marginalized citizens into the nation and into the productive economy. Chalatenango became the site of a flurry of postwar "reconstruction and development" attention beyond the hard-won battle for land. Indeed, it was the time of reconstruction and development *as* democracy with the accompanying

FIGURE 3. Repopulation, Chalatenango. Early 1990s. Photograph courtesy of the Sprenkels Melara family, © Ralph Sprenkels.

hegemonic discourse of reintegration. For the everyday rank-and-file Chalateca and Chalateco—the backbone of the insurgency—that search for economic justice, along with a call for truth and accountability (for human rights abuses), was eclipsed by this national and local framing that emphasized a material rebuilding and new vocabularies of *reinserción*.

Residents in these communities had been off the grid, long excluded from national policies, and then they had been agents in the rejection of local and national governments during the war because political, social, and economic life was organized through popular armed organizations. Their reintegration focused on access to land and infrastructure—electrification, potable water, and the building of new roads and cement-block housing. Microcredit programs, arts and crafts projects, and cattle, pig, and hen farming initiatives aimed at "gendering" development were also instituted within the nation's neoliberal turn. Much of this was handled through new forms of governmentality, through an explosion of NGOs, many deeply politicized, in the early throes of professionalization and emergence from insurgent collective action. My first book explored the unintended tensions and consequences of this time that often disempowered women and communities and fomented an everyday disillusionment evidenced in the circulation of a discourse of deceit. After so many decades into postwar life, it's clear that the model of reconstruction produced unintended consequences, with a nation territorially unmoored and the struggle for truth, justice, accountability, and an end to impunity ongoing.

In the early period—postwar, postconflict—all things "post" were actually experienced as temporally very present. Salvadorans were in the midst of transition, and the meaning and practices of *la transición* and everyday trust in the possibilities of democratization were new and lived differently across scales. For some sectors of the population who had struggled militarily and politically for social change, the FMLN *en poder*, "in power," meaning winning the presidency, was still a rallying cry and part of sustained political organizing, not a historical fact as evidenced in the election of two FMLN presidents: Mauricio Funes in 2009 and former FPL (Fuerzas Populares de Liberación/Popular Liberation Forces) Comandante Salvador Sánchez Cerén in 2014.[109] Thirty years have passed since the signing of the peace accords, and yet El Salvador continues to be framed within the arcs of war and postwar. This is also why I deploy the term *longue durée*.

This long postwar in northeastern Chalatenango is rooted in a historical narrative of oppositional politics, in local histories of violence and martyred leaders, in wounded bodies and heroic figures, and in a vision of the revolution as one that would result in socioeconomic justice, which has not occurred. But as new work offers, this *longue durée* of postwar has recurred to new regional articulations around the category of victim, rather than survivor as my early work showed. Indeed, new calls for truth, reparations, and justice move across generations in interesting ways. For example, anthropologist Adriana Alas's work on "children of postwar" shows how youth with no lived experience of war and who were born after the 1992 peace accords (and, I would add, born after the early transition of postpeace) exhibit more "tolerant memories." Alas uncovers a regionally valued "local regime of suffering" that is predicated on the intimacy of historical wartime suffering in relationship to insurgency, death, and the attendant binaries of Left versus Right and of good versus evil. Alas focuses on how the children of postwar seek to create more open and tolerant spaces based on their search for silenced stories and hushed memories about what really happened to their kin—when, where, how, and by whose hands did they die? In their questioning of regional truths and stories about insurgent accountability, they open space for some provocative political moves in terms of which political parties to support or when and if political allegiances even matter.[110]

Getting back to where this project began, I have conducted ethnographic research in the municipality of Las Vueltas and the *cantón*, or small community within the municipality, that I call El Rancho. I have written extensively about families in El Rancho in *Everyday Revolutionaries*, attentive to people's theories of explanation, their aspirations, their loves, and their losses. Nanita, who opens this book, repopulated with her family to El Rancho. She was not originally from El Rancho but settled there along with her neighbors and engaged in the backbreaking work of reclaiming a destroyed landscape, bit by bit.

Reader, throughout this book, I'll be providing ethnographic stories that took place mostly in El Rancho in the early to mid-1990s. I hope that you will be able to imagine the richness and complexity of everyday rural life at the turn of transition. For now, I want to share that in 1997, according to a hand-recorded census conducted by the Unidad de Salud, there were 343 homes and 1,486 residents (753 men and 733 women) in the municipality.[111] Today, we know that Las Vueltas stretches across the diaspora, as many residents have migrated across the United States,[112] and in some cases, to Europe. A 2007 census has the municipal population decreasing to 940 residents (453 men and 487 women) with only 32 percent living in the "urban" part of the municipality (as opposed to 44.6 percent in the 1997 local census).[113] This is a population decrease of 36.7 percent. At this writing, a new census is pending, but a 2014 Ministry of Economy report estimated that the population would further decline to 608 by 2020, a decrease of 59.1 percent from the 1997 data and a decrease of 35.3 percent since the 2007 census.[114] We'll turn shortly to thinking about numbers as narrative tools that encrypt or encipher violence (*violencia encifrada*). For now, though, I want to point out a cycle of depopulation, repopulation, and back to depopulation. Or is it? According to anthropologist Adriana Alas the local story is a bit different. Data

FIGURE 4. Reclaiming the fields, Chalatenango. Early 1990s. Photograph courtesy of the Sprenkels Melara family, © Ralph Sprenkels.

from a 2009 local study along with sources from the Instituto Geográfico Nacional "Ingeniero Pablo Arnoldo Guzmán" recorded the total population for the municipality at 4,246. And though for sure the story is one of wartime depopulation and the legacy of this violence, Alas indicates that in 2005 there were 1,314 residents, in 2007 there were 1,656, and in 2008 there was a slight increase to 1,750 residents.[115] More on numbers in chapter 2.

Migration

By the late 1990s, when I was wrapping up my doctoral research, the torrent of reconstruction aid was dwindling, and rebuilding the war-torn landscape waned, peaking again only during times of environmental disaster, such as the earthquakes in 2001. It was around this time, at the turn of the twenty-first century and nearly ten years into the transition to democracy, that Chalatecas and Chalatecos began an unprecedented mass migration to the United States. In doing so, residents of repopulated communities joined a longer and older wave of Salvadoran migrants in the United States whose labor and remittances are estimated to have reduced the national poverty rate by 7 percent.[116]

Indeed, scholars argue that migration has become a key aspect of El Salvador's national development plan.[117] According to the Pew Research Center, an estimated 711,000 Salvadorans lived in the United States in 2000, and 2.3 million Salvadorans lived there by 2017.[118] This data shows that Salvadorans are the third largest population of Hispanic origin residing in the United States.[119] Ample research and policy data illuminate how this population's remittances—the money and goods they send back home to their communities—keep the nation afloat, as we will see in chapter 2. And so, while my project started out with a focus on the everyday rural protagonists of war, over time I have been able to develop transnational diasporic networks across generations. I have aged along with insurgent parents, and I have sent condolences to the families of those who have died in times of peace. I have also marveled at how the young children I first met in the 1990s now have babies of their own. This is all part of a mapping that in *Everyday Revolutionaries* I theorized as an unanticipated obligation of migration, an outcome that was neither an aspiration of war or of postwar life nor about securing justice and equality.[120]

I continue to wonder if can we read these moves as another iteration of a history of displacement and dispossession where migration becomes a political act.[121] Can we read Chalatecas' migration as a creative endeavor?[122] Amparo Marroquín Parducci suggests just that—that a regional (Central American) perspective must attend to the spaces of creation and cultural work that happen via migration[123] and act as a "collective resistance against the projects of extractivist capitalism throughout Latin America."[124] This highlights how migrants make hope from despair.[125] Scholarship by and about "U.S. Central Americans,"[126] or "Central American Americans,"[127] corroborates this call and points to the importance of generation and the need to move analytics beyond civil war framings. Rather, scholars suggest focusing on "emplacement and social justice within the United States"[128] in order to write against the flattening of representations, the silencing of difference, and the violent stereotypes around the labeling of diasporic Central Americans as "traumatized people."[129]

And so, I ask, what has come of the Chalateco search for *una vida digna* (a dignified life), this war and postwar aim and human right referred to repeatedly during my research in Chalatenango? Indeed, for the Salvadorans I worked with, this was a rallying call that seemed pretty clear at first: ownership of productive land, fresh water and electricity, a decent home, fair pay, education and access to health care for their children, and the ability to have clothing and food—shoes, a clean Sunday shirt, a gold cross, that white dress for a daughter's communion, and something to eat besides tortillas, beans, and salt.[130] This would require an end to histories of abusive patron-client relations, the creation of democratic openings and economic opportunities, and an end to the militarized rural landscape. As political scientist Elisabeth Wood's work makes clear, there was affective pleasure in insurgent participation; she calls it the "pleasure in agency."[131] But the war, its hardships and opportunities, and the unfulfilled promises at its end have led many to leave Chalatenango seeking *una vida digna* in other places, from neighboring Central American nations to the United States, Italy, Spain, and Australia.

Let's hold on to that—to the pleasures and joys of a dignified life—and ask what that looks like years later through unanticipated diasporic paths and across generations. As one young Chalateco migrant we will meet shortly explained to me, he never anticipated the everyday relative ease of eating an eight-dollar hamburger or how he was able to work three jobs, send money back home so that his mother could have a smartphone and install a flush toilet, save up and help his partner with liminal legal status (TPS, or Temporary Protected Status), purchase a home, and buy all those toys for his beauty of a baby girl who he says should call me *abuelita*.[132] He also hadn't anticipated getting sick or needing surgery, and he thanked his faith and the love and strength of his new family for getting him through. We'll focus on illness and bodies in chapter 3, because as I see it, that's also a key part of a story that tethers befores and afters full of agentive debilitated bodies and an ethics of collective care that speaks back to corporal pain. So, to wrap up this chapter that has been a lot about setup, I want to share three before-stories. Two are the kind, maybe, that readers would expect about battle, injury, courage, and loss. The last story entangles my own "ethnographic before." It's about 1990s fieldwork, spaces for anthropological responsibility, and revisiting what I'm now calling the 1.5 insurgent generation.

WAR STORIES: BEFORE THE FLOOD, BEFORE AK-47S, AND FOR THE CHILDREN

In my walks through El Rancho in the 1990s and in the years after, stopping by local stores punctuated my everyday life. Teresita's home-front store sold staples like bags of salt and sugar and delicious plum tomatoes to add to rice. Teresita also sold homemade treats for children such as chocolate-dipped bananas, or *chocobananos*. I would buy tomatoes for Nanita, who was an extraordinary cook, and a *chocobanano* for myself and for whatever group of children that happened to be at the store when I stepped in.

Teresita had an expansive family, with more than eight children. I have a series of photographs of the family lined up in descending height order starting with Teresita, holding a newborn, followed by her twelve-year-old son, who was the eldest, and continuing down to the smallest toddler girl, chubby and grinning. I would come to spend a lot of time at that store and with Teresita's family. Early in 1997, Teresita's father, noting the big Sony tape recorder at my side, asked if I wanted to interview him about the war. I wasn't quite ready. Following an interest in naturally occurring speech, I hadn't yet planned on interviewing residents. True, I had spent months in 1993 and 1994 in El Rancho, but I was still getting my bearings and focusing much more on where participant observation would take me. But of course, Reader, I agreed and then had an open-ended exchange.

Reflecting on the interview and its transcript years later, I see more clearly Don Gilberto's positioned offer to teach me about the past, about what happened, *before*. His was an expansive history lesson—Braudel's *longue durée*? On the audiocassette his voice sounds forceful, and the resulting transcript reads as staccato. Specifically, Don Gilberto created a periodization of "before" that commingled, or swept together, three things in a continuum of violence: (1) biblical, religious time, (2) El Salvador's colonial history, and (3) a Marxist analysis of class inequality. Thus, Don Gilberto produced a powerful theoretical framework for understanding Salvadoran history as protracted, penetrative, and with ample intergenerational violence and injustice. Poignantly, Don Gilberto started at *one beginning*. He told me that it had all started with "the Flood," when El Salvador was first discovered. He stated, "Cuando el diluvio. Cuando se descubrió este país." He explained further that it had all started "when the powerful from other countries, the millionaires, came to discover and take ownership of the land. This is when the country suffered. It didn't cost those people not even one cent to become owners of the land." Through pointing to a history of systemic violence, Don Gilberto united biblical time, conquest, and colonialism with Marxist, world-systems critiques.[133]

His powerful history lesson also walked me through Indigenous rights and resistance—placing him at the vanguard of this conversation at a time when Indigenous rights as a concept in El Salvador was not quite emergent and for a region (Chalatenango) often described as being comprised of "white Indians." Don Gilberto explained that from the start "los Indios," Indigenous peoples, advocated for justice, for the right to own and work their land. We should note that Don Gilberto deployed the term "Indian" not in a racist, pejorative, dehumanizing framing as historically used in El Salvador, if not also across the Americas.[134] As a result, Don Gilberto explained, they were massacred; 35,000 people were killed. I wondered if he was referring to the 1932 massacre of Indigenous, "communist" coffee workers in the western region of El Salvador, an event known as La Matanza.[135] In the transcript, Don Gilberto dismissed my question about chronology and the naming of massacres and foregrounded the power of oral history. He emphasized that his grandparents had told him these truths, that Indians and workers had fought with sticks to contest the "millionaires" only to be called communists by the government. He knew something of this tactic and offered a theory of violence stemming from the biblical flood through conquest to his own 1972 insurgent participation. As he explained it, agricapitalism was just another iteration of deeply exploitative and extractive relationships[136] where "all of our sweat was for the rich," where standing on the side with their arms crossed "con los brazos cruzados" was met only with "matazones en las calles," with massacres in the streets, a flood of violence.

For Don Gilberto, the arming of the guerrilla was a direct outcome of this *grosería*, the vulgarity of the prewar violence from which children and the *gente de masa*, or "the grassroots base," had to be protected. Like other residents across conflict zones, he explained that at the time there were really just two paths, *dos caminos*, and he asked me to imagine the paths. You could choose the guerrilla or the Salvadoran Armed Forces. He explained that most residents chose the guerrilla because they didn't massacre the civilian population; specifically, they didn't assassinate children. Emphatically, he taught me that "no nos quedaba otra" (we didn't have another choice). Don Gilberto cited the example of one community in Chalatenango that had tried its hand at neutrality and had failed: "Esa pobre gente no se metía en nada y cuando venía el ejército los terminó toditos. No dejaron ni un alma y esa gente no se metía, no les daba ni a la guerrilla ni al ejército." (Those poor people didn't get involved in anything and when the army came, they killed them all. They didn't even leave one soul alive, and those people didn't get involved in anything. They didn't give to the guerrillas or the army.)[137]

Don Gilberto was already in his early seventies in 1997. Was it ageism on my part that kept me from centering Don Gilberto and his generation in the narratives about El Salvador that I was there on grant-funded doctoral research to focus on? Because listen to his elder wisdom: he placed himself first before the war, as a descendant of intergenerational trauma (that is, La Matanza), and then squarely in it, through the language of a respectful and righteous collectivity, in the "we," which we'll return to in later chapters. For example, he explained local history and insurgent military action in Las Vueltas as predicated on integrity and respect: "Aquí tomamos Las Vueltas. Aquí se respetó a la gente. Toda la gente que estaba, solamente al ejército se aniquiló. Y se respetaba a la gente." (Here we occupied Las Vueltas. People were respected here. Of all the people that were here, we only wiped out the army. And the people were respected.) Documents declassified through the National Security Archives mention the occupation of Las Vueltas in the early 1980s.[138] A March 1981 document noted, "The purposes of the occupations are to harangue and terrorize the townspeople, recruit new members, carry out selected assassinations of security officials and landowners, loot stores and destroy property."[139] A Department of State unclassified incoming telegram reviewed by R. Valas and dated October 14, 1982, reported, "Many heavily armed subversives yesterday attacked the town of Las Vueltas, Chalatenango Department, with light artillery. From several points around the town the extremists detonated six dynamite charges to terrorize the inhabitants, whom they ordered to leave their homes so that they might be occupied and the town turned into a guerrilla camp."[140]

Like Don Gilberto, the folks that I met across Chalatenango most often presented a radically different description than did this archive of declassified documents produced during the Cold War. For many Salvadorans, insurgency was an everyday kind of work, full of quotidian tasks described as *tareas*. In fact, Don Gilberto asked me to imagine it, to put myself in their shoes, to really think about if I had been in a "campamento de guerrilleros" (a guerrilla camp). For him, because of his already advanced age during the war, he wasn't asked to carry a rifle. Rather, he was involved in searching for supplies to maintain the guerrilla and in transporting goods—no easy task. He explained, "If they chose you and said, 'You, go and deliver this mail,' that was your task. There were thousands of tasks that the war demands. For example, *vaya*, here is someone who got shot, *un baleado*. You had to *echarlo al lomo y llevarlo a curar*, you had to throw him upon your back and take him to be healed. That was the task that had to be done." Reader, please hold onto this quote, for later.

Also among Don Gilberto's tasks was the making of explosives for bombs and mines. He didn't explain much about that work because after about an hour, the interview ended abruptly with several comments by him about the unexpected high cost of living in postwar times. I have tried to unpack if I said something to end the interview; did I offend in some way? Were there just too many memories excavated by an inexperienced anthropologist fumbling through ethical listening? Maybe. His daughter's narrative in chapter 3 may be a clue. Still, I need to own the raw space of that exchange. Don Gilberto concluded that despite the more than twenty years of war and the many that died, there was hope for the future "because God is all powerful, we liberated ourselves" (*como Dios es tan poderoso nos fuimos liberando*).

After my interview with Don Gilberto, his son-in-law, Nelson, requested to speak with me, also on record. He too wanted to teach me about life *before the official start of the war*. We had spoken many times starting in 1993 during my first visit to El Rancho. I had been tracking his growing business. Unlike the interview with Don Gilberto, our interview was scheduled and more formal. Nelson dressed up for the occasion in a pressed white long-sleeve shirt. As we sat in the main room of his home, he shushed his little ones who were standing nearby. One of his little girls sat on my lap. Like Don Gilberto, Nelson's narrative started before 1980. He located the before of war to the 1960s, to a slow, clandestine development of war, to a before of what would become the FMLN. He explained that back then, "No existía guerrilla todavía, así, conocida, pues, ¿verdad? Era una guerrilla que operaba con el nombre FPL." (The guerrilla didn't exist yet, well known, right? It was a guerrilla operating under the name FPL.)[141] He explained that first there were important early groups like the UTC and FECCAS,[142] followed by a consolidation of the Bloque Popular Revolucionario (the BPR)[143] and ultimately the armed guerrilla to contest the military's repression by presidents Colonel Arturo Armando Molina (1972–1977) and, subsequently, General Carlos Humberto Romero (1977–1979).[144]

Complementing Don Gilberto's historical analysis, Nelson provided a more detailed exposition of these organizations that by 1979 had formed *milicias populares*, or "grassroots militias," insurgents that "were inside the communities, personnel that was inside of *las bases*." I suppose that same declassified document from March 1981 corroborates:

> In mid-March 1980, the FPL was organizing and arming the Popular Liberation Militias (MPL). The FPL planned to use the MPLs as local security/defense units. By July 1980, MPL units were engaging in village raids. The FPL considers the MPL to be one of the three operational levels of the FAPL, the other two being the "guerrilla units" (FPL cadre), and "regular soldiers" (FAPL troops).[145]

Nelson located this past of early armed organizing in a geography and a protagonist generation (youth) that I was familiar with. He explained, "The community of El Jícaro had a base. The community of Los Calles was another base. There you would find the *masas populares* which was the population, children, women, the elderly. It was the youth that was mostly involved in the guerrilla and the *milicias—la juventud más se dedicaba a la guerrilla y a las milicias*. Young women also formed part of the militia. Those that formed part of the *masas* created barricades to stop vehicles."

Nelson participated in the first offensive in 1981; he called it "el primer levantamiento que es la insurrección del 10 de enero," and he explained that by then, years in, they had a "guerrilla preparada" (a prepared guerrilla) with weapons such as M16, Fales, G-13, carabines, pistols, and other kinds of ammunition of their own invention.¹⁴⁶ But before this, he clarified that the insurgent weapons were homemade, crafted out of their own Chalateco ingenuity—and entrepreneurship, I would add—for battle making. The list of homemade weapons is long, including *papas* (potatoes) and bombs made of sugar, soap, oil, and other things used to ignite. Papas were also filled with little stones that would explode when they hit the ground. They were tricky and dangerous, easily set off. Nelson explained that many "compañeros se jodían. Unos se volaban las manos" (comrades got screwed up. Some even lost their hands because the contact [he slapped his hands] was with the ground and that's how they exploded). "Entonces, se quitó eso." (So, they stopped with that.)

Other weapons included versions of Molotov cocktails and mines to destroy electrical towers and disrupt the Salvadoran economy. Nelson spent some time describing how with one mine they could recuperate close to ten rifles from the Salvadoran Armed Forces. Indeed, he detailed how important it was to confiscate weapons and how they came from the United States. He recalled the early specifics: "We got M16 and R15 [Remington]. *El ejército salía con la M16.* The army would patrol with M16s." But here comes the interesting part, the hidden part, a before that can come out only in the after—even this early after. After telling me about the confiscated M16s provided by the United States to the Salvadoran army, Nelson followed with the word *entonces*—translated as "and so, as a result, or because of." He said, "Entonces, nosotros tuvimos también una ayuda y ahí se compraron armas. Ahí se compraron el AK" (As a result we also received some help and that's when arms were bought. That's when the AKs were purchased). In my hours of tapes and transcribed material, had I missed this? Intentionally so? Was this the "help" that campesinos and campesinas linked to international solidarity movements had denied for years? To note is the passive voice of the sentence, the ambiguity of who bought the insurgent guns.

Though I appear surprised in the interview, I push a bit and ask where the money had come from to purchase the AK47s. Nelson responded, "Maybe it was from the very *solidaridad.* Entonces, viene la ayuda para ayudar a la misma guerra. No decir, compren armas, si no, pero como había la necesidad, de ahí mismo se agarró una parte para comprar armas. Y las guerrillas de otros países también colaboraron con nosotros." (So then comes the help for the war. It didn't come to say go buy arms, but because of the necessity, you took from that help to buy arms. And guerrillas from other countries also collaborated with us.) This blurring or ambiguity, this question or hierarchy about who can know what and when, is also a characteristic of a before. To note, by 1985 and 1986, according to Nelson, they were a "complete army" and felt strong. Indeed, that declassified document from 1981 kind of got it right: "The FPL reportedly has used rifles made in Czechoslovakia. It also fabricates homemade bombs."[147] Regarding finances, the document adds, "The FPL is a wealthy organization. It funds itself primarily from armed bank robberies and kidnappings."[148]

As we wrapped up the interview, Nelson discussed his approved temporary leave from the guerrilla—not desertion, he clarified, because that would have carried a death sentence, or what was called euphemistically or culturally coded as *ajustamiento* (adjustment). Nelson spent several months in the Honduran refugee camp in Mesa Grande to address an illness. The time in Mesa Grande prompted him to reflect on the difficulties of losing grassroots support, comprised of so many families with young children, the elderly, and the infirm. Reader, I ask you to hold onto these bodily (and psychological) vulnerabilities for just a little bit longer. We'll get to them in chapter 3. Regardless, the displacement to Mesa Grande was tough on the guerrilla, and he invoked all those same *tareas* mentioned by Don Gilberto. For instance, it was harder to get the tortillas to the *guerrilleros* and build those human and material barricades. He said that "the people were the mountain of the guerrilla," and that this was lost with the flights to refugee camps. For both *bandos*, or bands, as the FMLN and the Salvadoran Armed Forces continue to be referred to, the people as the sea or as the mountain were critical.

I want to disclose that at the time, I was troubled or maybe unsure about the interview. I write about that in my fieldnotes. I was already attuned to the everyday gendered conversations that emerged in development projects and contested the hegemonic and masculinist logics around military battles. I didn't know what to make of the long list of weaponry, just as I ultimately have never known how to share the nearly fifty recipes that I spent hours transcribing with Nelson's neighbor Kasandra. These are stories about war and survival, about guns—stealing them and buying them. It's about how we all perhaps tell our stories, our survival narratives. Battles for some, cooking for others.

Angel-Ajani's call for an ethical listening and Thomas's insistence on the politics of recognition push me to share these stories and those that follow with an openness to where they may lead us to imagine. I have shared with you these befores, quotidian, from everyday rural former revolutionaries, old and young, that we can read as either reframing historical time or reproducing an expected trope of insurgent grit and ingenuity. Don Gilberto and Nelson were for sure not at the peace-process negotiating table, but they do represent what historian Joaquín Chávez analyzes as the critical role campesinos played in the revolution—particularly in Chalatenango.[149] Sharing their stories leads to more questions. For example, what to make of the haunting honesty about civil society as the guerrilla's human barricade, the underbelly of that Cold War counterinsurgency logic? Because the vulnerable bodies of children of war were deployed both as shields and invoked as the raison d'être of the struggle for a just and hopeful future, the fruit of the revolution. Does this paradox embody a legacy of war? What does thinking across generations reveal about that search for a dignified life? Because there are memories here too—some would argue intergenerational trauma that underscores everyday life.[150]

POSTWAR BEFORES: THE 1990S AND THE 1.5 INSURGENT GENERATION

By the early 1990s communities like El Rancho were simply full of young people, infants through teens. The Salvadoran 2007 census, for example, indicated that the largest percentage of the nation's population consisted of 10–14-year-olds, a result of the spike in births from 1992–1997.[151]

Across the repopulated communities, little ones tagged along to their mothers' literacy workshops and to gender and development trainings. They were carried on hips, scolded for whining, given a soda and a piece of *pan dulce* as a special treat, or left at home to tend the fire and make the tortillas for their activist parents. When they were a little older, they attended local schools staffed by insurgent teachers who had won the hard battle for

FIGURE 5. Children in the afternoon, El Rancho, Chalatenango, 1997. Photograph by Antonio Rossi.

national accreditation. They were also the subject of much postwar development effort from an array of NGOs. Indeed, Plan Internacional was a longtime partner in the municipality of Las Vueltas and focused their solidarity and development work squarely on children.[152] In August 1997 I attended one of their many trainings and workshops. One was on water safety, latrine use, and garbage collection. Ten months into fieldwork, I was amazed by the large community attendance, given the diminishing number of participants at other more political and community organizing meetings.

The meeting took place in El Rancho's *Grupo Escolar*, a modest cinderblock three-room school complex painted an aqua blue. Improving children's health outcomes and decreasing parasitic illnesses and childhood diarrhea centered the workshop's agenda. These were everyday preventable childhood deaths. In 1990 the rate of infant death was 46.0 out of 1,000 live births. By 2013, this had declined to 10.2.[153] In any event, there was active participation by caregivers, mostly mothers, and the representative admonished, "When you leave this *charla* [talk or meeting], *que sean más conscientes*" (you should

FIGURE 6. Children waiting in the Grupo Escolar, El Rancho, Chalatenango, 1997. Photograph by Antonio Rossi.

be more aware). *Consciente* in this community harkened back to a militant wartime discourse of organizing and protest. Attendees were reminded to take care of their children by purifying *agua bastante mala* (bad water), and several mothers provided the correct strategies to deploy, from boiling water to putting twenty-five drops of bleach into a jug that could hold twenty-five bottles. Plan Internacional's regional representative reminded the audience that of course these jugs also had to be cleaned "por el bien de los niños porque ellos son los que más sufren" (for the good of the children because they are the ones that suffer the most). Caregivers agreed with this health regiment but admitted that sometimes they didn't have the money to buy bleach, sometimes they forgot to boil the water, and sometimes the little ones were just too fast and didn't wait for the purified water and drank straight from the (unpurified) tap. With the room packed, kids were clinging to the school's wire windows and looking in as day turned to dusk. On my way out, I walked by several little boys urinating directly into the gutters that surrounded the school's perimeter. So much for that latrine usage.

Reader, what's my point? As a category, the children of war and early postwar (again, what I'm calling the 1.5 insurgent generation) were key subjects of interest in the rebuilding of the nation. From access to standardized education, nutrition, and wellness programs to children's rights, they were also the indirect beneficiaries of development projects aimed at empowering, rehabilitating, and reintegrating their kin. Decades later, their political identities are of interest to academics, policy makers, and political parties alike, both in El Salvador and across Central America more broadly.[154] Decades later they are at the center of diasporic conversations regarding questions of memory and belonging. As Susan Bibler Coutin documents in her study of youth who migrated to the United States during the Salvadoran civil war, their practices of "re/membering" contest the rampant processes of "dismemberment" that emerge from "civil war, displacement, emigration, the denial of legal status, and removal."[155]

And so, although not the central focus of my original study, I was attuned to the topic of kids and youth as it would come up quite a bit in the everyday talk across El Rancho. When delegations traveled with more frequency across the municipality, several children could be mobilized as victims or survivors of the violence, orphaned or with shrapnel in their bodies. Indeed, critical human rights work has documented the horrific deaths and disappearance of children during military operations, evidenced in the groundbreaking work of organizations like Pro-Búsqueda.[156] Gloria, an NGO worker in Chalatenango explained it best to me. She was originally from the neighboring Department of Cabañas. When I asked her why she hadn't returned home after the war, she shared that while in part it was because she had followed a new partner to Chalatenango, it was also the weight of the past. Her first husband and infant son had been killed early in the war, in their home, by soldiers. She asked me to ponder, "Do you think I could go back there, to where my little baby was just learning to crawl?" For Gloria, the past was too full of memories, too full of death. "It's too painful. Better to start here," she said.

As my earlier work has shown, stories of survival were gendered, and many women contextualized their emergent transition into postwar lives through narratives about caregiving and their children. Many of these stories conveyed the horrors of *guindas* when mothers literally and figuratively carried the weight of their children. As one mother, Irma, explained to me, she had just given birth to her newborn, and her womb was still healing, still bleeding, still cramping. She had to leave the little ones, the pair (*la parejita*), the boy and the girl, with their sleek black hair and so-round faces, ashen from drop by drop of sugar water, by the side of the path, by that tree. Her husband scooped them up, one in each arm, dropping the cornmeal, the bit of tarp, the bag of beans. Father arms. She didn't know it at the time. It wouldn't have made a difference. But they lost not a child in the war and made more in postwar. Of those children, I know that Facundo is a man now. He was already a strapping teen in the late 1990s rumored for his virility. He left El Rancho for Maryland in the mid-2000s, raised a family *a la distancia*, lost a wife to illness, mourned his parents' death across borders, and sent money for the everyday-living kind of stuff and to buy land for his big entrepreneurial dreams of factories and fast food in his community. But I'm getting ahead of myself. More on after-stories in the book's last chapter.

My fieldnotes are full of references like these, that span memories, narratives, and participant observation of family life, with the 1.5 insurgent generation at the periphery. It's not like I missed these kids; remember the photograph request that I delivered to Elsy. And I wrote up rigorously detailed and descriptive fieldnotes that tried to get it all in (perhaps what Jackson would call ethnographic hubris). It's that my focus was on the "protagonists" of insurgency who were still being asked to mobilize and leverage their radical identities and histories for a society still to be made. When I did ask specific questions around generation, socialization, or memory practices (today we might say storytelling), about how Chalatecas and Chalatecos were teaching their kids about the war, about what had rooted their own original mobilizing, about their hopes and dreams, people's answers were often quite short and thin on detail. It was not a topic readily addressed, and I didn't push.

Sometimes mothers responded with comments about teaching their kids about FMLN loyalty—and I wonder if we can see the fruits of this political education in the consistent FMLN electoral victories in Las Vueltas. Other times, mothers shared that of course their children knew about the war; many had experienced it as infants, through what we would now theorize as embodied trauma. Because imagine it: reflect on what it could mean

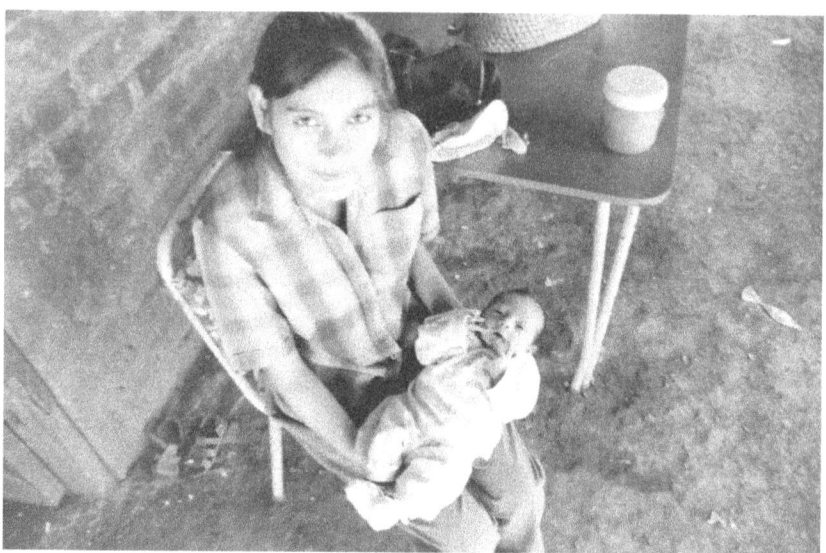

FIGURE 7. Infants of postwar, Chalatenango. Early 1990s. Photograph courtesy of the Sprenkels Melara family, © Ralph Sprenkels.

to be born during a five-day escape through the mountains, miraculously survive a fall, and slip out from under your mother's strong embrace, only to witness your grandmother's assassination by members of ORDEN (Organización Democrática Nacionalista, or Democratic Nationalist Organization), the paramilitary group often comprised of one's neighbors. In my fieldnotes, I summarized this war story and underscored how this mother juxtaposed her baby's experiences of suffering against his, at the time, preteen, war-free life. How in fact "he didn't remember anything" because he had been "tiernito" (a newborn), a "tenderling."

I think about stories like this one often, these experiences of violence and survival and the care of tenderlings. To note, the tenderling who fell through his mother's arms is now a local politician in Chalatenango, advocating for repopulated communities—still. I wonder what he would make of Nanita's folktales, those trickster characters and gender-bending thieves, in the context of Chalatenango's long history of battle that keeps unfolding.[157] He is for sure an example of the diversity of the 1.5 insurgent generation and that hope for a collective future that emerges from the experiences of "radicalized" youth who were socialized into, from, and out of an embodied experience of insurrection, flight, and peace building. He represents one of the *caras de la misma moneda* (the other side of the same coin), of diasporic 1.5 insurgent generational pathways. I end this first chapter that has walked us through different moments and my thinking on the *longue durée* of postwar by calling out attention to generational shifts, diasporic moves, anthropological responsibility, and a commitment to recognizing the power of people's narratives. These are threads that I'll pull on throughout the upcoming chapters. The next one will look specifically at a range of stories told through numbers, full of a politics of "statistical panic"[158] for El Salvador and beyond—what I'm calling *violencia encifrada*.

CHAPTER TWO

NUMBERS

THIS IS AN ETHNOGRAPHIC ACCOUNT of *violencia encifrada*, a concept that I coined to refer to a codified, encrypted violence made possible by numbers that are entangled with storytelling and memory.[1] This is a chapter on numbers but not a conventional one that seeks to prove or disprove numerical facts or do the crucial work of contextualizing statistical data or "making better numbers" that we all desperately need.[2] And so, I'm not making a claim to getting the numbers right. Instead, I want to look at how "the numbers" circulate in nonlinear, eruptive ways—often cherry-picked, decontextualized, and consumed by a range of audiences at different times—and how they come to hold the promise of "truths" about El Salvador. Numbers matter, and this chapter doesn't escape the partiality of the numbers or the hegemonic US-centric violence around them. While other people do in fact give other numbers and tell other stories about them and make powerful arguments about their validity,[3] I argue that numbers acquire an everyday weight that can terrorize, anesthetize, and inspire their producers and consumers as they reify the act of counting itself. Mine is an affective approach to numbers that I hope can lead us to a more radical sense of what counts that is grounded in everyday life. At times my intention is for us to feel that barrage of numbers that I have personally experienced as dizzying, overwhelming, and paralyzing but that pushes me to think and act in the service of solidarity. We'll begin by juxtaposing some often-circulated contemporary numbers, the stories about them, and the making of *violencia encifrada*.

During the summer of 2014, US president Barack Obama declared the unaccompanied border crossings of minors an "urgent humanitarian situation," as the number of detentions was dramatic and on the rise.[4] Indeed, Customs and Border Protection (CBP) of the Department of Homeland Security reported the capture of 68,541 unaccompanied minors in 2014, a 77 percent increase since 2013. Of these children, 75 percent were from what policy makers describe as the Northern Triangle—the Central American countries of El Salvador, Guatemala, and Honduras.[5] At the time, this was a breaking news story, one that we now know global reporting has continued to expose. But back then, for the first time in decades, news about El Salvador and its people entered the front pages of mainstream media, particularly in the United States. With this reporting came the televised images of disheveled, dirty, and panicked children warehoused in shelters. This image-making framed unaccompanied Central American youth, in part, within a conception of vulnerable humanity rooted in what Didier Fassin illuminates as the moral compass of our time.[6] For others, however, in the heated politics of immigration reform and border security, these same bodies were read within a continuum of dehumanizing illegality spawned both by neglectful, amoral parents—who allowed their children to travel alone despite the well-known dangers of the desert and the infamous cargo trains known as *La Bestia*, where they could be raped, trafficked for sex, kidnapped, and murdered—and by President Obama's compromised immigration reform of June 2012 for undocumented youth.[7] Deferred Action for Childhood Arrivals (DACA), which granted liminal legality and deportation relief to a generation of undocumented youth between the ages of sixteen and thirty, supposedly had opened the floodgates.[8] Data compiled by the US Citizenship and Immigration Services indicate that 18,700 Salvadoran youth received this status from August 2012 to September 2013.[9]

By the spring of 2015, another set of "alarming" numbers dominated the international public sphere. There were 635 homicides in El Salvador during May, 667 in June, and 911 in August.[10] Reports highlighted that these numbers marked a peak in the violence, the highest since the end of the Salvadoran armed conflict (1980–1992), with one murder every hour. At the time, analysts were consumed by these numbers, prognosticating that if the homicide rate continued at this rate it would exceed 90 per 100,000 people in 2015, the highest in the world.[11] Indeed, recent analyses indicate that there were 103 homicides per 100,000 people in 2015.[12] To analyze this surge of violence, significant discussion has focused on gang violence. Reports focused on how a truce between the leading gangs Mara Salvatrucha (MS-13) and Barrio 18 and former FMLN president Mauricio Funes's administration dramatically lowered the murder rate, which then only escalated when the truce failed.[13] Gangs have been compared to ISIS,[14] though less coverage exposes the hidden violence aimed at gangs perpetrated by El Salvador's police forces.[15] Overwhelmingly, accounts highlight the immediacy of everyday anger and insecurity felt by so many Salvadorans who see no solution outside of historically right-wing Mano Dura (Iron Fist) policies.[16] Unlike those unaccompanied minors, there is no humanitarian project here, though ample reporting clearly illuminates the forced conscription of minors into gangs throughout El Salvador.[17]

Reader, I've started off this chapter with two examples of how discussions about El Salvador often get filtered through numbers and are dominated by a torrent of numbers and how these quantifications tell some stories and not others. In part, I do so to invoke the words of anthropologist Laurence Ralph. Writing about police torture in Chicago, he reminds us, "The numbers themselves are astounding enough, but they offer only the surface of this horror."[18] Not being a numbers person, as I have often been told, when I first started analyzing "the numbers," I was drawn to Sujatha Fernandes's work on the emergence and rampant circulation of "curated stories"—that (re)packaging of storytelling in neoliberal times that masks deep inequalities and is so often leveraged for a Western public. Fernandes documents how storytelling gets "refashioned" and reduced for particular ends and with particular "predetermined storylines" that are often about the mobility of self-reliant, entrepreneurial subjects.[19] Fernandes is hopeful, though, about the possibility of recuperating practices of storytelling in which storytelling can be reclaimed, transgressive, and transformative.[20] For El Salvador, I argue that "the numbers" have become a key aspect of its curated story, both domestically and internationally, and that they too can mask inequalities and other forms of truth-telling—because the process of collecting numbers and curating them in narratives can separate them discursively from the very realities they are tethered to and change their meanings or what they claim to represent in infinitely reproducible ways.[21] They come to stand in for "El Salvador." Hegemonically, across perspectives, consistently, and resoundingly, El Salvador is numerically depicted as a contemporary, bloody, terrifying, and insecure place nearly three decades into the postwar period. Importantly, this chaos threatens to "leak" into the United States—those disheveled and panicked kids, in and out of cages, and the transnational gangs organizing crime and violence across borders.[22] In this chapter, my intention is for us to feel the sensorium of these numbers that the *violencia encifrada* produced and consumed. We'll be traveling together through some of these expected numbers, reading alongside them and against them, and always trying to keep up with the numbers, what they represent, and for whom.

I'm struck by how these embodied numbers juxtapose both numerical vulnerability and numerical violence. I'm also struck by how quickly numbers become dated. But some things appear to stay the same. The earlier numbers, for example, on migration, remain contextualized by a history of US nativist, xenophobic, racist, and white supremacist logics laid bare by the legal practices and policies that were explicitly forwarded by the Trump administration that have local and global consequences.[23] They persist, despite a change in the US presidency with the election of Joe Biden. What also doesn't change is a responsibility to keep up with the numbers and what they may elide and to hold at bay the systemic violence that reduces people and lives into numbers. Not keeping up with the meaning of numbers enacts an ontological privilege and an epistemic violence. I have the privilege and power to look away and to not count.[24] As anthropologist Diane Nelson reminds us, on the one hand, what roots all this counting is the question "whose lives 'count'—whose lives are meaningful and valuable?"[25] And on the other hand, we need to think about who gets to, "literally," count.[26]

This chapter will unfold, like the previous one, ethnographically and historically situated across times and places. Our aim will be to complicate the numbers and understand their agency and how they get deployed in stories about postwar life in El Salvador—because if numbers have become key to the cultural production of El Salvador's postwar subject, it's important to consider what anthropologist John L. Jackson Jr. describes as the always already racialized and embodied "overdetermined markers" that are deployed to tell a story.[27] Enumerated violence is an example of this "overdetermined marker" for Salvadoran postrevolutionary and postwar bodies. We'll start off by thinking along with Diane Nelson's theorizing on the accounting of genocide in Guatemala. With this framing, the chapter develops an argument around numbers in what I'm calling *violencia encifrada*—that relationship between storytelling, memory, and violence that is translated into or through numbers—codified, encoded, encrypted, enciphered.

Subsequent sections of the chapter build on my ethnographic research. We'll turn first to practices of radical counting in war and peace in Chalatenango. This will lead us into hegemonic tropes around reintegration and reconciliation that have always been about more than just the numbers. A third ethnographic section returns to where this chapter erupted—in the statistical panic felt across diasporic communities. Specifically, we'll explore quantitative data such as Salvadoran opinion polls about insecurity as well as the compiled record of deaths made available in an "atlas of violence."[28] Finally, we'll juxtapose these numbers against two singular stories, one from El Rancho and another from Los Angeles. These stories offer an alternate reading to *violencia encifrada* through an everyday of living through it. These are stories that (ac)count for violence *and* the paradoxical or unexpected spaces of forgiveness, still laden with brutality, impunity, and still without reconciliation.[29] Ultimately, we'll come to see how numbers flatten regional and local histories, erase both lived experience and larger geopolitical forces, are used to justify and produce new cycles of violence, and condemn a nation and a people for the production of just so many outlawed bodies. To counter,

I ask, what other narratives can be told about El Salvador's history of prolific and proliferating violence and insecurity? What else counts in postwar truth-telling?

KEEPING UP WITH THE NUMBERS

Reader, I'm not alone in arguing against a facile account(ing) of a Salvadoran culture of violence as a legacy of war.[30] I agree with leading scholars of peace building that contest this "cultural" framing and who instead urge us to consider the historical formation of state and society power relations that underscores the social reproduction of violence.[31] I also point to the very risks regarding enumeration and what, for example, the numbers of homicides can elide or conceal, such as "non-lethal violence" that we'll ethnographically explore at the close of this chapter.[32] Nelson's work on the "after-math," on the "mathematics of death and life after genocide" in Guatemala, proves instructive in reading El Salvador's curated story about the barrage of bloody numbers. Because, indeed, these numbers are everywhere. Nelson argues that they can do the work of generalizing, of equivalizing, of mapping out the relationship between the past and the future—like the exponential generational losses that come from a son's death or the unexpected gains in neoliberal times.[33]

In this way, counting can also be a moral act rooted in memory work. Nelson suggests that accounting and the making of an aggregate can create collectivities of strength as survivors demand accountability and justice for war crimes. Additionally, an aggregate can rehumanize and underscore the importance of a life, can make visible the particularity of the horrific loss of a loved one.[34] Of course, as many others have written, numbers can also dehumanize, alienate, anesthetize, stereotype, and reduce. They can be decontextualized or recontextualized to tell some stories and not others. And sometimes, in "Latin America, not all bodies are counted," as the ongoing reality of "disappearance" makes clear.[35] Indeed, a Human Rights Watch (HRW) report cites findings from the Inter-American Commission on Human Rights (IACHR): 3,289 people were "disappeared" in El Salvador in 2018, as were 3,030 in 2019.[36] El Salvador's National Civilian Police (PNC) force registered

10,800 disappearances from 2010 to August 2019, "more than the estimated 8,000 to 10,000 disappeared during the civil war (1979–1992)."[37] Thus, as Nelson offers, "numbers are deeply entangled in *both* violence and amazement, oppression *and* emancipation."[38] She offers that numbers have power—all this measuring in the aftermath of genocide aimed for the future that is everyday also can be qualitative, relational, embodied, and exchanged, can work for justice, and can be linked to historical memories.[39] *Violencia encifrada* accounts for these expansive qualities of numbers and the multiple ways that numeric power can be leveraged, not simply to horrify but also to demand recognition, particularly for historically disenfranchised groups faced with the possibility of obscurity, oblivion, and misrecognition. We can see this relationship between enumerated violence, vulnerability, and agency in our first ethnographic section in what I describe as Chalatenango's radical numbers.

RADICAL NUMBERS IN WAR AND POSTPEACE

In October 1997, Chayo served in leadership positions on various community committees. She was also raising three small children, maintaining a bustling and much-needed local store, attending her own seventh-grade classes, volunteering in her children's school to cook the government-funded lunch meal, and serving as El Rancho's community teacher for returning students—those teens and young adults whose education had been interrupted by the war. Since part of my doctoral research explored spaces of intersection between emerging national apparatuses and wartime popular organizing, I was thrilled when Chayo invited me to one of her classes. The rainy season was ending and so were the frequent and powerful afternoon and evening storms, although midway through the lesson it started to rain, and Chayo's oldest daughter brought her an umbrella. I wrote this down in my fieldnotes because at the time, most residents in El Rancho didn't have umbrellas. I also wrote this down because it showed the affective care in Chayo's family between mother and child and a respect for gendered, intellectual labor. In any event, Chayo's daughter joined for the rest of the lesson, sat down beside me, and did her own math homework. Twenty years later I would meet Chayo's daughter in New Jersey, a successful entrepreneur just like her mother.

That early evening, the *grupo escolar* was quiet and dim, with the recently installed electricity of bare lightbulbs that flickered on and off. Chayo's lesson was an intimate one; there were just two young male students on the cusp of adulthood. Both young men had been orphaned during the war. One had survived by feigning his death as he lay beside his dead mother and baby sister. Both also spent most of their day doing agricultural work, tilling others' fields for modest pay. They attended the lesson after a quick game of soccer in the school's adjacent small field.

As a diligent student, and, again, not a numbers person, I took copious notes during the lesson. It was on statistics. How did I miss this before?! Chayo explained that statistics can serve to tell us the meaning of a total and that statistics can be visualized through tables and bar graphs. Building on El Rancho's history of popular education in which instruction is predicated on a liberatory model that brings everyday realities and critiques to bear on each subject, Chayo's lesson plan focused on the number of daily cases of diarrhea seen at the municipal health clinic in Las Vueltas.[40] She disaggregated this data for each community within the municipality. It illuminated the power of numbers to speak truth to power, to reveal a public-health crisis with a liberatory and transformative agenda at its core. After attending her own morning class, Chayo explained to me that she had worked from 11:00 a.m. through 2:00 p.m. designing the session and mastering the concept. Here we have an answer to Nelson's invocation of who has the power to actually count.

Like Chayo's students, I worked with the table and bar graph titled "Datos estadísticos de casos atendidos por diarrea" (Statistical data on diarrhea-treated cases) that she had carefully crafted for the class. She explained the representation of maximum and minimum cases across the communities and asked the students to respond to a series of questions that interrogated the numbers. Chayo asked us what else the numbers could teach us. She ultimately asked her students to ponder what other issues could be read through numbers and to what end. I raise this ethnographic example among many that I could now offer about the place of numbers in the ordinary moments of postwar lives. I read them today as an urge to quantify, to reckon, and to settle the score.⁴¹ And I offer them also as part of a wartime continuum, in which numbers counted and were counted and could lead to significant ends—how many insurgents really were there in Chalatenango? How many women were recruited and became part of the rank and file? How many guns were confiscated? How many towns occupied? How many children kidnapped? How many killed during a massacre? How many green pants did Chayo's husband sew for the insurgency and hide in his home?

Writing for the *New York Times* in December 1985, journalist James LeMoyne offered an interesting clue about the everyday wartime survival and strategy predicated on numbers. Reporting on insurgent strategies, he writes:

> The subregional junta has a university-trained accountant, whose job is to travel the region with calculator and account books, estimating the size of the harvest and the needs of farmers in the new season.
>
> The accountant, who gave his name only as Eric, said the rebels depended on financial aid from rebel sympathizers in the United States and Europe to buy fertilizer and seeds each year to distribute to villages for planting.⁴²

This is not a banal entry. I want to read it as an example of *violencia encifrada* in which accounting predicated in rural lifeways has always been part of El Salvador's war stories. Mostly though, I am troubled by LeMoyne's mocking tone regarding the very category or possibility of a "rebel accountant," as if this is not a radical act, an insurgent count, or perhaps a pejorative wonder on who can count. Regardless, like the ethnographic vignette about Chayo's statistics lesson, LeMoyne's description illuminates the profound space of radical counting, of radical numbers, of numbers in the war ledger. In the postwar context I believe we can see the everyday power and legacy of a radical (ac)counting, with or without the "university-trained accountant."

Here's just one more example. During one of my very last bus rides from El Salvador to Chalatenango in late December 1997, my conversation was full of a counting up (and down). I traveled beside a woman from the capital of Chalatenango whom I had never met. She gave me her phone number, something that most folks didn't have at the time. Her narrative was full of an accounting, mostly a series of losses on a balance sheet that she quantified as "pérdidas." First her husband was *perdido*—but that wasn't such a loss given

FIGURE 8. Travel in Chalatenango, 1997. Photograph by Antonio Rossi.

that he was "un hombre malo" (a bad man) who had served in the Guardia Nacional during the war. Second, her daughter was *perdida*, by the guerrilleros who had taken her. She never saw her again. Third, her son was *perdido*; at twenty-six he had become *un marihuanero* (a pothead). I wondered if that was code for *marero* (gang member). I didn't ask. Two of her children had moved to Colorado. That's why she had given me her number. Perhaps I could take things for them.

In her measuring up, she placed the greatest hope on her seventeen-year-old daughter who was still living with her in Chalatenango and was graduating with her *bachillerato*, her high-school degree. My bus companion wondered if I knew how much it would cost to buy fifteen pieces of chicken from Pollo Campero—the Guatemalan national fast-food chain exceedingly popular in El Salvador and renowned for its delicious fried chicken that has only grown as an iconic symbol of transnational belonging[43] and the making of a "Salvadoran imaginary."[44] Her daughter's dream was to serve five hundred pieces of Pollo Campero at her graduation party. I apologized for not knowing the answer but could imagine the festive spectacle and sensorium of all that crispy chicken brought from San Salvador. During fourteen months of fieldwork in El Rancho, I knew of only a few families that had been able to buy this coveted meal, of no more than six pieces for sure. In the early to mid-1990s in El Rancho, there were still very few young people on their way to getting a *bachillerato*. More on that soon.

REINTEGRATION: PAST, PRESENT
AND BY THE NUMBERS

It's not a neat connection between rebel accountants, students counting cases of diarrhea, and a bus companion's desire for five hundred pieces of fried chicken, yet I see them all as intimately tethered to the contemporary challenges of reintegration in a postwar deterritorialized nation still characterized by impunity. This other-numbering of Chaltenango's radical count is grounded in everyday life, and I argue that it is also part and parcel of how we can think about a Salvadoran story. Because examples of Chalatenango's accounting link up to the early postwar period in which the search for economic justice—good, fair, equal, shared numbers along with a call for truth and accountability (for human rights abuses)—was eclipsed by a national plan and a local experience of postwar life as reconstruction: development as democracy, with the FMLN at the helm. Political power was seen as the key to peace building. In the *longue durée*, in the felt temporality of decades of postwar life, it is clear that the hegemonic model of reconstruction as peace building produced unintended consequences, with a nation territorially unmoored and still in search of truth, justice, and repair.

Recall that across El Salvador but especially in former war zones, the torrent of reconstruction aid was over by the late 1990s, and the global peace industry shifted to new sites.[45] With internationally funded projects dwindling, an agricultural economy marginalized, and a series of "natural disasters" having caused devastation,[46] ten years into the "transition" Chaltecos and Chaltecas began an unprecedented, mostly clandestine migration, or displacement, to the United States.[47] I highlight two things: (1) this migration was not the expected reintegration plan, and (2) we are back to the numbers and a compulsive counting. This compulsive counting brings with it promises about future interventions, subsequent evaluations, and enlightened decisions driven by longitudinal data sets that will materialize on the horizon. *Violencia encifrada* recognizes these implicit promises and draws attention to how the numbers can also become agents used to justify the terrorization and dehumanization of the very bodies being counted and measured. Here are a few thoughts on some numbers that entwine reintegration and migration, what I see as a characteristic of the *longue durée* of postwar life.

Estimates from 2017 underscored that 2.3 million Salvadorans live in the United States and send remittances home, keeping the nation afloat.[48] Indeed, the Pew Research Center states that "since 2000, the Salvadoran-origin population has increased 225%, growing from 711,000 to 2.3 million over the period. At the same time, the Salvadoran foreign-born population," all those migrants, "living in the U.S. grew by 142% from 539,000 in 2000 to 1.3 million in 2017."[49] Precarity roots these numbers. Estimates from 2012 to 2016 indicate 665,000 unauthorized Salvadoran migrants in the United States.[50] Comprehensive statistical reports by the Migration Policy Institute lay out further trends about migration. In FY 2014, the US CBP "apprehended more than 239,000 migrants from the Northern Triangle, a fivefold increase over FY 2010."[51] This was the first time that "non-Mexicans" were the majority captured. Although analysis of capture and deportation at the US and Mexican borders suggests that Salvadoran migration then slowed,[52] in FY 2018 the CPB "apprehended more than 38,000 unaccompanied children and nearly 104,000 people traveling as families from El Salvador, Guatemala, and Honduras at the U.S. Mexico border."[53]

Reader, we're back to the topic that opened up this chapter. By June 2019, CBP "apprehended more than 363,000 migrants traveling as families."[54] An HRW report contextualizes that between 2009 and 2019 the United States apprehended 557,000 Salvadorans, while Mexican authorities apprehended 175,000.[55] Across the globe, media coverage focused on the phenomena of "Central American Caravans" and the multipronged attacks by the administration of then US president Trump on immigration policies, including a desire to dismantle asylum.[56] In this equation, Mexico, led by President Andrés Manuel López Obrador, effectively became the new border, or as some stated, "Trump's wall," enacting the US administration's punitive immigration policies.[57] In the first seven months of fiscal 2019, apprehensions in Mexico increased by 32 percent in comparison with the previous year. Thus, 10,000 Salvadorans were apprehended in Mexico from January to July 2019.[58] Multiple sources also reference the 26,000 Salvadorans with DACA who are at risk with the threat to the program[59] and another 195,000 Salvadorans with TPS who were also targeted by the Trump regime's immigration policies.[60] On February 6, 2021, the Biden administration announced the immediate suspension of these asylum agreements and began processes to terminate them.[61]

Regardless of legal status, Salvadorans in the United States have been critical in maintaining El Salvador's national and local economies through their remittances. As a UNDP country report makes clear, the municipality of Las Vueltas was altered by this new migration that erupted between 2001 and 2004; it was a response to a crisis in the agricultural sector[62] and ultimately a product of the violence of neoliberal economic policies already underway before the peace accords.[63] The numbers keep climbing. El Salvador received $5 billion in remittances in 2017,[64] and $5.7 billion in remittances in 2019, comprising 21 percent of El Salvador's GDP.[65] As research has now long shown, migration has become a key aspect of El Salvador's national development plan.[66] But the everyday narratives and testimonies of former insurgents from Chalatenango clearly indicate that emigration was not an aspiration of war, of postwar life, or of securing justice and equality. It was not an anticipated path for reintegration. We can read these moves as another iteration of a history of violent displacement, or as others remark, migration as a political act.[67]

These numbers travel. They hold an urgency, a life-and-death empiricism that map out a cartography, or geography, of violence.[68] Just in the numbers intentionally selected and cited earlier, we can see that Salvadoran, Mexican, and US government institutions are tasked with quantifying crossings. And in response, a range of domestic and international migration policy institutes, humanitarian organizations, and human rights groups react to these official counts. We see this in the ample news reporting that has exposed the human rights atrocity of family separation policies and of "kids in cages"—perhaps not the foreseen humanitarian outcome first noted by President Obama—and that has launched both quantitative and qualitative human rights work and calls for action that target the US carceral, capitalist detention system.[69]

Indeed, Amnesty International went to great lengths to access the official numbers and reported that in 2017 and 2018, the Trump administration separated approximately 8,000 family units.[70] The Southern Poverty Law Center created a timeline of the Trump administration's family separation policies that continued despite the June 20, 2018, executive order that instructed the Department of Homeland Security (DHS) to end them.[71]

All these embodied numbers and circulations that I've introduced push us to think through the ongoing politics of reintegration predicated on that promise of the count. This is a reintegration now multiple temporal and political administrative waves in, from the early United Nations–brokered laying down of guns discussed in chapter 1 to the historic FMLN presidencies to the (violent) quarantining of deported Salvadorans amid a global COVID-19 pandemic under Salvadoran president Nayib Bukele.[72] What I mean is that there are new calls in El Salvador's postpeace to "reintegrate" citizens into the nation—a rhetorical and practical move from wartime *guerrilleros* to postwar returning migrants. For example, by 2015, a new politics of *reinserción*, or "reintegration," was aimed at a different generation of outlawed bodies—Salvadorans deported from the United States, or "removed," as discursively constructed by DHS.[73]

In El Salvador this population is known as *los retornados*, "the returned." As the director of the Dirección General de Migración y Extranjería stated on its Salvadoran government website in 2015, the work ahead involved facilitating deportees' reintegration "to work so that the returned understand our economic environment so that we can facilitate their reintegration. We are in a very different context than what they had in the United States. That requires an adaptation."[74] Early ethnographic research with *retornados* in the municipality of Las Vueltas indeed pointed to the diversity of their experiences and the difficulty of "integrating" often urban, service-sector skills—for example, those of a bartender in downtown Washington, DC—into the rural spatial and temporal geography.[75] For now, let's note that there are multiple ways to count, such as by apprehension, detention, and categories of removal. Recent numbers from ICE (Immigration and Customs Enforcement) on removals by country of citizenship indicate that 15,445 Salvadorans were removed in FY 2018, and 18,981 in FY 2019.[76] The count is consistent.

This "deportation regime,"[77] and the making of "deportability,"[78] was concretized through the 1996 passage of the Illegal Immigration Reform and Immigration Control Act (IIRIRA), which dramatically increased deportations to Mexico and Central America. By 1999, the numbers had tripled (from 1995) to 180,101 people deported.[79] With the post-9/11 reorganization of the immigration apparatus in 2003 to DHS, "deportations became a primary objective of the new bureau of Immigration and Customs Enforcement (ICE). Deportations underwent a quantum jump under the administration of ICE and reached 438,421 in 2013."[80] From 2014 to 2018, "the U.S. and Mexico [deported] about 213,000 Salvadorans (102,000 from Mexico and 111,000 from the United States)."[81] And according to another set of numbers, 26,479 people were returned to El Salvador in 2018.[82] More numbers. The International Organization for Migration (OIM) announced that 32,705 persons were returned to El Salvador from January to October 2019. The majority of those people reported that economic factors, insecurity, and family reunification had motivated their original migration.[83] Disaggregating for age and gender, scholars show that 55 percent of deportations to El Salvador were young adults between ages 18–30 in 2014.[84]

HRW further contextualizes that approximately 900,000 Salvadorans live in the United States with either legal precarity (temporary status) or "without papers." This population, along with the thousands still attempting to cross into the United States, live with an everyday risk of deportation.[85] HRW's *Deported to Danger* states its thesis in the very title of the report. Through a systematic analysis of 138 cases of death after deportation and more than 70 cases of sexual violence, the organization's findings illuminate the violence that awaits deportees, the very condition from which most were escaping.[86] It is in this context that the call for *reinserción* continues and is bureaucratized through various efforts that officially call for the inclusion of "connacionales."[87] For example, on the Ministry for External Relations of El Salvador website, services include "the economic and psychosocial reintegration of people returned to El Salvador,"[88] which benefited 147 "returned migrants" through microenterprise projects and psychosocial support. The aim is one of (re)incorporation and also to "avoid a possible re-migration."[89] We can't escape these numbers, although now they are qualified by attention to mental health—an aspect woefully absent in the transition to postpeace.

My interest in a politics of an affective or radical count asks us to pause and take in the workings of this *violencia encifrada*, with all of its abstraction and disembodied numbering that simultaneously inundates us with what we are supposed to "know" about what is happening in El Salvador. You may feel anesthetized to (or through) these numbers, but let's keep asking if we can deploy them to tell a more humanizing story that links a before and an after, because these numbers can help us to think about reintegration from the arc of early postwar through the current deportation regime.[90] We could look at some of the reintegration numbers of former combatants that took place in the early 1990s. There was anxiety surrounding these numbers at the time as well. Demobilization figures indicate that 15,009 FMLN combatants and political cadre demobilized with the peace accords, as did more than 20,000 from various units of the Salvadoran Armed Forces (FAES), with a total of around 40,000 people demobilized across both forces.[91] Analyst Alexander Segovia situates these numbers by noting that of the demobilized, many joined the new PNC.[92] The security apparatus was already being mapped out amid the recognition and contestation of the violence of wartime numbers.

As the United Nations' Truth Commission report announced to the world, of the twenty-two thousand investigated cases of human rights violations, 85 percent were attributed to FAES and to paramilitary groups and death squads clearly linked to the state. Ten percent were attributed to unknown perpetrators. Five percent were attributed to the FMLN forces. Amelia Hoover Green's work in *The Commander's Dilemma* helps to explain these figures through her analysis of "repertoires of violence . . . , the forms of violence frequently used by an actor, and their relative proportions."[93] She unpacks the data around the low levels of FMLN violence (including sexual violence) and is most interested in illuminating what she unmasks as the "Commander's Dilemma," the ability to not lose a war through commanding "restrained" violence.[94] Through a study of the institutional biographies of wartime armed groups, she demonstrates how the FMLN's political education kept insurgents from committing atrocities against noncombatants.[95] She's got the numbers to prove it.

On the heels of the publication of the Truth Commission report that disclosed these numbers, a General Amnesty Law was passed in March 1993 that prevented investigations and prosecutions of war crimes and shielded those involved in crimes against humanity (on the Right and Left) during the war. Thus, a window was dramatically closed in the search for truth and justice and for redress, and instead a path was charted for institutionalizing impunity. The hegemonic Salvadoran national discourse emphasized that it was critical to forget the war, to forget the past violence in order to move beyond it and to forgive and reconcile the nation, because remembering the bloodshed would create festering wounds and deepen a polarized political field, the body politic toxic. As Sprenkels reminds us, the amnesty law benefited not only the leadership on the right and the FMLN but also the human rights organizations that were historically closely aligned with the FMLN.[96]

Across sectors in El Salvador and internationally, though, the pressure mounted to remove the amnesty law,[97] from the Spanish National Court's pursuit of justice in the Jesuit Massacre case[98] to then FMLN president Mauricio Funes's public apology for the El Mozote Massacre and the acknowledgment that the military committed serious human rights violations[99] to the July 2016 Constitutional Chamber of the Supreme Court's ruling that the amnesty law was unconstitutional. This opened a legal path for the investigation and prosecution of major human rights abuses during the civil war, as exemplified in the case of "Proceso Penal 238/1990," known as "Masacre El Mozote y lugares aledaños" at the Juzgado Segundo de Primera Instancia de San Francisco Gotera by Judge Jorge Guzmán Urquilla.[100] Still, in El Salvador the majority of perpetrators have not been prosecuted, reparations programs have not been institutionalized, and many argue that there is no justice.[101] The long fight to end impunity continues. In February 2020, the Salvadoran Legislative Assembly approved a controversial new law, the Law for Transitional Justice, Reparation, and National Reconciliation. Human rights organizations vehemently contested this law, characterizing it as a "de facto amnesty" that seals impunity.[102] Thus, we can see, as provocatively suggested by historians Rey Tristán and Lazo, that reintegration takes shape through "el modelo de 'reconciliación' vía impunidad" (a model of reconciliation via impunity) that spawns "una reconciliación sin reconciliados" (a reconciliation without the reconciled).¹⁰³ This framing is extremely compelling. I wonder if the numbers support this story—those insurgent numbers that defy an easy reintegration so many decades after. What does it mean to have reconciliation without the reconciled?

INSECURITY IN THE LONG POSTWAR PERIOD

One way to think through this question is to analyze Salvadoran public opinion polls about violence, policy research on the "prevention of violence," and census data on violent deaths. These are among the most obvious examples of *violencia encifrada*, numbers about terror that also terrorize, numbers about death that are used to justify killing. As the internationally recognized Instituto de Derechos Humanos of the Universidad Centroamericana José Simeón Cañas (IDHUCA) explained in one of their analyses, "Prevention is always better than to cure; when the disease is present—in this case, violence—it should also be addressed so that preventive measures are able to reduce or eliminate the risk of the appearance of violent events."¹⁰⁴ What interests me most about this opening passage is the metaphor of the diseased nation to be cured—in part, the report suggests, by the government's "strong political will" to combat the multiple causes of delinquency. A diseased nation comprised of delinquents and the wartime unreconciled? We'll look specifically at metaphors around injured bodies in the next chapter but for now we'll focus on the numbers.

It is true that violence has been rampant in El Salvador, ranging from everyday extortion in neighborhoods to assassinations and gender-based violence to the assault of local buses.¹⁰⁵ The response has been decades of zero-tolerance anti-gang laws in El Salvador known as Iron Fist policies: Mano Dura, which was passed in 1993, and Super Mano Dura, passed in 2004. Both of these pieces of legislation consolidated the ARENA party's political power and left the underlying causes of gang memberships untouched.¹⁰⁶ Critical scholarship continues to expose the deep contradictions and unexpected consequences across political parties of these security policies, including former president Salvador Sánchez Cerén's "Plan El Salvador Seguro"¹⁰⁷ and the extension of "extraordinary measures"¹⁰⁸ through what President Bukele calls the Territorial Control Plan.¹⁰⁹ We now know that restriction on the rights of suspected criminals made gang membership illegal, compromised fair trials, and dramatically, in a reversal of the peace accords, introduced the military into everyday policing.[110] As a result, between 2004 and 2005, of the fourteen thousand Salvadoran youth arrested, ten thousand were released. Shouldn't we be highlighting those numbers? Reports indicated that it was during their incarceration that youths were subsequently recruited into gangs.[111] And while homicides decreased during a controversial truce between gangs and the Salvadoran government led by Mauricio Funes, the homicide rate has consistently remained at what the World Health Organization terms epidemic levels.[112] It is the violence committed by gangs (for example, the PNC reported the figure of 60 percent in 2015) that is the curated story—that embodied, enciphered marker of what we think we know about El Salvador.[113]

According to sociologist Steven Osuna, anti-gang security discourses and apparatuses and transnational moral panic entwine neoliberalism and the militarization of the police. It is the global capitalist economy that propels the panic around deported youth who are the "relative surplus population that ruling elites, through the capitalist state, must regulate and control."[114] We have seen this clearly during the COVID-19 pandemic through an array of President Bukele's announcements, often via tweets. On the one hand, almost daily, Bukele has broadcast coronavirus statistics such as tests administered, cases confirmed, quarantines and releases, deaths, and so on (fig. 9).[115]

On the other hand, as much human rights and media reporting has noted, Bukele deployed the COVID-19 pandemic to increase authoritarian practices by criminalizing and jailing quarantine violators and authorizing the police and military in their use of lethal force against them.[116] Indeed, Bukele showcased the violent performativity of his regime through the global circulation of a photograph of imprisoned gang members in the Izalco prison—they were all men, tattooed and not socially distanced, row upon row of bowed heads, spread-apart legs, and sexualized bodies pressed up against one another. The sheer number of their bodies does the epistemic work of Foucauldian control.[117] As Osuna writes, the "*marero* has become a hegemonic interpretation of the violence in the country"[118] and, I would add, a marker of *violencia encifrada*—massified bodies codifying past and present violence, because

FIGURE 9. Tweeting official numbers.

the photograph was taken following the highest homicide rate observed under Bukele's administration (seventy-seven murders between April 2–27, 2020).[119] This spike in homicides circulated in the media and arguably provoked Bukele's authoritarian act. It was a numeric trigger for the story of state violence in the name of security.

Reader, some would argue that I'm writing outside of my scholarly expertise and that I should leave the numbers to the experts—and I point to their work (that of, for example, José Miguel Cruz, Pamela Ruiz, and Roberto Valencia and the work of Sala Negra of El Faro) throughout this chapter. I respect this critique, but I am a consumer of this data like so many of us, and perhaps you, like me, have questions about these quantitative estimates, the validity of these numbers, and the accuracy of these estimates.[120] In El Salvador, one could posit that the state's infrastructure for exercising due diligence in an investigation of homicides is lacking and outpaced by the desire to count and analyze. The numbers are being fetishized despite serious questions about their validity. Counting is happening on top of poor infrastructure.

To support this argument, I point to the work coming out of the Universidad Centroamericana José Simeón Cañas's (UCA) Maestría en Estadística Aplicada a la Investigación, which produced its first graduating cohort in 2016.[121] A collaborative thesis by Mendoza Posada, Orellana Herrera, and Pocasangre Portillo homed in on homicide rates in El Salvador using mixed-effects models for longitudinal data.[122] Working with data provided by the attorney general's office (Físcalia General de la República),[123] they uncovered a curious finding: the homicide rate in San Salvador systematically decreased during electoral periods. In other words, if the numbers are valid, they tell us that you can decrease homicides in San Salvador by having an election. Obviously, the real question is why this happens. Are corrupt politicians paying off gangs around the time of an election? Are politicians telling police to stop counting? Are the numbers being manipulated for good public relations after they are being collected? Either way, the finding points to how the number is produced in the first place. It leads to basic questions surrounding the accuracy of the estimates, which undermines the validity of the homicide numbers themselves.[124]

This conversation on numbers is explicitly linked to an everyday of insecurity that negotiates ideas around a Salvadoran culture of violence or "culture of democracy."[125] And there are public opinion polls that explore precisely these experiences of insecurity.[126] For example, Córdova Macías, Cruz, and Seligson's analysis of 2013 public opinion polls indicate that political tolerance (seen as a sign of a healthy democracy) was lower that year than in 2004 and that Salvadorans listed insecurity as one of the key fundamental problems across the nation.[127] Researchers based at Fundaungo[128] have followed up with a series of studies on crime and violence that continue to produce a biopolitical population through this reporting. The numbers are, again, dramatic in terms of pointing to the degree of people's everyday concerns. For example, 52.5 percent of Salvadorans in one study reported that violence and delinquency are at the heart of national problems. Six out of ten Salvadorans stated that crime was the country's main problem.[129]

Disaggregating this opinion poll data is crucial. For instance, the study further points to a rural-urban divide. While the problematics associated with violence are noted as the primary factor generating insecurity in urban areas, it is the economy that is perceived as key to people's everyday insecurity for Salvadorans in the rural countryside.[130] This supports my ethnographic findings on the unanticipated obligation of migration for so many of the Chalatecos and Chalatecas I have interviewed. People's perception of insecurity also appears to be strongly linked to their feelings of confidence in various institutions. Thus, whereas 81 percent of the Salvadorans interviewed felt the highest level of confidence in churches, followed by the Instituto Salvadoreña para el Desarrollo de la Mujer (73 percent—a striking number—perhaps indicating success in gendered issues), they were least confident in those institutions actually charged with ensuring citizen security (in other words, the Policía Nacional Civil at 61.4 percent, the Corte Suprema de Justicia at 61.6 percent, and the Central Government at 61.2 percent).[131]

The *Atlas de Violencia en El Salvador (2009–2012)*, the third atlas produced since the turn of the twenty-first century, yields some striking data. The *Atlas*, a collection of tables, charts, and glossy colored maps rigorously compiled from a range of national sources, provides a detailed statistical breakdown of homicides at the national, departmental, and municipal levels.[132] Accordingly, we know nationally that in 2011 and 2012 the most vulnerable age group was 15–19. This age group constituted 20 percent of the nation's homicides in 2011, followed by youth between the ages of 20–24, comprising 19 percent. In 2011 and 2012, people in the 25–29 and 30–34 age groups each comprised 14 percent of homicides.[133] A recent 2019 fact sheet produced by Fundaungo provides a similar finding, significant in its pattern of lethal violence. On average, from 2012 to 2018, youth between the ages of 15 and 29 constituted 52.4 percent of homicides, and people between the ages of 30–59 made up 41.8 percent of homicides.[134] In the *Atlas* gendered data is also available, although no substantial analysis follows regarding femicide.[135] Comparative departmental data is available as well.[136]

I see these charts as instructive in their work of documenting and representing El Salvador. They can push us to ask questions about the geographies of postwar violence. For example, why is it that Morazán and Chalatenango, two departments that compete in ranking for poverty, marginalization, destruction from war, and war organization (Morazán via the ERP [Ejército Revolucionario del Pueblo/People's Revolutionary Army] and Chalatenango as FPL), have the least number of homicides, ranking thirteenth and fourteenth respectively?[137] Is organizational capacity, despite disillusionment, a contributing factor? Is it a legacy of Hoover Green's statistical analysis and institutional biographies regarding the key role of political education for the FPL and ERP insurgent political-military organizations? Are we back to asking who is counting and what are the resources available to count? Is it, as Garni and Weyher suggest in their comparative study of two Salvadoran towns, that it is the "kind" of experiences of wartime violence that matter? They offer that "direct" wartime violence leads to more cohesion in the postwar period.[138] These experiences, they theorize, can confront the violent, individualizing processes of neoliberalism, the "estrangement" that casts violence in the bodies of individuals rather than in "situations."[139] This ranking remains consistent when we disaggregate for gendered data. Women were killed proportionately less in Chalatenango and Morazán. In 2012 in Chalatenango, 3.7 women were killed out of 100,000 inhabitants, compared to 16.7 per 100,000 in San Vicente (the highest in the nation).[140] After a peak in homicides in 2010, there was a steady decline in Chalatenango.[141]

The *Atlas* also provides further breakdowns for each department, tracking homicides at the municipal level from 2009 to 2012.[142] These are the local numbers that I'm interested in. In both the *Atlas* and the 2019 updated fact sheet, analysis of this data indicates that former organized conflict zones, the repopulated communities at the heart of much theorizing on the war and the postwar period, have remarkably low homicide rates. For instance, the oft-touted model insurgent municipality of Las Flores had no recorded murders from 2009 to 2018.[143] Compare this to the region of Nueva Concepción, which had the highest murder rate in Chalatenango[144] and is known as a key narcotrafficking route (*el caminito*). In the municipality of Las Vueltas, where I conducted my research, no one was killed in 2009, 2010, or 2011, according to the *Atlas*, although one person was killed in 2012.[145] I've reviewed my fieldnotes and my personal communication with families in Las Vueltas and El Rancho but never learned who was killed. But I did piece together a hazy story about the near murder of a former insurgent. Like so many, his story and that of his kin don't quite fit the numbers outlined in this chapter. He was "lucky" in that he did not become a statistic in the *Atlas* and survived a coma. As his rumored story reveals, he embodies the entanglements of victim, perpetrator, past, and present in the interstices of insecure Salvadoran spaces. I'll end the chapter with a few ethnographic stories that reveal spaces of hope within *violencia encifrada*.

ESMERALDA AFTER WAR

In February 2012 I returned to Chalatenango and engaged in follow-up visits with many women and men I had not seen in fifteen years—though in many cases I had met their kin in the United States. A significant number of women were still single heads of household; others had left their partners or had been left by them because of migration. For instance, Esmeralda was in a new home, displaced from her former house and plot of land when she left her husband, a local *curandero* (folk healer). I'll call him Julio. She told me he had gone crazy again, from war and from drink. There were just too many beatings. I was unclear if she meant hers, or his from the war. Esmeralda had given birth to many children, all of them with deep, almond-shaped, wide-set eyes, just like hers. The youngest was cognitively disabled and motor impaired, and really, no longer very small. When I stopped by Esmeralda's home, he was at the center of social and familial life, sitting in a hammock between two sisters. Esmeralda has nurtured ten children. Remarkably, none died during the war or during infancy. Many of her adult children live in the United States. I saw her eldest last when he was twelve, a wiry, strong little boy working his father's carpentry wheel. He is a man now, in Kentucky of all places. Esmeralda's third child, Raquel, her first girl, had a six-month-old baby boy who was round faced and had a hearty cry. As we visited, she asked my advice about when it would be best to cross the border with her baby. With the infant's father already in the United States, she surmised it was only a matter of time before the relationship ended. "When would it be best to cross?" she asked. She had heard that when infants turn one, border crossings separate mother and child. Younger infants can travel with the mother but are heavily sedated, limp and loose on their sides. Years later, knowing what we know about increased repression and migration under Trump's regime, her question is more prescient than ever.

I don't know if Raquel crossed alone or with her baby. We lost touch along the way, through the years. I did learn about Raquel's father, however, a local *curandero*, carpenter, and artist whose vibrant paintings on smoothed slabs of wood depict military attacks against rural communities. Like others, he produced these in the early 1990s for the wave of postwar solidarity delegations in search of recently retired revolutionaries. His art still graces my office wall.

But news in the diaspora travels. Only six months after my return trip to Chalatenango in 2012, when I was conducting ethnographic research in a diasporic community in New Jersey, stories about Julio emerged. Rumor had it that Julio was consorting with some questionable new residents in El Rancho—not really maras, but this too was unclear. A former neighbor, now living in New Jersey, had heard that Esmeralda had kicked Julio out of their home. According to the narrative, he was seeking revenge and planned to kidnap her for ransom. While extortion is common across El Salvador, it appeared to be much less prevalent in repopulated communities.[146] As the story goes, Julio had planned the kidnapping with some local youth and "unos muchachos Hondureños" (there is some reporting of illicit movement of Hondurans escaping the law into this region of Chalatenango).[147] Rather than capture Esmeralda, however, the "muchachos" (also a term used to denote the insurgents of the past) turned on Julio and brutally assaulted him with knives, leaving him for dead in a pit originally dug for his wife. At least, that's the rumor.[148] A farmer discovered Julio on his way to his own field. After months in a coma in the department hospital, Julio was released, minus one eye.

Reader, I keep returning to the archive of photographs I have, a duplicate of all those photographs that I took of and for families in the 1990s. I have many photographs of Julio and his sons laboring, of Julio and his wife, of all his children. I search through them, excavating this unanticipated future of Julio's injured body and fractured home. I suggest that Julio's circulated story of near death embodies those always already overdetermined markers that do the cultural work of packaging El Salvador as simultaneously violent and vulnerable, comprised of massified bodies to be contained and disciplined at borders and checkpoints or counted in atlases of the dead. As Michael Taussig offers, "Sometimes when you write fieldnotes time stands still and an image takes its place."[149] Although Taussig does not suggest an analytic paralysis, that is a concern. For there are so many halting images of the postwar period: migrants' desolate homes in El Rancho that cost over $35,000 to build and that are vacant because unauthorized migrants can't return, and Julio, as I imagine him, one-eyed and crazy (*enloquecido*) and without kin, his severely impaired son laying on a hammock rocked by his mother.

Julio's story of postwar, nonlethal violence doesn't fit so neatly into the rubrics that quantify and seek to measure how, where, and why people feel insecure or what deaths and near deaths matter. Why did this story—true, fictional, or, more than likely, somewhere in between—move across borders, through former kin and neighborhood ties? Was it a story about "everyday insecurity"? Perhaps. As Ellen Moodie's work has long shown, it's not necessarily people's direct experience with crime or the truth about the alarming numbers that matters; it's about the stories that circulate and what they do—the uncertainty and not knowing that create patterns of insecurity.[150] Anthropologist Daniel Goldstein, writing about Bolivia, suggests that people "occupy a habitus of fear and uncertainty that is at once social, psychological and material," and in which insecurity is "a sense that the world is unpredictable, out of control, and inherently dangerous, and that within this chaos the individual must struggle desperately just to survive."[151] As a result, a citizen security constructs naturalized evil criminals and delinquents to be cleansed.

Ethnography can help us theorize Salvadorans' insecure and precarious lives and link the interpersonal and the structural. As Goldstein observes, we can understand the "disposition of the neoliberal subject in this security society" as "one of perpetual alertness" in which citizens are always on guard, ready for emergencies and for threats around every literal and figurative bend.[152] For the variously positioned protagonists of the Salvadoran struggle, I wonder if we also need to think about embodied experiences of agentive alertness. Here I am thinking of postcolonial theorist Frantz Fanon's discussion in which "the colonized subject is constantly on his guard. . . . The muscles of the colonized are always tensed. It is not that he is anxious or terrorized, but he is always ready to change his role as game for that of hunter."[153]

For the Chalateco and Chalateca self-identified revolutionary combatant and supporter, this alertness was linked to a revolutionary security—a security of territory, a control over geographical perimeters—areas counted. The securing of insurgent spaces was scaled up by the disciplining and regulating of obedient bodies. These bodies were indeed targets of violence but also agentive actors. This is a key tension that in turn raises questions around the legacy of postwar violence. What happens to obedient bodies in disobedient times? In a context of reconciliation without the reconciled, are there spaces to contest embodied insecurity across generations and geographies?[154] Below, I answer with a cautious "yes." Reader, we are wrapping up this chapter on arguably ominous numbers with a story of a family numbered at four, five, or six, depending on how you count and depending on who counts.

IN THE AFTER

Maybe it's just one more migrant story, a counternarrative to precarity, insecurity, and injustice as lived through the frictions of postwar life.[155] I offer it from my complicated work and friendship with Salvadorans in the diaspora,[156] where I am struck by the everyday intimate negotiations that unexpectedly rub against the profound lack of accountability in postwar life. This is the everyday of the unreconciled who reterritorialize reconciliation through *practices of forgiveness*, without justice, in the aftermath of war.[157] These practices of forgiveness take place in the apertures of daily life, across generations and across polarized political fields of the past. These practices trouble the insecurity that structures transmigrant's lives—all those numbers referenced earlier. They also link up to Ruth Elizabeth Velásquez Estrada's work on the "practices of coexistence" in El Salvador in which ex-combatants contest state-led definitions of "reconciliation" and offer instead "grassroots alternatives for peaceful coexistence."[158] This is a "convivencia" that marks postwar efforts to "reconstruct social networks."[159]

So, shortly after my time in El Rancho and Las Vueltas, I traveled to Los Angeles, where I visited Flor, who I had first met in Chalatenango when she was nine years old. I have written about Flor in the past because she blazed the trail for her family, as now all of her siblings live in the United States—some faring better than others. I have written about how her life trajectory embodies waves of clandestinity, from being a child of the FMLN to her unauthorized migration—agentive yet pained in the chronic unfolding of her multiple losses, from the death of her insurgent father to the violent death of her firstborn son when she was only sixteen; a stray bullet killed him during a gang-related bus holdup.[160] I have also discussed Flor's "transborder mothering,"[161] as she has been separated for more than ten years from her now teen boy in El Salvador because of her inability to return home. In the meantime, Flor has built a home in California, created ritual kinship ties within the diasporic Salvadoran community, and given birth to two US-born children, although their father was later deported.

From Flor's vulnerable space, it may be the configurations of ritual kin that have provided respite from insecurity. During our visit, as I shared with Flor photographs (that she had already seen posted on Facebook) of her son's birthday party, which I had attended during my time in El Salvador, I was struck by an unexpected and hopeful story made possible through migration. Like so many Salvadorans, Flor and her partner worked multiple jobs and long hours. We spent quite a bit of time discussing their work schedule. Flor and her family shared a home with a Salvadoran couple who had become their daughter's godparents, *compadres*. In talking about daily life and how she juggled what we would call the gendered work-family balance, Flor shared a compelling story about making family. Specifically, one of her daughter's kindergarten assignments was to draw a picture representing her family. According to Flor, young Jennifer drew a picture of herself with her "two moms" and her "two dads": the parents who took her to school in the morning and the ones who picked her up at the end of the day (in other words, her biological parents and her godparents). Only later, during another conversation, I learned that Jennifer's godfather had served in the Salvadoran military during the war. In fact, he had been stationed in the northeast of Chalatenango at around the same time that Flor's insurgent, platoon-leader father was ambushed and killed.

Institutional, historic enemies in the past, both Flor and her *compadre* claimed that the past, the war, and their war stories never came up. Jennifer's godfather explained that Flor was simply too young to remember. I don't believe this is the case. Among the first objects Flor requested from El

Salvador, many years ago now, was a copy of a picture of her father in olive green with two guns strapped on his back. In 1997, she had also shared with me her memory of waiting for her father to come back from a *tarea*. When he did not, she realized that he was dead. This is the knowledge of the child of war, of the 1.5 insurgent generation. Indeed, before I wrapped up my doctoral fieldwork and headed back to New York City in December 1997, I had accompanied Flor and her mother to place flowers on the site where her father had been killed. Like other stories, this one is silenced, and in that space there emerges a way to survive and make sense of an everyday insecurity, away from what Sprenkels describes as "militant memories" that are complicit in maintaining a polarized political field.[162]

Recent work supports this theorizing, such as Adriana Alas's ethnography on the children of postwar in Las Vueltas and their quiet insistence on recuperating silenced memories that can break apart a politics of Left versus Right, or Velásquez Estrada's findings on alternative "grassroots" peacemakers whose work has "the potential to plant the seeds for a much-needed social healing that could support a lasting democratic peace."[163] I offer that these intimate domestic, corporal spaces between former warring bodies erupt with new negotiated postwar truth-tellings, because across the diaspora there are new spaces for accommodating reckonings that take in but move beyond the *violencia encifrada* that this chapter has outlined.[164] Alas's work on the sequelae of war wounds and the unexpected alliances across veterans' organizations also makes this clear.[165] In part, by thinking through Adriana Petryna's framing of biological citizenship in the wake of catastrophe,[166] Alas demonstrates how injured former insurgents and former soldiers contest the state's reductionist quantifications of their war wounds, aging injuries, and concomitant disability status through making claims to time—to the *longue durée* of their wounds, their enumeration, and what they mean.[167]

Reader, we've traveled through, within, against, and alongside the numbers. In the next chapter, we'll keep focusing on the everyday diasporic realities that contest humanitarian logic's emphasis on urgent, bounded crises and on the suffering body.[168] For the Salvadoran case points instead to suffering that, to quote Philippe Bourgois and Jeff Schonberg, is "chronic and cumulative" and both personal and structural, a framing that will guide our next chapter.[169] Ultimately, this is living in the after-maths despite or because of memories of war, across generations and across geographies, so that, for example, a little girl can have two moms and two dads, at least for a while. We'll continue to think through the reemergent discourse of reintegration of migrants and former fighters, the entanglements across spectacular and chronic violence in our next chapter on bodies replete with difference, before and in the after. We'll start by turning back to El Rancho.

CHAPTER THREE

BODIES

>I didn't make it to Andresito's *velorio* (wake), her little boy—her third child to die in postwar. His mother, Rosario, said it was from a brain aneurysm. Jennifer, the international volunteer, said Andresito died of malnutrition like his siblings before him, like what Jennifer expected for Rosario's youngest baby, living in waiting for death. The baby girl was so thin the last time I saw her. She was listless in the hammock when I brought the kids a big bag of pan dulce.[1] The community council decided to stop giving Rosario the extra assistance provided by the international development program. No more supplemental milk and vitamins for the children. She'd been selling them back to the local stores.
>
>—FIELDNOTES, OCTOBER 1997

I LOVED TERESITA AND NELSON'S STORE, with its big open window to the street. It was one of the first tiendas to have an enormous refrigerator stocked with the plastic-wrapped, commercially produced brand of *Pollo Indio* from the Chalatenango supermarket; they then resold this packaged chicken to their neighbors at a slight profit.[2] They were also the first tienda in El Rancho to bring ice cream and cones to sell alongside other treats: delicious homemade pink-milk *charamuscas* tied up in plastic bags, and remember those crisp, cold *chocobananos* on a stick from chapter 1? Gerardo, their oldest boy and all-around helper who now lives with nearly all of his siblings in the southeastern United States, was in charge of the store on a Sunday afternoon in October 1996 when I stopped by. Teresita was resting against a woven plastic rainbow-colored chair. Her baby girl was asleep in a soft infant-sized hammock. The small black-and-white TV was on, the sound low in the background. Teresita had been tired as of late. Her forty days of *dieta* had just ended.³

In the thick-thin description of my fieldnotes, I described how the girls wore pastel-colored cotton dresses with simple bows tied in the back, polyester slips, and flip-flops. The boys wore work boots, thin pants, and button-down shirts. The kids moved in and out of the house, out front to the street, and out back to a small yard, and sometimes, they paused to rest a hand on their mother's shoulder and listen to her speak. I didn't have my audio recorder. For many, it was a day of rest. I had just stopped by to say hello and buy a soda on a Sunday afternoon. It was unexpected, then, when Teresita invited me to sit a while so that she could share the story of her younger brother's death early into the war. He had been injured and killed during a bombing by the Salvadoran military. She told me that she didn't speak about his death much, but she wanted to tell it to me given that I was there, living in El Rancho, studying, and learning about their past. Her story has traveled with me through thinning description, though no less powerfully. It was an intimate exchange. Only while writing this book did I find the traces of her father's detailed description of the very beginnings of the insurgency. I had missed this before. Recall his words that I cited in chapter 1. Don Gilberto explained, "For example, *vaya*, here is someone who got shot, *un baleado*. You had to *echarlo al lomo y llevarlo a curar*, you had to throw him upon your back and take him to be healed. That was the task that had to be done." Reader, keep those words present. This chapter is about bodies, and it starts off with another war story.

It was the early 1980s, before Teresita had her children. According to Ralph Sprenkels and Lidice Michelle Melara Minero, who built on findings from the United Nations Truth Commission report, 1980 was the most violent year of the armed conflict, with 39.5 percent of wartime homicides and 138 massacres registered and nearly 200,000 Salvadorans displaced.⁴ They underscore a key pattern of violence: the state-sponsored, systematic enactment of scorched-earth counterinsurgency policies that disproportionately impacted and targeted residents in the countryside.⁵ Recently, scholars Amelia Hoover Green and Patrick Ball reassessed that 1982 was the most violent year, particularly in the countryside.⁶ Regardless, Teresita never gave me a date for her story—the story of her brother's murder. I'm not sure if I asked or not. Already, I was aware of what I would now call temporal unease; my interlocutors would most often tell their stories without reference to a year. They would provide a month, and sometimes days, a before or an after that contextualized or framed the episode of extreme violence. They would explain that they weren't quite sure of the year. My temporal questions often felt invasive, so I stopped pushing about chronology. My notes also don't provide an exact location for her brother's murder. Am I complicit in homogenizing a placelessness to wartime violence that happens "over there," or was I giving the narrative breath and contesting human rights insistent and empirical questions of what, when, and where?⁷ Now I wonder, was this the Río Sumpul Massacre (May 1980),⁸ or did the murder take place during what is known as the Guinda de Mayo (1982),⁹ or, or, or? Sprenkels and Melara Minero synthesize the Cold War logics and practices of extermination as well as the scorched earth, "quitarles el agua (population) al pez (guerrillas)" counterinsurgency; both were "frequent and regular," particularly from 1980 to 1984.¹⁰ This story for sure is an outcome of these logics.

Teresita explained that she was young at the time and lived with her husband, her parents, and her siblings. When the bombing from the Salvadoran military started, they were all separated. She described the utter chaos and terror and how people in the community ran in multiple directions for the hills, escaping and desperate for cover. This was when her father lost sight of his adolescent son and assumed that the teen was keeping up right behind him. But with just a turn of the head he was gone. Teresita reported that her father found his son gravely injured in a crater made by one of the bombs. His legs were severed in the bombing and his intestines fully exposed. Alone, the father wrapped his son up in a shirt as best he could and hoisted him on his back. Does Don Gilberto's refrain about the kinds of insurgent labor haunt you in the violent space of what is not said? Remember, I told you to hold onto his words: "For example, *vaya*, here is someone who got shot, *un baleado*. You had to *echarlo al lomo y llevarlo a curar*, you had to throw him upon your back and take him to be healed. That was the task that had to be done."

They walked this way for several hours until they found a group of people also fleeing from the military operation and heading to an insurgent camp in the mountains of Chalatenango.[11] In my contemporaneous fieldnotes, I wrote that Teresita's brother was fourteen years old. In my notes I call him a young man. Am I translating from Spanish into English? Did Teresita say "muchacho" or "joven"? I read this now and pause. Thinking like the mother I've become, I feel he was a boy.[12] They placed the adolescent on a hammock-like stretcher typical of the time, and Teresita recounted that her brother received an operation in the insurgent camp.

(I need a parenthesis here, Reader.)

A 1985 *New York Times* article covering the war in Chalatenango describes one such hospital. Reporters had been blindfolded and met with four doctors who moved through "three carefully concealed hospitals." One doctor gave his name as "Francisco," brought the journalists to a field hospital, and told the reporters he had worked with the "rebel forces for four years." During that time, he had "learned how to carry out an amputation by flashlight, as well as use a broken door with tree branches for legs as an operating table."[13] Because of patterns of army violence against insurgent medical camps, the units were mobile and equipment was kept in backpacks. The *New York Times* report continues, "Dr. Francisco, who is 35 years old, said the most common ailments are parasites, malaria, and malnourishment among children. He has chosen to work with the rebels, he said, because he feels politics is inseparable from his practice as a doctor. 'We are not going to cure hunger and disease with medicine,' he said. 'We have to fight to change this system or else our profession will be the useless giving of pills.'" And here we see Dr. Francisco's insightful critique of what Philippe Bourgois later documents as a continuum of violence,[14] that linking of political violence to structural violence that predates anthropological theories on the pharmaceuticalization of health[15] and anticipates Jasbir Puar's theorizing on the "right to maim"[16] that we'll explore later.

Reader, can you imagine the field hospital and Teresita's brother in it?

Shortly after the surgery, Teresita's father went in search of his remaining extended family, not knowing who had survived. He left his son in the hands of the camp doctors and medics. Tragically, while Don Gilberto was on this journey, Teresita's younger brother died. As the story goes, someone in the insurgent camp, taking pity on the muchacho's pleas and his thirst, had fed the boy a few ripe oranges. He had been begging for them despite the doctor's prohibition. Teresita spent a long time describing those oranges and explaining the wartime local knowledge around fasting with abdominal injuries. I can picture Teresita's brother. I envision him with his sister's angular cheekbones, looking like her own tween son at the time. I picture his abdomen sutured and his legs amputated. And alongside his injured adolescent body, I smell those round, juicy oranges beckoning in a time of extreme pain, violence, and abject poverty. This is the assemblage that dooms from the $6 billion dollars of US aid provided to El Salvador over the course of the war.[17] In my notes I included Teresita's pauses and silences and the palpable sadness that lingered as her ten-year-old son, Gerardo, rested his body against the chair, taking in the last parts of her story.

I start this chapter with attention to wartime corporal injury in order to honor both Teresita's story and her brother's life. I also start here because I'm deeply invested in exploring how bodies in and out of war—agentive, suffered, traumatized, and always replete with difference—comprise another node in El Salvador's "curated story,"[18] that *longue durée* of the nation's embodied injury and the making of the Salvadoran "chronic body." I come to this work by returning explicitly to the now historical-ethnographic archive of everyday life and the narratives of loss that I collected from 1993 to 1997.[19] I connect this to my interest in generational arcs, and as a result, the chapter unfolds by tracing out how these stories, first told in the early postwar period, link up with the trajectories of the 1.5 insurgent generation—youth that were born into and socialized through a radical, collective project *and* its aftermath. This generation, I argue, holds the hope for our global futures—even as I am wary of the weight and perhaps sentimentality inherent in putting the onus of (saving) the future on young people. In working through this material, I'm most interested in what the field of critical disability studies can offer analyses of post-conflict societies, and so, we'll be traveling through that literature too. There has for sure been groundbreaking work on injury in times of war,[20] with recent explorations focusing squarely on the sequelae of trauma and how Salvadoran wounded war veterans mobilize for their rights and make claims for compensation of their aging, wounded bodies that are in need of continual care.[21] This work is complemented by a potent literature on violence, injury, disability, and death on the migrant trail, as Jason De León's exposition on "necroviolence" has shown.[22] Or as Wendy Vogt argues in her analysis of the "anthropology of transit," "A missing foot, a scabbed ear, an empty belly—these are a few examples of the ways the violence of migration becomes inscribed onto people's bodies."[23] These are not "random" violences but rather are "produced by local and global political-economic forces that create social conditions in which such violence is rendered natural, expected, and even to be regarded as deserved."[24]

What I'm offering is a bit different. I turn to disability studies in the sense that scholars Michele Friedner and Karen Weingarten suggest.[25] They beckon us to "disorient disability" and to consider disability as a method. Building on feminist writer and critical race and queer theorist Sara Ahmed's work on the "politics of disorientation,"[26] they push us to disrupt how we "do" disability studies so that it is much more about mode than about conventional objects of study.[27] That's why this chapter isn't necessarily focused on conventional stories around Salvadorans' experiences of disability. This emphasis aligns with scholars such as Robert McRuer, who theorizes the work of "cripping," where "'to crip' like 'to queer,' gets at processes that unsettle, or processes that make strange or twisted."[28] McRuer writes against "straightening,"[29] as "*cripping* also exposes the ways in which able-bodiedness and able-mindedness get naturalized,"[30] while disabled bodies and minds are excised from the center of the discussion.

And so, I've structured the chapter in the following way. First, I begin with my own disorienting entrance into disability studies and how this engagement has changed the questions that I ask. Second, I attend to how my earlier work may have elided a focus on trauma and the experiences of lives as full of chronic and cumulative suffering, and I turn to how disability theory can help us think through the arc of war and postwar.[31] From there, I move through various sections and stories in order to juxtapose the spectacular violence and chronicity of war and postwar via Chalateco/a narratives of bodily pain, injury, and disability. We'll honor the stories of survivors, and we'll honor the dead, those who aren't with us anymore and whose lives touched ours. Theoretically, you'll see that I build this chapter on the trope of bodies to illuminate the ways that violence evokes an affective response, an ethics of collective care for many of the Salvadoran families that I have known over twenty-five years. Ultimately, I argue that these stories can lead us to new conceptualizations of disability, extending what scholars discuss as debility,[32] and the making of a dignified life for the 1.5 insurgent generation and their kin.

BODIES, TRAUMA, DISABILITY, AND AN ANTHROPOLOGIST'S PATH

I have been at once thinking about traumatized bodies and resisting this categorization before I even had a term for it, as anthropologist Kirin Narayan cogently reminds us about our positioned intellectual formations.[33] These entanglements of war, migration, illness, and bodily difference have long been at the center of my development as a "South American gringa" daughter, sister, partner, friend, and mother. Please bear with me as I weave together some disorienting threads.

Among my earliest memories are those of my Argentine mother. At night, I would sometimes catch her—dark-haired, fair-skinned, and ethereal—in a thin chiffon sky-blue nightgown. She would skim across the wooden floor from her bedroom to the bathroom as she cried into the night. She moved through dim hallways with all those tears for a country, with such longing. Now we have words (and pharmaceuticals) to categorize her loss: "anxiety," "depression," "OCD." Or was it "chronic sorrow," the supposed "natural," or at least normative cumulative daily pain that parents feel for their sick children?[34] Sadness that keeps you on your feet. Sadness that I came to know from the other side, years later.

By the age of four, I knew for sure about my brother's miraculous yet medical survival—and about what we termed my mother's *brujería*. There are few pictures of my brother, as I imagine him from the family *cuentos*, pale, skeletal, and blue-lipped, but there are plenty of the cherub he would become. The night before his X-ray at the Hospital de Niños in 1960s Argentina, the one that found his pneumonia (those blue lips), that found his tumor, my mother dreamed her worst dream. I hear this all in Spanish—my first language, the language of my own 1.5 generation. It was a story that I begged her to repeat. Before my brother's diagnosis, my mother envisioned "una araña inmensa" (a giant spider) crawling across his "thorax" (my father added, with his medical terminology), right on the spot where his mass of cancer was detected. For years I would look at my brother's surgical scar and imagine that black spider. I wore his survival as a badge. It was mine too. Now we know that illness cuts across kin,[35] that it is social, that illness carries meaning,[36] and that historically, narratives around illness emerge as a genre by the mid-twentieth century.[37] In retrospect, I loved the commingling of my mother's prescient vision, the miracle of infant survival that beats the odds (invasive surgery at twenty-eight days old, in 1960s "developing" South America), and most importantly, the unproblematic promise of my father's science.

I did not foresee turning back to questions of anomalous bodies in times of war or peace. But then, many years ago now, I became a young mother, and I have spent the better part of the last two decades raising a child with a compromised body, with difference, with fragility, and with love.[38] As that young mother, I felt my baby's and my own diminished personhood[39] forcefully, externally, with an ever-unfolding worry, and with rage. Time has not changed this. Across the world, difference, disease, and disability compromise one's humanity. This is not merely a theoretical statement. I am not alone in fighting it and protecting against it. Contesting this dehumanization is the hallmark of a radical disability rights movement in the United States, which has won a series of legal battles through the Americans with Disabilities Act and continues to mobilize against a biomedical, pathologizing model of disability.[40] Disability justice is also global, as evidenced in the United Nations Committee on the Rights of Persons with Disabilities and the Convention on the Rights of People with Disabilities.[41] For years now, critical-disability theorists and activists have pushed against a deficit-based medical model predicated on people's impairments. Instead, they have advocated for a range of perspectives that highlight how societies create the obstacles that are disabling. Disability is thus not rooted in people's bodies or minds. This view is most clearly evidenced in a social model of disability that has exposed the political and economic forces at play and illuminated the historically contingent and socially constructed processes that create what is understood as "normal" or "natural."[42] As more recent work has shown, though, sometimes it is important to bring bodies and minds back into the conversation.

For the Salvadoran context, I wonder what happens if we hold onto the social model of disability but foreground the injured, traumatized body, visibly or invisibly disabled, and take seriously the critiques of ableism?[43] Because there are narratively driven connections here between disability studies and the scholarship on violence and war in El Salvador. In some disability literature, there is a real insistence, interestingly enough, in personal narrative as a way to explode the pathology inherent in the biomedical model. These are testimonies of surviving, of resilience. These individual illness narratives, like the Central American *testimonio*, do similar work. The individual's story stands in for the collective to make truth claims, in this case writing against problematic assumptions that people "suffer from" particular conditions. Often these are narratives about bodies "that *defy* medicine to fix them, even if it can."[44]

In any event, motherhood pushed me squarely into the field of disability studies and to think about my projects, such as the making of chronic bodies and the care around them, in new ways. Motherhood also made me painfully aware of the ways narratives can become an excess, a violence in medical (and human rights) attempts to heal always already anomalous bodies that supposedly tell a story—how many times have I had to retell the story of my child's condition? Under what context? Through what lens? What of the circulation and performance of gendered human rights activists standing in to represent their suffering, their resistance, their cause—what Ethel Brooks has documented around the contradictions of "living proof"?[45] I suggest that the wounded (social and political) body and the congenitally atypical body are both produced and excluded. As anthropologists Faye Ginsburg and Rayna Rapp explain, "Disability is not simply lodged in the body, but created by the social and material conditions that 'dis-able' the full participation of a variety of minds and bodies."[46] For them and many other scholars, "Disability is a profoundly relational category, always already created as a distinction from cultural ideas of normality, shaped by social conditions that exclude full participation in society of those considered atypical."⁴⁷ At the same time, Rapp and Ginsburg illuminate the increasing narratives across media spaces that have expanded what they call the "social fund of knowledge about disability."⁴⁸

While a triumphalist narrative (of overcoming) at times inflects disability studies (similar to the romance of resistance for the Salvadoran civil war), disability studies scholars must reconcile the tension between structural forces and exclusions and the trajectories of atypical bodies of "stigmatized difference."⁴⁹ Alison Kafer's work here is instructive precisely because she brings the body back in through a "political/relational model of disability." For Kafer, "the problem of disability is solved not through medical intervention or surgical normalization but through social change and political transformation."⁵⁰ At the core is a challenge to the presumption that "we all desire the same futures"⁵¹ and most importantly a call to imagine disability futures (always already denied) that make us live differently in the present. I've disclosed my entrance into the field of disability studies, or how the field "found me," so to speak, so that we can think together about the making of a more inclusive humanity and what centering disability can tell us about the trajectories of postwar and how to imagine different futures. I'm trying to close a circle. There is a connection between these threads, and I believe it is in that relationship between spectacular violence; the emergence of injured, chronic bodies; and the attendant labor of collective care.

METAPHORS OF DISABILITY

It may still be provocative to entangle injury with disability, but I find it often in my readings on El Salvador. Take anthropologist Philippe Bourgois's reflections. He explains that in an effort to contest the Cold War's counterinsurgency logics, he "oversimplified and understated the ramifications of terror in a repressive society torn by civil war."⁵² In 1982, Bourgois testified before Congress about the military bombardment he survived in the countryside of El Salvador. In "The Power of Violence in War and Peace" he returns to his fieldnotes to think through some of his representations; the language he used to describe the violence and the deaths of babies, child soldiers, and the old and feeble; and his own survival.⁵³ He suggests that this violence of war has led to a "traumatized silencing" of what one had to do to survive the counterinsurgency and that it is related to other forms of intimate violence.[54] I love this work. A new generation of scholarship continues to excavate this past and to recuperate silenced stories about insurgent lives.[55]

Implicit in these reflections is the place of difference in bodies of war. Who survives and escapes with Bourgois? He states, "Thus it was the young, healthy and fleet-footed who had the best chance of surviving."[56] I pause in considering the place of compromised bodies of war—the injured—like Don Gilberto's son carried on his father's back—the malnourished, the ill, the vulnerable, the young, and those with atypical bodies. I wonder: What if I had paid more attention to my ethnographic data on guerrilla combatants serving with what today I would write about as chronic illnesses (such as epilepsy), on those who had "gone crazy" and deserted their posts, or on those who supported insurgency efforts beyond the ideal, gendered body, like the narratives around a deaf young man problematically called "el mudo" who in postwar taught leatherwork for women's arts and crafts projects aimed at international solidarity markets?[57]

Striking also is Bourgois's language that documents his return to El Salvador in 1994, a few years after the war ended. He writes how the land and the people of postwar are injured, angry, and disabled.[58] He shares excerpts from his fieldnotes: *"Due to land scarcity the villagers are forced to farm steep, rocky terrain. As if to add insult to injury, badly healed wounds from the war make it difficult for many of the young men to hobble up to their awkwardly pitched milpas [plots]. Even the earth appears disabled and angry: carved by rivulets of runoff from exposure to the heavy rain and pockmarked by sharp protruding stones."*[59] We could ask: why the commingling of the two—bodies and land?

Bourgois is asking us to bring trauma back into the stories we tell about El Salvador, to recognize that the insurgency was steeped in a deeply traumatic violence. It is interesting that he relies on metaphors of disability to make his case. He writes that his urgent call to denounce human rights abuses "blinded me to the internecine everyday violence embroiling the guerrilla(s) and undermining their internal solidarity. As a result, I could not understand the depth of the trauma that political violence imposes on its targets, even those mobilized to resist it."[60] Blindness here stands in for what he missed. What he did not see. To be sure, *trauma* is a tricky word. In my own research in the 1990s, Chalatecas and Chalatecos did not circulate the term much. I have evoked trauma from time to time as I interpret regional narratives around strength, suffering, disappointment, and the practices of postwar. But mostly, in the early postwar hegemonic narratives, Chalatecas and Chalatecos were agents or heroic insurgents (or subversives), rarely traumatized victims, though often they were paradoxically told they were lazy in the forgetting of their past collectivity.[61] Trauma creates victims, and ultimately that troubles the metanarrative of collective action.[62] But in the *longue durée* of the postwar period, in that making of a chronic Salvadoran body, the category of victim has emerged as salient and entwines with the surge of interest in recuperating historical memory across Latin America.[63] We'll explore here some of these Chalateca war stories, as they are entangled with everyday injuries and ailments.

CHRONIC BODIES

In part, I resisted war stories in the 1990s because I didn't want to reproduce the kind of *testimonios* that had circulated in the solidarity movement and that inadvertently flattened people's lives.[64] I have been careful about negotiating the expectation of the war's spectacular violence, that mediation between suffering victim and agentive fighter all predicated on intimate bodily experiences. But also, my project was based on respecting the talk of everyday life and in engaging in the quotidian. Today's local interest in historical memory and efforts at truth, justice, and reparation in places like Las Vueltas and El Rancho were not at the heart of repopulated communities' organizing efforts in the early and mid-1990s.[65] It was a time consumed by discourses, practices, policies, imaginaries, and struggles for the *reinserción* (reintegration) of diverse wartime actors into everyday life, as the previous chapter made clear. What I mean is that narratives that framed injury in terms of victimhood were not the stuff of everyday. The everyday political battle was for economic justice and political representation. The scars of war were leveraged symbolically for the ongoing struggle—in political party rhetoric, for international solidarity consumption as delegations visited, or in everyday community life when former male veterans, for example, would return from a day of laboring in the fields with their shirts off and wounds of war visible.

But something else was also going on, embodied and corporal in the everyday. Alongside the narratives of wartime injury and disablement, my fieldnotes are chock full of descriptions about "ordinary" ailments—mostly women's and children's body-minds, and my own—sick with fever, twisted ankles, *ronchas* (hives), parasites, gastritis, falls from guayaba trees, stitches, miscarriages, hunger, and yes, sometimes the "everyday" of death.[66] I haven't mentioned it yet, but the epigraph that opens up this chapter is just one example of a little boy's arguably preventable death that happened in the early postwar period. Anthropologist James Quesada, writing about post-Sandinista Nicaragua, extends this further by unpacking the everyday life, logics, agency, and sacrificing of a "suffering child" living through postwar's abject poverty.[67] Although I was not investigating the cultural politics of childhood,[68] El Salvador's insurgent history of child soldiering,[69] or the impact of "youth and the post-accord environment,"[70] I'm surprised by just how often I mentioned children and their illnesses and injuries in the context of family life in my fieldnotes.

For example, I have a long entry about a little girl who was run over by the Las Vueltas bus. I couldn't take pictures of her open casket, although I was asked to. My own cultural formation, silences around death, and relationships to dead bodies, along with sociohistorical ideas about the innocence of children and their expected futurity, clearly kept me away. I was staying with Elsy at the time (recall her from chapter 1), and she had a detailed conversation with a neighbor about the accident, about the little girl's internal injuries, about the tire tracks on her body, and about how it was the parents' *descuido* (carelessness—we'll get to care soon) that caused her death. I also have notes about the multiple times Elsy's son Miguel was injured. He was an adventurer. Once, he fell from a tree; another time he split his lip on a rock in the river and needed stitches at the clinic, and then later, he sliced his foot on a barbed-wire fence during a festival in Las Vueltas. Mothers often narrated their children's illnesses alongside their own—parasites, diarrhea, malnutrition, exhaustion after a miscarriage, irregular periods, and all-over body pain. I also have ample notes about folk medicine and the many families who were forgoing the Las Vueltas clinic for a new folk healer, a *curandero* and *naturista* who had entered the repopulated communities circa 1997 and offered traditional healing practices such as stomach massages (*sobadas*) and internal "operations" to remove illnesses without any cutting.

It is only recently, however, that I have recognized the relationship between everyday and extraordinary injury because of my more recent experiences and relationships with the 1.5 insurgent generation. In 2017 I received a series of unexpected images by text of a little three-pound baby boy born in Maryland. He was wrapped up in cozy fleece and was wearing a purple pom-pom hat. He also had a breathing tube taped to his cheek. In the photos, his premature and prenatally diagnosed, rare-diseased body was attached to monitors, and he was surrounded by members of his extended family. The last pictures I received were of the baby placed in a wicker basinet on his mother's hospital bed, unhooked from life support, his last resting place.

Reader, I need to pause. As I have said, I know something about sick babies, the weight that this brings, and how it can push us to think more expansively about humanity and the value of a life.

So, when I received those images, I felt deeply for the young Chalateca I will call Camila. I have known Camila since she was a cherished and adorable toddler splashing in the communal *chorro* in El Rancho. In the 1990s I learned much from her mother. I felt deeply for her family, for Camila's parents in El Rancho who would never meet the baby, and for her brother and sister who took the risk and crossed state lines, thankfully from a state that had issued them driver's licenses. Receiving those photographs included me in ritual kin ties predicated on love and support and, I will argue shortly, brought me into an ample Chalateco understanding of the humanity and worth of atypical, compromised, injured, disabled body-minds that moves across generational arcs of war and peace through a cultural politics or ethics of collective care.

DÉBIL Y DEBILIDAD

Earlier in the chapter, I invoked anthropologists Faye Ginsburg and Rayna Rapp's reminder to write against the long, pathologizing medical model of disability that sees the problem of impairment as lodged in the body, with all the deep stigma associated with this impairment.[71] Several waves of disability studies and hard-won legal battles for disability rights have clearly critiqued this model and laid out for us a social model of disability that argues instead that larger social and structural barriers are disabling.[72] Poet and scholar Eli Clare adds to this calculus and offers the concept of "brilliant imperfection," which "is rooted in the nonnegotiable value of body-mind difference. It resists the pressures of *normal* and *abnormal*. It defies the easy splitting of *natural* from *unnatural*,"[73] and it also defies the medical ideology of cure and the triumphalist narratives of overcoming (one's disability) that are still quite hegemonic. All of this framing informs how I want us to approach these stories of injury.

But for critical scholars like Jasbir Puar, the concept of disability remains steeped in a Western, white, heteronormative, colonial, and capitalist politics of identity.[74] In her book *The Right to Maim*, Puar builds on the work of writers such as Lauren Berlant on "slow death" and the "physical wearing out of a population" as a tactic of biopolitical control, and Julie Livingston on the invocation of debility.[75] Significantly, Puar pushes the concept of debility beyond the category of disability as identity politics and asks questions about the making of social exclusion and injury for particular populations. This is a conversation beyond social-structural barriers and accommodations that I mentioned earlier. Puar explains, "Debility addresses injury and bodily exclusion that are endemic rather than epidemic or exceptional, and reflects a need for rethinking overarching structures of working, schooling, and living rather than relying on rights frames to provide accommodationist solutions."[76] This statement makes me think about the relationship between Teresita's brother's severed body of war and Camila's sick baby in that unexpected postwar displacement decades after the signing of peace. I see this as an example, a connection, the embodiment across generations of the making of the Salvadoran chronic body, the making of a curated story about chronicity.

Specifically, Puar builds an argument against the before and after racialized logics of disablement and offers instead that we consider processes of debilitation. Debilitation happens because the very possibility of the disability category is foreclosed for particular populations.[77] Thus, debility is not an identity; instead it moves us away from the "normalization of disability as an empowered status" toward a focus on the biopolitical processes that are "a form of massification."⁷⁸ I wonder too if here we have the imbrication of the tropes of numbers and bodies for El Salvador? Among Puar's examples are the ways that state-sponsored violence enacts or sanctions what she terms the "right to maim." For instance, she discusses Israel's policy in Gaza that includes the intent to cripple. She writes, "Maiming thus functions not as an incomplete death or an accidental assault on life, but as the end goal in the dual production of permanent disability via the infliction of harm and the attrition of the life support systems that might allow populations to heal from this harm."⁷⁹ Puar argues that maiming is a requirement of war, "not merely a by-product of war, of war's collateral damage."⁸⁰ In 2019 in the United States, we learned about perhaps another invocation of this right to maim when the *New York Times* broke the story that President Trump first "suggest[ed] that soldiers shoot migrants if they threw rocks." Upon being alerted this was illegal, "aides recalled, he suggested that they shoot migrants in the legs to slow them down."⁸¹

I have been thinking a lot about these terms—*debility*, *debilitated*, and *debilitation*—and their entangled processes for the Salvadoran families and communities that I know and the narratives they have shared with me over time. Of course, we could consider the rich research on disabled body-minds produced by war, such as anthropologist Zoë Wool's writing on life at Walter Reed, the US Army's flagship medical center. Her analysis homes in on the contradictions between the iconic public figure of the injured US soldier and the everyday care that takes place in the remaking of their lives.⁸² For the Salvadoran context, Adriana Alas provides, as the preceding chapter highlighted, one of the first ethnographic analyses of wounded veterans' bodies through specific attention to their changing corporal experiences and quantification around their aging injuries. Ralph Sprenkels too, in *After Insurgency*, maps out the postinsurgent struggles, conspiracy theories, and patron-client relationships that infuse postwar El Salvador through an attention to veterans' often disabled lives. Most recently, interdisciplinary scholars, including anthropologists and epidemiologists, are trying to understand the epidemic of chronic kidney disease of unknown origin (CKDu) in rural farm-working communities, as "diseases of the genitourinary system are the leading cause of hospital deaths in El Salvador."⁸³ So, in part, this chapter pushes me to mine my ethnographic data for the times that I "missed" disability, from the wounded war veterans to the debilitated everyday of chronic illness that punctuated an abundance of my field journal entries.

To do this work is not a call for recuperating a more medical model of disability, but it is a recognition that injury, trauma, and debility meet up in bodies and minds.[84] Take Laurence Ralph's instructive work. Regarding disability in the context of gang violence in Chicago, Ralph's *Renegade Dreams* proffers a radical reading of injury and disability in which "within this violent world, wounds become the precondition for enabling social transformation."[85] Ralph's ethnography exposes how disabled gang members "living through injury" recur to the medical model because in fact "for members of racial groups who are prone to debilitation through gun violence, drawing attention to the broken body is a political act."[86] Injury was also entwined with community dreaming—of everyday kinds of dreams, like getting to school safely—that had what he terms a "renegade quality,"[87] that were an "act of defiance,"[88] and ultimately that showed narrativizing one's injury could be leveraged "as a resource for resilience."[89]

I bring Ralph's attention to bear on the terms proposed by Puar. In doing so, I code-switch into Spanish. Growing up, speaking *castellano*, as they said in my Argentine household, I was socialized into a particular affective stance regarding debility—a compassionate view of *debilidad* and *de una persona débil* and what this signified. This prompts me to take up a different reading of Puar's debility through Chalateca narratives of wartime loss along with the everyday, endemic unfolding of injurious chronic life.[90] Let's turn to the terms in Spanish. According to Real Academia Española, *débil* can be defined as follows: "De poco vigor o de poca fuerza o resistencia" (of little vigor or of little strength or resistance). *Debilidad* is defined similarly, as "falta de vigor o fuerza física" (lack of vigor or physical strength) and as "carencia de energía o vigor en las cualidades o resoluciones del ánimo" (lack of energy or vigor in the qualities or resolutions of the mood), and interestingly includes an entry on *debilidad* in regard to affect, explaining with a sample sentence: "Sentía por él una gran debilidad." (I felt for him a great weakness.)[91]

It is this affect, this positionality of what debility can make someone feel and how it can make someone act toward another that I find compelling.

Imagine it, Reader: "I felt for him a great weakness." If *debilidad* is weakness, lack of vigor, or physical strength that can move someone to enact solidarity, this links up to what feminist philosopher Eva Kittay develops in her classic work on the ethics of care and the labors of love. Kittay dismantles hegemonic Western conceptions of personhood predicated on an a priori ableist concept of independence and argues instead for the ways in which we are all dependent. In doing so she develops a theory of interdependence and caregiving.[92] What prompts her theory? In part, the interdependence and humanity that marks the life of her severely cognitively disabled daughter.

Where am I going with this? Well, I want to build on the work of scholars such as Puar, Ralph, and Kittay and think about the *ethics of collective care* that I argue is foundational to the making of insurgent survival in El Salvador during the war, during the long postwar period, and across diasporic generations and geographies. *I argue that in the Chalateco case,* debilidad *produces an affective response of collective care that can contest the logics of the "right to maim."* It is an ethics of collective care that at first supports a *débil* insurgency, those first clandestine and risky militant organizers we learned about from Don Gilberto. It is an ethics of collective care that takes the leap and accompanies those first fighters who were armed with only nails hammered into wooden slats. It is an ethics of collective care that confronts the debilitation of the countryside and the injured, *débil*-made soldiers. I believe that it is also this ethics of collective care that roots the successful arcs of the 1.5 insurgent generation, that next generation prognosticated to be debilitated.[93] We will see this more clearly in chapter 5, "After."

To make my argument more explicit I explore that which I originally resisted: spectacular war stories. Specifically, we'll turn to a long audio-recorded interview I conducted in December 1997 with Camila's mother, whom I'll call Pacita. I haven't written about this before. The interview is an open-ended life history and moves through episode after episode of loss, punctuated by love and solidarity. I'm struck by how she described a sequence of moments of physical and emotional care of debilitated neighbors, kin, insurgents, and lovers—victims and survivors of both chronic hunger and spectacular violence that prompted individual and collective efforts to contest the continuum of biopolitical tactics of control, from scorched-earth policies to that right to maim. Pacita's words show how injured bodies are spared, healed, and mourned. Weakness and resistance are in tension. It is not so facile a binary. Does *debilidad* make one weak or strong for another?

GOING BACK TO WAR STORIES

During the open-ended interview, Pacita narrated how she preferred being in the *monte* (the mountains) with her guerrilla *compañeras* (intentionally gendered) as opposed to her time "encarcelada" (imprisoned) in the Mesa Grande refugee camp in Honduras: "Pues a mí me gustaba—so I liked it [the mountains] because we shared time with the other compañeras who were from far away, from other departments." She explained how she had voluntarily joined the FPL, a branch of the FMLN insurgent forces, when she was fifteen years old and that she was quickly moved into the position of *sanitaria*, where her role was to care for injured insurgent soldiers. My research in the repopulated communities evidences that this was one common gendered path for young recruits.

Already in 1997 Pacita wanted to make it clear that she had not been forcibly conscripted. It was her choice. Yet, she explained that back then, they didn't know *"que se iba a tratar de tantas las guindas que iba a ver*—that there were going to be so many guindas. The imperialists started seeing that they weren't going to win so they started with the operatives."[94] Back then, she reflected, they hadn't anticipated their bodily exhaustion: "Look, what really upsets us is that those of us who really suffered the war, *que sufrimos la guerra*, in those times [she means early on]—because *cuando anduvo mi papi*—when my dad participated [literally walked], when my uncle participated, when the majority of the people first participated, so many of us were screwed, because in that time they [here she means the clandestine movement/leadership] didn't even give you a pair of shoes. It had to come from you, from your own debility—*de uno salía, con las debilidades de uno.*" Make a note about shoes; they'll come up again soon in another former guerrillera's story. The insurgency and their supporters started out from a position of debility contextualized by chronic exhaustion—chronic bodies historicized. Pacita described the long treks across the mountains "a pura pata" (all by foot) where she had to rest along the way because she often fainted: "Me sentaba y lo que hacían los demás era esperarme. Hasta que reaccionaba un poco y seguía caminando." She fainted, but people waited until she was ready to walk again. An ethics of collective care.

An ample literature unequivocally documents the "infrastructure of oppression," the state-sponsored terror that comprised the overwhelming majority of the human rights abuses during the war.[95] Pacita's narratives about the *guindas* emphasize extraordinary exhaustion, extraordinary hunger, and extraordinary suffering and loss. She started our conversation by describing one of the most memorable ones, or as she stated, "Habían guindas más favoritas." She laughed and then continued, "Por ser más pesadas—there were the favorite guindas . . . for being so brutal." She couldn't remember the year, but her "favorite" took place during the month of October, when she spent fifteen days without eating, fifteen days barely drinking, fifteen days without sleep, and fifteen days during which she became critically ill and could barely move by the end of it.[96]

Guindiando or not, Pacita also explained that from the start of it all, she was quite good at her job as *sanitaria* and quickly got over her fear. She never really felt a visceral disgust in the healing of violented bodies.[97] Indeed, one of her first loves would let only her attend to his wounds—no one else. He was injured three times in battle before he was sanctioned for desertion and before he was killed in an ambush. Pacita explained:

> *Ya nos íbamos a acompañar.* We were about to be a couple when they told me, "Verónica [her wartime pseudonym], go to camp because Pablo just arrived and *está bien jodido*—he's pretty messed up." And I came, and I'd just arrived when he tells me, "Verónica, I want a lemonade." And I approached him, but I was afraid to see his leg.

That lemonade reminds me of Teresita's brother and his last taste and desire for juicy oranges. Pablo's leg was severely injured, bone exposed, muscles and tendons exploded. Pacita asked me, in a moment that perhaps sought to breach difference, "¿Ha visto cómo queda un balazo de G-3? ¿No? Queda como. . . . Have you seen what a G-3 wound looks like? No? It looks like, how to describe it? Where it enters it's very thin, but where the explosion exits it opens up like a rose, like a big, red, flowering rose. You should see how ugly it is." Reader, should we think about the aesthetics of injury too?

From Pacita's account of healing Pablo's multiple injuries emerged a story that she let me know she'd never really shared. It was about a miscarriage during her fifth month of pregnancy, when, as she explained, she was so young and inexperienced that she really didn't know what it meant to be pregnant, just that she had stopped menstruating. It happened shortly after that fifteen-day *guinda* in October. The account is striking in its detailed description of her loss and the detailed description of her first love with Pablo. Pacita and Pablo shared intimate aspirations and hope for their future child. She explained to me how much she had loved Pablo, how kind he had been to her. She told me, "A pesar de que era de la guerrilla, él era un hombre formal." (Despite being a guerrilla, he was a formal man.) What is in this despite? Is it a reference to the lived experience of gendered violence and hierarchies during the war?[98] He didn't drink, he was monogamous, he called her "hija" (daughter) and dreamed up imaginary scenarios where he presented their soon-to-be baby to his own mother and taught the boy, the baby imagined as a son, to play *futból*. Pacita told me, "Sí que él era bien buena gente. Bien buena gente. Estaba cipotona yo." (Yes, he was a good person. A really good person. I was just a kid.)

A baby's breath. A baby's death. That *guinda* and "la aguantada de hambre" (the bearing of hunger), Pacita explained, caused the miscarriage. And in an expansive Chalateco conception of life, death, and love, Pacita described her miscarriage and the baby, who was indeed a boy. I quote her loving description of the baby in Spanish below and then offer a summary:

> Bien con los huevitos salió. Todito bien formado. Era varón. Mire—que igualito salió a Pablo. Era chiquito. Bien bonito. Y fíjese que yo vi cuando cayó el niño que abrió la boquita, como era de cinco meses. Bueno como yo no sabía . . . le hubiera cortada la tripa . . . le mandé llamar a una señora que vive en Las Vueltas, entonces vivía en ▬▬▬▬. Ahí la mandé a llamar para que ella fuera a ver. Solo llegó ella y le cortó la tripita y me salió la placenta y ya lo arregló ella.

Pacita's tone was full of emotion and affection for the beauty of the baby, who looked just like Pablo, who was perfectly formed, testicles and all. She had seen him open his mouth for an instant. She called for a midwife, who helped her deliver the placenta, and that night Pacita wrapped her dead, premature baby in one of her blouses (it had been pretty and a gift). She didn't have clothes for the baby or cloth diapers. She slept with him through the night, and her brother buried him the next morning, not in the cemetery but near their house, under a tree, in a little cardboard box. That's why most people didn't know about her loss.

> Lo tuve ese día y así en la noche lo hice dormir conmigo, así muerto. Y como no tenía ropa ni pañales, una blusa que me habían regalado, era bien bonita, ahí lo envolví. Y ya en la mañanita no lo fui a enterar en el panteón. Es que la mayoría de la gente no se dio cuenta. Le hicimos un hoyito y ahí lo enteramos. Mi hermano, él fue a buscar flores, la cajita de cartón.

Pablo, though, never got to meet the baby. He was sanctioned for desertion, for throwing away his rifle right after that very *guinda* of October. Pacita explained that perhaps he had gone crazy: "Se enloqueció y botó el fusil." He was locked up for two weeks, and then on his very next *tarea*, he was ambushed and killed.

TRAUMA AND *ENLOQUECER*

To go mad. To be crazy. To be driven insane. Pacita's narrative demands recognition, to imagine it—her baby and her partner's humanity cut short. We need a moment to pause and pursue this line. Disability studies would push us to interrogate the stigma and assumptions that underscore definitions of madness through an intersectional lens[99] in ways that complement the interdisciplinary literature on the sequelae of trauma;[100] genocidal, historical trauma;[101] and the suffering of war that question the hegemony of diagnostic criteria around post-traumatic stress disorder (PTSD).[102] I didn't push hard and ask questions about the madness of war. This was an intentional decision, rooted in solidarity and empathic listening. I didn't push for the spectacular stories of trauma or the experiences of madness; furthermore, I didn't want to retraumatize. While people did sometimes mention how their kin or their neighbors went mad during the war, most didn't talk about their own experiences with madness or deploy a discourse around trauma. More common were stories of suffering and survival that circulated to either bolster hegemonic tropes about heroic insurgents or critique the lies and deception of war. Still, in El Rancho I heard stories about a man in a neighboring community who went mad after he discovered that his entire family had been assassinated by the Guardia Nacional; they were pulled from a bus, placed face down, and executed—down to the baby. Rumor had it that he was still crazy more than a decade later. Residents also talked about the woman whose madness killed her; she died shortly after learning that all three of her insurgent children were killed on the same day, all in different places of battle, all doing different *tareas*. At the time, though, in that early and intermediate postwar, calls for mental health support were not yet in the reconstruction imaginary, not yet a space of repair.

Beyond exploring these fieldnotes, I've returned to some of my original transcripts for these new-old stories and wonder if in my efforts to intervene in debates about social movements and collective action I wrote trauma out, problematic as the concept is shown to be. For example, in *Everyday Revolutionaries* I've written about a former insurgent I've called Hugo. I have highlighted his agency, his intellectual capacity, his wartime leadership, and his postwar fatigue. I haven't included yet his stories of near capture by the Salvadoran military, his hiding of revolutionary pamphlets among balls of soap, his interrogations, and his extreme fear. At one point he qualified and used psychological language to describe his imprisonment: "No me golpearon, pero amenazas psicológicas sí—They didn't hit me, but I was threatened psychologically. They didn't tie me up. But I was captured, completely in their hands."[103] Hugo's words echo martyred academic Ignacio Martín-Baró's prescient analysis on the psychosocial trauma of El Salvador's war.[104] Martín-Baró emphasized how "the situation of war produces a psychosocial trauma, that is, the traumatic crystallization in people and groups of dehumanized social relations. Polarization tends to become somatized, and the institutionalized lies precipitate serious problems of identity, and violence leads to the militarization of the mind."[105] Institutionalized lies. The militarization of the mind. This too, one could argue, is wrapped up in the making of chronic *débil* bodies. Martín-Baró included an urgent call to action, a resistance through the "psychosocial task of depolarization, de-ideologization, and the demilitarization of the country."[106]

What doesn't get said? Another example; it's important. In my conversations with Chayo, the mother, student, and popular education teacher from chapter 2 and her statistics class, I wonder what my analysis would be if I had focused on her affective statements, full of anxiety and terror, alongside her critical reflections on the meanings of development in postwar times. For instance, during a long interview, Chayo contextualized her experiences with an early postwar development project, a local "women's" store that ultimately failed, as follows: "But Lotti, when I had to work from six in the morning to seven at night I would go crazy [Yo me escapaba a enloquecer—a literal translation would capture her word choice, her act of escaping to go mad] because I didn't have the time to develop myself. When I would leave the shop I would say, 'I have to wash the corn, sweep, cook the beans for my children. . . . I was always so worried.'" On another occasion she shared that she was always terrified and anxious while her husband was encamped for two years during the peace process. In the transcript, Reader, I focused on chronology. Like, really, was it two years that he was in the demobilization camp? I hadn't heard that before. "No, one year," she corrected.

To think about stories like these, we can turn to Didier Fassin and Richard Rechtman's *The Empire of Trauma*, in which they argue that today the concept of trauma has gone global, so to speak, and shifted for a variety of larger social factors, including our changing relationship to time (tragic and anxious), and because of historical shifts in the practice of psychiatry. For example, they demonstrate how neurosis, or shell-shock, moves from being seen as a product of an individual's weak, suspect constitution—the wounded soldier who is stigmatized for his neurosis—to being seen now, a time when suffering is at its core, as "an experience that excites sympathy and merits compensation"[107] and is understood as legitimate and produced by *external* events, universalized through the category of PTSD. Fassin and Rechtman brilliantly map this out as a complicated and never equal shift in a moral economy of trauma. In this framing, we can all be traumatized, individually and collectively. We can all be victims and thus have access to reparation. Or can we?

In any event, what Fassin and Rechtman show is that the politics of proof, in the body and testimony, and that search for disappearing traces works out better in theory than in practice. The individual psychiatric proof of trauma is often not enough to instantiate the category of victim. Does trauma need victims? In the circuits of human rights work, such as the trauma portfolios at the heart of Erica Caple James's work on insecurity in Haiti,[108] the answer is yes—even as trauma "obliterates experiences" through its flattening.[109] And so, what I'm most interested in is that tension between the agentive and suffering body and how that gets played out (and masked) through a chronicity that is embodied, cumulative, personal, and structural. It is this idea of chronic as traumatic that most interests me as a different iteration of a "sequelae of trauma," the lingering, secondary effects of injury and disease evidenced in the politics of proof of the testimonial body.[110] Anthropologist Janis H. Jenkins's work complements this framing through her research on "extraordinary conditions," from mental illness to surviving war, that she maps across personal, social, and political spaces. In doing so, she writes against a pathologizing model and argues for a continuum of experiences rather than bounded categories such as "ordinary and extraordinary, the routine and the extreme, the healthy and the pathological."[111] Let's foreground, then, the injured, traumatized body, visibly or invisibly disabled, we could say in this production. What affective response is generated? Let's get back to Pacita's stories.

CARE AND LOVE OF DEBILITATED BODIES

The interview with Pacita was heavy. It ranged from her miscarriage to Pablo's death and then to the death of nearly every single one of her compañeras: "Todas esas bichas, mis amigas [pause]. Todas murieron. De todas mis amigas son las raritas las que quedamos. Haciendo puesta las mataban." (All those girlfriends, my friends [pause]. They all died. Of all my friends, only a rare few of us survived. They killed them while they were on patrol.) Her recounting of a sequence of losses can for sure be read as a trauma of war, as the earlier section suggests—an affective count, as chapter 2 showed. *But they also point to my argument about the collective affective logics of care that contest the state's right to maim through a recuperation of debility.* I have pored over her words and can identify the multiple stories that disclose a politics of love for debilitated bodies. Because part of Pacita's analysis of the legacies of wartime violence included a listing of disabled veterans and their suffering, after. She told me about the (at the time recent) suicide of a disabled former insurgent, who had first lost his arm (as a *sanitaria* she had been responsible for keeping his wound clean) and then lost most of his sight. He'd been treated either in Nicaragua or Cuba, she couldn't remember, but there he met his future wife, also blinded by a bombing during the war. He was, as she explained "choco de un ojo y cuto de un brazo."[112] The young man, who had remained armed (or rearmed) in the transition to postwar, had killed himself in late 1997 after his mother had suddenly died of an illness. Mother and son were close, Pacita explained. His mother had done everything for the blind couple, helping them raise their children. Pacita wondered if he had gone mad from missing his mother too much. It would be up to the community to step up and support the disabled widow with her two small children. This care, in the after, is something we'll return to in chapter 5.

I've been building up to one last story from this long afternoon interview with Pacita. It's about Pacita's mother and her serendipitous survival. I can't tell if this story documents the horror of a scorched-earth operation that took place right after that fifteen-day guinda, another time before, or another time after. Again, the temporality of the narrative is vague, and remember, I didn't push. I don't push now. But imagine this: on her way to a *tarea*, Pacita passed by her family's home and warned her mother about an impending military operation. As an insurgent she had access to this military intelligence, and part of her own *tarea* was to warn the civilian population that supported the struggle. Pacita begged her mother to drop everything and leave immediately with her. Pacita's mother, though, said that she needed to wait for her neighbors and kin who were just about finished cooking the tortillas for the insurgents and the masses. Recall all that labor needed, the number of tortillas required to feed an insurgency. So, Pacita left on foot and made it to safety up the mountain, but when she turned around, she saw the smoke. A bomb had landed right on her home. Pacita explained how she was paralyzed from fear and couldn't move. She didn't know if there were any survivors. Soon the injured were carried on stretchers, but she couldn't find her mother. One of her compañeros told her, "'¡Callate vos! Que en tu casa, toditos están muertos,' me dijo. 'Va,' le dije yo. Y yo me paralicé, ¿va? No di para arriba ni para abajo. Me quedé ahí sentada." ("Shut up, you! They're all dead in your house," he told me. "Okay," I told him. "And I was just paralyzed, right? I couldn't walk up or down [the mountain]. I just sat there.")

Miraculously, luckily, by chance, an object saved Pacita's mother's life. Reader, hold on to the stuff of war because objects is the theme of our next chapter. And yes, indeed, although Pacita's mother didn't have much, she had recently purchased a *peineta*, a beautiful ornamental comb. She didn't want to lose it. Pacita explained, "Se la quitó porque estaba nuevita y le daba lástima perderla. Se la quitó y fue a echarla al costal." (She took it off because it was brand new and it pained her to lose it. She took it off and went to place it in the sack.) She put the sack on her head, and in that physical move from storing the *peineta* to placing the heavy cloth bag on her head (how women often carried things), the bomb dropped on her home. A corridor of blood separated the living and the dead.

Pacita lost most of her family that day. Her mother made it out of the community with just one little nephew by her side. Pacita, helping me imagine it, described what he looked like—*bien bonito* (in this case meaning "light-skinned"), just like her own son. The little boy witnessed the death of his mother and was just standing there over the bodies. Pacita's mother found him and asked him what happened. Actually, she asked him, "¿Qué tiene?" (What do you have?) He responded, "Ay Abuelita, lléveme." (Oh Grandmother, take me.) Pacita's mother took pity on the little boy because he had often helped her hide her *piedra de moler*—the stone used to roll out the masa for tortillas. Remember, military operations in the early 1980s were a key part of El Salvador's state terror. Hiding a *piedra de moler* was vital to living after bombings, integral to the making of food for survival. Let's listen to Pacita's story:

> "Vámonos" (Let's go), my mom said. So, she grabbed his hand and they darted up the mountain. But because of all the suffering and affliction, she

didn't really take a good look at the little boy. She grabbed his hand and just kept walking. When they passed by Niña Rosario's home, the little boy said, "Ay Abuelita, si ya no aguanto." (Oh Grandma, I just can't bear it anymore.) "¿Y qué tenés, Juancito?" (And what's wrong, Juancito?) "Mire" (Look), she said that he said. And when she turned him around she saw that he was missing a buttock (no llevaba una nalga). Literally, he didn't have one buttock. The shrapnel from the bomb had cut it off. The whole thing, all of it. And so how was he going to bear all that walking? (¿Y cómo iba aguantar a caminar?) So, they put him in the hammock and kept going up the mountain. But he had lost just too much blood. When they were nearing the peak of the mountain, he died. So, the little boy died, his mother died, his baby sister died. They all died. Eleven people died that day. Only my mother survived. Es una gran historia porque púchica, imagínese. Quedar una viva entre todas. (I mean, that's one great story, because dang, imagine it: to be the only one left alive out of them all.) Laura, dándole de mamar al niño quedó. Así quedó, ahí muerta. Dándole chiche al niño." (Laura, nursing her baby, that's how she ended up. That's how she died. Nursing her baby.)

I ask us to pause with the pulse of this story and then to breathe in the sensorium of its telling. From what lens are you reading it? In what ways can we honor it? Know that Pacita wrapped up this last account by invoking the importance of, at the time, an imagined documentation: "That's why I'm telling you, Lotti, if you start thinking about it, it's enough to make a book. A ver de cuantas hojas, Lotti, lo hiciera." (Let's see how many pages, Lotti, I [or is it "you"?] would make it.) In the telling of these stories, in the call for compiling a book of these stories, in the hiding of a grinding stone, in the fleeing together, in the surviving together, in the taking care of injured bodies and the dead, I argue that we witness an ethics of collective care that contests the state's logic of a right to maim. How many pages to fill a book, Pacita asked in 1997? That too is a call for archiving injury through caring for stories.

So, we are back to the arc that I hope bends toward a politics of love, recognition, and accountability[113] and that expands across geographies and temporalities. These are positioned accounts of loss and injury and debility and care. Because while Pacita and her daughter Camila's maternal losses are of course quite different, the 1.5 insurgent generation carries with them the pain and joys born from their kin's radical projects, as I argue throughout the book. I believe many scholars of historical memory would agree. They suggest that we consider the cultural ways that pain and trauma are transmitted through generations. For example, Carol Kidron offers us the term "trauma descendants" and emphasizes that specific cultural perspectives need to be understood.[114] Marianne Hirsch directs us to analyze "postmemory," the "relationship that the 'generation after' bears to the personal, collective, and cultural trauma of those who came before—to experiences they 'remember' only by means of the stories, images, and behaviors among which they grew up."[115] And Kimberly Theidon's work on reconciliation in Peru points to the embodied intergenerational trauma transmitted through the senses and substances—"la teta asustada" (the frightened breast)—to think through "toxic memories" and the transmission of violence across gendered bodies and reproduction.[116] Theidon also suggests, however, that while terror gets passed on through the maternal body, everyday spaces of healing also exist through the work of *curanderos*.[117]

For El Salvador specifically, anthropologist Julia Dickson-Gómez discusses how traumatized war survivors often pass on trauma symptoms to their children—such as anxiety, isolation, and fear.[118] Puar discusses this too, pointing to the research about "cognitive and psychological injuries that have long-range, traumatic effects that potentially debilitate any resistant capacities of future generations."[119] She discusses this as "targeting youth not for death but for stunting, for physical, psychological, and cognitive injuries."[120] Where does Juancito fit in here, nearly the sole child survival of a bombing? How about Andresito, dead so young from chronic, systemic, structural violence, whose mother bartered his vitamins for what? A tomato, an egg, a small bag of rice, an onion, a soda, or some soap to do the wash? Puar focuses on the Palestinian case and how this stunting is a "biopolitical tactic that seeks to render impotent any future resistance, future capacity to sustain Palestinian life on its own terms, thereby debilitating generational time."[121]

Reader, I do not mean to be facile here, or romantic, or write generational trauma out in my depictions. But my longitudinal research does offer another mapping. As I've written, when I first met many 1.5 insurgents, they were little, living in makeshift tin-roofed homes in repopulated communities in rural former war zones. They attended local schools staffed by newly accredited teachers whose training first began in the revolutionary popular-education schools. Meeting them again in their late teens and early twenties, mostly in the United States, in the homes they had bought, in the new families they had formed, prompts me to think about the legacies of *debilidad* and the ethics of care that contests the right to maim and that positions them as the hope for our global futures. Think back to our last chapter, to Flor and her practices of forgiveness and how she makes a rich diasporic home.

To close up these stories, a few months ago Camila invited me to celebrate her son's first birthday. It was an enormous backyard party attended by her extended intergenerational family and friends. She had made the most delicious ceviche from a recipe she learned here in the United States from working in restaurants, not from a Salvadoran recipe from the mountains of Las Vueltas, for sure. Camila beamed as she walked across the lawn with the baby in her arm. Missing was her first son, born in Las Vueltas and raised by her mother-in-law. And, of course, missing was the premature baby who had died. The music was blaring. Camila reminded me so much of her mother when I had first met her, although she was rocking a very different outfit. No flip-flops and skirt below the knees. Camila was wearing tight jeans and a frilly top. And her wedge heels were amazing. She was all light and air. A snapshot. Of. Celebration. The arc of her life. The tears for her sons, one dead and one in Las Vueltas, shed with me just the week before, were wiped, at least for now. She stepped toward the birthday cake with the baby in her arms, and we all cheered. In the next chapter, we'll turn explicitly to what and who gets carried in times of war and decades after. This is affective, generational work full of embodied memories of love and loss, pain and hope.

CHAPTER FOUR

OBJECTS

> They carried all they could bear, and then some, including a silent awe for the terrible power of the things they carried.
>
> —TIM O'BRIEN, *THE THINGS THEY CARRIED*

NOVELIST AND VETERAN TIM O'BRIEN captures the weight of war from the perspective of US soldiers' everyday war making during what scholar and fiction writer Viet Thanh Nguyen clarifies and corrects as "the American war in Vietnam."[1] In O'Brien's account, soldiers carried objects from the mundane to the deadly, from light to heavy. Soldiers, or "legs" or "grunts," carted, lugged, and ported their "necessities," from pocketknives, gum, and rations to canteens of water and lighters.[2] They carried fifteen to twenty pounds of stuff before the weight of ammunition and weaponry. Soldiers also carried an existential weight. O'Brien writes,

> They shared the weight of memory. They took up what others could no longer bear. Often, they carried each other, the wounded or the weak. They carried infections. . . . They carried the land itself—Vietnam, the place, the soil—a powdery orange-red dust that covered their boots and fatigues and faces. They carried the sky.[3]

O'Brien's focus on materiality and the intimacy of bodies and land—on the stuff of war and the meanings attached to things that become corporal, worn on, remembered and of the body, like the dust that penetrates the skin—offers us a particular lens through which to ask questions about the arcs of war and postwar.[4] In this chapter, we'll explore both the embodied acts of carrying—objects and people—and things themselves as they come up in different ethnographic moments of everyday life both in El Salvador and in the diaspora. Rather than pursue a direct comparison, let's say, between objects of war and objects of postwar, an interesting and worthy project, I once again ask you, Reader, to think with me along a more open path—from the iconic war imagery of carrying the injured to the meanings and care that Salvadorans in the diaspora place on the everyday objects that they keep. This focus on objects illuminates another key trope for how we build truths about El Salvador. As we do so, we'll think about O'Brien's invocation of the objects carried, of the weight of memory, of what it means to carry the earth and the sky.

EXPLORING AN ETHNOGRAPHIC ARCHIVE FOR THINGS

As my ethnographic archive of the early postwar period documents, Chalatecas and Chalatecos talked about surviving the war in the 1980s via *guindas*.[5] People walked, carried, and sometimes left things or each other behind as they escaped aerial bombings and military operations. My notes are full of the essential objects for survival: tortillas, salt, a lime, a mango, a *cántaro* of water, a machete, a cloth to wrap up a newborn or the ill. All of these things were sometimes dropped midflight to catch hold of a child who was losing speed, because of hunger and thirst or because their tiny little limbs couldn't keep up. Small children were swung on a brother, a cousin, a mother, or an uncle or on a neighbor's back. Sometimes kin were embraced one last time and then left behind. People walked over mountains and through rivers that also carried massacred bodies.

These regional insurgent narratives emphasize survival through displacement and illuminate the entwining of objects and bodies through the land. We could think about that *peineta* that saved Pacita's mother's life. We could think about Don Gilberto carrying his son in his arms, on his back. People and things were carried and hidden. Things were lost and longed for, and things were sometimes recuperated, curated, and archived in the long postwar. When we bring objects (their loss and sometimes their gain) back into a story of displacement and dispossession, what work does that do? Because people had stuff. Saved their stuff. Hid their stuff before fleeing if they could. They used their stuff to survive and like many of us, had desires for things—a pair of shoes that actually fit or a second dress to send a daughter to school. This is not to diminish the ample literature that documents Salvadoran human rights atrocities, the annihilation produced by scorched-earth policies, and the struggle for justice for the victims of massacres where the counterinsurgency logic was to inflict a reign of terror and destruction of the land, the people, and their things.[6]

Anthropologists have long been interested in material culture, in the "social life of things,"[7] and in the biographies, networks, and circulation of objects.[8] In the archive of my fieldnotes, my annotations reference people's memories of the social lives of things but also, with a careful reading, can provide a catalog or description of the value of things from the early to intermediate postwar period. What I mean is that I wrote descriptively in two ways: (1) about people's memories of their past objects and (2) about what people actually had—what women cooked with, what they fetched water with, what *corvo* men labored with, what kids played with, what little ones slept in, how many forks a family had, and so on. Most residents in El Rancho didn't have much. The popular-education schools were not full of pedagogical materials; there was no abundance of markers, crayons, or colored paper. Not all homes had electricity and lightbulbs. Latrines were just being constructed, and most people did not have commercially packaged toilet paper. Few homes had more than two stools, one pot and a frying pan. Very few had a television set, but consumption practices were changing. Markets were opening up in Chalatenango, and merchants were bringing in new gear, like knock-off soccer jerseys for the boys and low-heeled strappy sandals for the teen girls—a real shift from women's rubber flip-flops. By the mid-2010s I was also documenting the tremendous changes in infrastructure and consumption—across the diaspora—where smartphones became the objects that reached across borders.

Let's travel together from Chalatenango to the United States, and sometimes back again, with the things that were carried. The chapter is organized in four parts and does follow the temporality of war to postwar and a generational arc. First, I start us off by analyzing more deeply the wartime act of carrying amid escape so eloquently portrayed in Sprenkels's early writing on the war's disappeared children and in the work of the Asociación Pro-Búsqueda.[9] This first section builds on O'Brien's metaphor to highlight the emblematic affective act of carrying in war. In this way it links up to our previous discussion on an ethics of collective care. Second, we'll move through a series of stories that dig into my ethnographic archive in order to think about the relationship between bodies, objects, and memories. We'll meet a friend, whom I will call Rubén, and his family, and I'll also discuss objects in Chalatenango in the 1990s.

The crux of the chapter, the third section, focuses on later fieldwork, on an ethnographic exchange that took place in the late 2010s with a young woman I call Nancy. Specifically, I focus on the things she carried back with her to Chalatenango when she was deported from Virginia, in the United States.[10] I invite you into this intimate and moving space that reaches for an expansive reading of what I call the *materiality of deportation*, on the things that *los retornados* take care to bring back with them. My aim is to contest the dehumanizing and stereotyped images that many hold about deportation. Inspired in part by Jason De León and his reading of artifacts and their modifications on the migrant trail, I ask, what happens if we take a look at the meanings around material culture, the objects, the stuff that people bring back to their land of origin as part of the deportation process?[11] What do these objects tell us about entanglements with borders and the state, with forms of violence, chronic lives, and aspirations—with the very *documentation* of the unauthorized? Papers and things become prompts for narrative unfoldings, and ultimately, the chapter suggests that we read them similarly to what Deborah Thomas argues is as an archive of violence.[12] I theorize this as an *archive of the returned*, the documents of deported life that complicate the contemporary Salvadoran call for the "reintegration" of a different kind of postwar subject, as we saw in a previous chapter. The fourth and last section wraps up with the deep love of objects, as a Chalateca migrant in the United States discusses the bounty of her realized dreams evidenced through her abundance of things.

CARRYING AND LEAVING

Stories Never to Be Forgotten by Ralph Sprenkels is a cocreated anthology that tells the stories of children who were separated from their families during the violence of war and who were reunited with their birth families years later, after the war, through the human rights work of Pro-Búsqueda. Andrea's testimony and her story of flight and separation comes early in the volume. We can learn much from her account about regional Chalateco processes and the experiences of what I've been calling the 1.5 insurgent generation. She was originally from a community near El Rancho and was severely injured during a military operation. Like Don Gilberto's son, she was carried by her father, with her sister in tow. Let's read together Andrea's description of flight and being carried:

> We did not experience any peace after the bombing. My father tied me to his chest with a cloth to carry me. The people headed to a mountain called Chichilco. The food quickly ran out, so we would spend days without eating while walking, during the night. In the middle of the flights, I had to get another surgery because the wound was not healing properly and the bone was sticking out. We couldn't walk during the day because the soldiers were on the edges of hills and the planes could detect us. In the daytime, we would stay in the tatúes that people had made in different locations in the area or in caves in the hills. As soon as it got dark outside, the people would come out and begin walking. The trails or paths were never used. If able to, people would walk downhill because the vegetation around the edges provided additional coverage.[13]

Andrea's testimony commingles bodily intimacy and interdependence—she is strapped onto her father's chest—with the paradox of the land's deprivation and power of protection. Anthropologists like Jason De León help us to understand this human-environmental assemblage as a "hybrid collectif" that can both aid and harm.[14] Here, the land is open for both as an agent in war. The climax of Andrea's narrative took shape when she was left behind, when she was no longer carried. She narrates:

> In Los Alvarenga, there was no escape route. There were tons of people, probably thousands, hiding in the vegetation on a small hill. . . . My dad had to

run through a shower of bullets with me tied to his chest and with Carmen in his arms. My mother ran with Argelia, and Arturo ran with my brother Luis, but there were so many people that they couldn't follow my dad. The people were running aimlessly. The dead were falling left and right.[15]

With one injured daughter tied to his chest and another daughter in his arms, separated by kin, Andrea's father made a weighty "choice":

In that moment, he decided to leave me behind. He untied me from his chest, gave me a last kiss, laid me under a tree next to the cliff, and jumped with my sister in his arms. Hours later, my mom, dad and Arturo found each other again. Everyone was safe but me.[16]

Reader, I trust you haven't skipped over these passages. They were intimately shared and carefully edited between Andrea and Ralph Sprenkels. They match up with so many narratives of war specific to Andrea and her family, and yet they are an example of the counterinsurgency tactics that defined the war and that targeted rural people. Stories like Andrea's have long, unfolding consequences that refute the epistemic violence of casting acts of survival as "unimaginable" or "impossible" or "choices" regarding what and whom to carry or what and whom to leave. Andrea continues:

My dad suffered the most from my loss. He spent months crying and lamenting his decision to leave me. He felt very guilty. Personally, I feel that the decision he made was the right one. However, it is a decision that no one, not any human being, should be forced to make—a decision about life and death, of saving one life or another. I am haunted by so many emotions as I confront this horrible decision that my dad had to make. Even now after having found each other and having experienced happiness again, he is still burdened by the weight of that terrible decision.[17]

And like so many survivors of war, Andrea returns to a familiar trope, stating, "My father was perhaps the bravest of the hastiest of the combatants. He fought for his family when the war was trying its hardest to destroy it."[18] Andrea's testimony of her and her kin's particular experiences illuminates, like the genre of the *testimonio* does best, larger collective and regional processes of war in Chalatenango. It moves us to honor and think about the legacy of carrying, to be carried, to be left. Andrea's account speaks to that existential, intimate weight of a father and daughter, of hearts beating across chests and then separated. I want us to hold onto Andrea's words as we dive into my ethnographic archive circa 1996 and the paper trail and digital archival research that it launched connecting the past and the future. What follows immediately here is a poetic pause from the ethnographic archive of my fieldnotes. It is a personal and positioned interlude about an urban 1.5 insurgent and his family's stories. I turn to them because they offer so much about war, displacement, trauma, care, and the objects that both memorialize insurgent arcs and quite literally support injured bodies.

MAMI, ¿Y YO QUÉ ME QUITO?

Claribel was my hero.[19] Her son, Rubén, was still thin from his time in Cuba, thin from the lack of stuff, like food and transport, during the economic crisis known as the período especial of 1991. Claribel and Rubén were all that I wanted my own Argentine family to be, meaning so clearly and solely political in exile in our migration. Yes, los Silber had emigrated because of the increasing repression in Argentina that would become known as the Dirty War, but we had also moved for my father's education and career. Claribel was the kind of revolutionary mother a South American gringa could easily covet. A professional (in multiple senses of the term) female revolutionary. She had so many stories. Together, the family had so many stories wrapped up in the small objects of their past. Rubén was also my entrance into the 1.5 insurgent generation in urban middle-class spaces.

In between my trips in the "field" in Chalatenango, I was a regular at Claribel's San Salvador home—their rebel home; their legit, Marxist, communist, revolutionary, intellectual home; a put-your-money-where-your-mouth-is, as the expression goes, kind of home. Their house in San Salvador was a haven, with a big dog protecting the entrance. It was a modest place on a quiet street near the university, and it had a breezy patio in the back full of hanging plants. By the mid-2010s, like so many middle-class neighborhoods, it was protected by a newly erected gated community with a twenty-four-hour private armed *vigilante* (guard). In the 1990s, I was in awe of their home and particularly admired their living room wall of framed war memorabilia: empty shells and magazines, portraits of the dead, and photographs of first *reencuentros*, or reencounters, that celebrated their return and belonging to El Salvador after years of familial separation. From the late 1970s Rubén's father had transferred his "urban" professional skills to the rural countryside and had risen to the rank of comandante. The children were raised in exile. Claribel moved from one political party position to another within one of the branches of the FMLN. I don't know the full reach of Claribel's political trajectory; folks in the 1990s were still peeling back layers of their clandestine identities: where had they been based, when, and what they had really done.

Years later, in my pursuit of declassified documents, perhaps fetishized research objects, I found Claribel and her husband listed in a mid-1980s CIA report on political actors across the political spectrum.[20] This declassified document has become part of an ethnographic archive that plays with my temporal understanding of the past. By chance, the report leaves a trace of Rubén's insurgent parents. I actually had been searching for another object of war: a photograph of Ruben's father that had been published in a book about the war. I first came across it in 1994, when I photocopied the image and mailed it to Rubén. At the time, the photograph generated a powerful affective response in me. I felt a personal rather than an academic relationship to the picture, and so I didn't cite it, file it, or what have you. I have looked for it ever since. Something about the image grabbed me. It felt paradigmatic, transcendent of time and place—a prototype of what a revolutionary leader should look like. Reader, this is super problematic, I know.

I recently found the photograph online, reprinted, recontextualized without original citation or a nod to authorship, and embedded in a relatively recent postwar interview on a leftist blog. I could include the photo, but it is traceable and I'm intentionally not naming Rubén's father. I'll describe part of it, though. Twenty-six years later, my relationship with Rubén and his family has spanned decades. I wonder where his family was when that picture was taken. Were they in Costa Rica or Cuba or Mexico or Nicaragua or Guatemala or Venezuela?[21] When exactly was that photograph taken and in what insurgent camp? Rubén's father looks dashing in the image, with a relatively crisp uniform and his gaze intent and off to the side. He is thin and strong. Why wasn't he armed? In Rubén's stories his father was always armed, his rifle an extension of his body. In the postwar his body ached for the strap of a rifle on his shoulder—thus the satchel he carried in peace. More questions: Who was the young man standing behind him, and who was the man by his side? Both are armed. Why the different hats? I wonder about their trajectories but have not pursued the extraordinary photo-elicitation work by Ralph Sprenkels that shows the varied paths of early campesino insurgents and the legacies of clientelism.²²

I don't have the answers to my questions about the photograph, this object between archived and forgotten. But I offer it as part of a story about the place of objects and archives for building truths about El Salvador. Because back at Rubén's home, alongside this published gendered, iconic photograph of a male revolutionary leader, there were other photographs that peppered that wall of war memorabilia. Claribel had curated much of that wall, and along with the shells and decommissioned magazines she had framed photograph after photograph of her many successes, images of herself across time receiving awards, first prizes, and multiple diplomas. As with the photograph of Rubén's father, one image from the past captured my imagination. This one was taken right after the peace accords. Claribel was not yet middle aged. She is wearing a vibrant dress, her hair is coiffed and abundant, and she is simply radiant, the embodiment of power and glow. Like an emblematic poster of "the revolutionary woman." Yes, I know, problematic, but *ni modo*.

That radiant photograph is the setup for a story that Claribel loved to tell about the embodied objects of war, a story I heard multiple times but never tired of. The context was the health clinic that Claribel ran while she was stationed in ▇▇▇▇ in the early 1980s with her small children—this was after her husband was released from his year in jail. This was after the soldiers put the rifles to her temple with her children in the car. This was after her son's memories of the assassination of Father Rutilio Grande, a liberation-theology Jesuit priest beatified in January 2022—Rubén remembers how the altar boy rang the church bells as a warning. Rubén remembers how that was followed by the *balazos* (the gunshots). According to Rubén, the altar boy was assassinated (by soldiers or by paramilitaries?) and then the priest. This is one of Rubén's first memories. He was three years old.²³

Ni modo. The health clinic in ▇▇▇▇ served a rather large number of *lisiados de guerra* in exile. This supports Pacita's narrative from chapter 3 about wounded war veterans in exile. The boundary between clinic and Claribel's home appears to have been quite fluid. In the marginalia of my archived fieldnotes I found a reference to extreme poverty. Rubén, during the 1990s, shared stories of his time in ▇▇▇▇▇▇ and in the health clinic and of his poverty. His memories were about making flowers out of newspaper to sell in the market. I wonder how it could have been that a representative on a (declassified) CIA list of important political actors was poor. Is this when Claribel abandoned the party? Did it have to do with a quotidian misunderstanding she had with the FMLN? I have a reference to that in my notes.

I don't have these answers, but the story interests me deeply.[24] I have carried it with me for more than twenty-five years, before my interest in disability, before I really understood and felt and cared intimately for vulnerable bodies. I can almost feel the Salvadoran evening breeze as I read my notes. I had joined Rubén's family around the wrought-iron patio table and chairs. The family was reminiscing about their past and sharing their stories with one another and with me. Claribel's stories captured a particular moment of the Salvadoran war across borders and the meanings attached to bodies, loss, masculinity, and normativity. Here's the climax of the story.

A female friend/colleague/insurgent came to "visit." Again, I don't have these facts. Was her friend another representative on the CIA list in exile? In any event, Claribel's friend was traveling with her young son, and they were staying in Claribel's home for a while. Each night the little boy would watch the *lisiados de guerra* get ready for their repose and unwind. The men, they all appear to be in men my notes, would end their day by resting their tired bodies and by taking off their assistive devices, removing a prosthetic limb above or below the knee, or a prosthetic foot, or an arm, or an artificial eye—all customized technologies.[25] And so, with days into the visit, this ritual, this object-body relationship replayed, the little boy turned to his mother and asked, "Mami, ¿y yo qué me quito?" (Mommy, and what do I remove?). Do you see what I mean about bodies, prosthetics, the things carried in war?

"Mami, ¿y yo qué me quito?" has become a refrain for me. It evidences the routes insurgents took and the geopolitical pressures, havens, and networks that extended beyond El Salvador. "Mami, ¿y yo qué me quito?" reflects the positionality of the 1.5 insurgent generation and the heterogeneity of what they experienced, discovered, and lived. While I know Rubén's trajectory, the little boy in my story-notes remains a little boy. I never knew his name. I don't know his path. I don't know if he made it, this 1.5 insurgent of war. "Mami, ¿y yo qué me quito?" was first told, perhaps, as a tender story of motherhood that exploded binaries around valued whole bodies and crafted another way to think about the norming of injured bodies and the ways that war corrupts an idealized vision of the innocence of youth. Imagine, Reader, really think about what it means for the removal of a prosthetic to be experienced as normal—more than normal, even aspired to—reframing the very way that a young boy (narrated as normative and whole in his body by Claribel) comes to understand his own corporality, as if growing up into a man necessarily involved a naturalized disability, a *débil*-made body, and an interdependence or reliance on prosthetics and their absence. This socialization is part of that foundational radicality of the 1.5 insurgent generation. It's simultaneously a beautiful story that marks an inclusive humanity and values disability and a tragic story of the violence and injury of the Salvadoran war. "Mami, ¿y yo qué me quito?" is a prosthetic imagination about the objects of war. We'll follow with a few more examples that I hope can displace some of our thinking on what Salvadorans carry with them in war and postwar and the concomitant meanings of those carried things.

THE THINGS OF WAR AND POSTWAR
There are various approaches to theorizing the importance of materiality, of objects, of things like prosthetics, photographs, and cloth and the memories or traces that cling to those things. Laura Levitt, for example, suggests that we explore the "afterlife of objects" or the "objects that remain."[26] She focuses on the artifacts of violence and tacks between intimate violence, her unsolved rape case, and genocide. Specifically, Levitt explores the objects stored and cared for at the US Holocaust Memorial Museum, such as how an iconic striped prisoner uniform is stitched together, how it was shaped by the body that wore it. The cloth reveals so much—it is witness to genocide much in the same way that the material culture remains across Central America expose massacres and wartime violence.[27] Levitt finds connections and relationships with others through "tainted" materiality, through what is absent, and through what is lost and invokes a reading of the power of their traces. She

is invested in showing how objects embody suffering, how they witness, and how they can heal and reckon outside the juridical.

We're back to another iteration of O'Brien's things they carried.

Recent work on El Salvador points to the saliency of Levitt's framing. For Adriana Alas, everyday, quotidian objects from "before" and from the war do different work across generations in the repopulated communities of El Salvador. She demonstrates that for youth born after the war, these objects provide a way to recuperate more nuanced stories about the past that holds the FMLN to account. Discovering these objects creates spaces for youth to learn from their elders across the historic Left and Right divisions of the war, but I wonder if it also might shift the ongoing struggle against impunity to a discursive backstage.[28] During my research in the mid to late 1990s, objects of war were often steeped in a deeply polarized political field. Take Santos, who had been on the front lines throughout the war. He met his insurgent wife in 1991 when they were demobilized. By my calculations his wife was fifteen at the time of demobilization. A child soldier? Recruited for the numbers? Santos had invited me to his house because he wanted to show me objects from the past. His was one of the many homes that had been built from a development project (FUNDASAL), but the interior looked a little bit different than most homes.

Inside his house there was one room that could be described as a local personal museum, alter, or archive.[29] It was like the wall in Rubén's home. Cemented into the block interior of the house were two empty magazines from an M16 and an AK-47. Most women I spent time with didn't have photographs from the war, but Santos had several. In one photograph he was kneeling, and hoisted on his shoulder was a missile. He explained that that particular missile was used to shoot down helicopters. Curated below the objects, in red marker and handwritten letters, Santos had captioned the war artifacts, dating them and naming the type of weaponry and site of battle. His youngest child woke up from a nap as Santos concluded the tour of objects. We were all standing in front of the empty magazines, and I asked Santos why he had taken the effort to place these objects the way he did. They were hung like pieces of art embedded into the living cement walls of his home. There was a permanence to the curation. Did it have to do with how he was teaching his children about the past? In fact, I asked, what was he going to teach them about the war? He didn't exactly answer. That happened a lot in fieldwork. In my notes I wrote his crisp response: "¿Qué no va a creer? Esperanza de criarlos en tiempos muy diferentes." (What do you think? I hope to raise them in very different times.) Indeed. Santos, like so many compatriots of his generation, migrated to the United States in the mid-2000s to support his family economically, although he returned after just a short while, missing his life in Chalatenango.

Stories about the objects of war, the evidentiary traces of the stuff of war, the deception around the stuff of war, and the desire for future postwar things abound in my ethnographic archive. As I examine this archive, I am reminded of Solimar Otero's work on "residual transcriptions" that comprise an "archive of conjecture."[30] Otero analyzed an institutionalized personal anthropological archive of a former anthropologist, Ruth Landes, and engaged with the marginalia of this archive—data found in the margins, on scraps of paper, and in annotated reflections, the "unofficial transcriptions" of the ethnographic archive.[31] For Otero, an archive of conjecture contests those anthropological pulls to construct "a neat timeline, to relate a linear narrative."[32]

I find Otero's framing useful, and I employ it to think through my own archive, as the temporal and spatial moves of this book make clear. I could talk about the making of life in war through discarded objects, like a baby bottle found in the Mesa Grande refugee camp dumping ground that was rescued and cleaned to feed an infant her formula because her mother didn't have enough breastmilk to nurse her. That's one space of the archive of conjecture. I could also talk about shoes. Did you see that coming? Ethnographic description of shoes comes up in asides and tangents quite a bit in my notes. I have written about *zapatos*, *botas*, *yinas*, and *sandalias de hule*, up through a 2018 trip when I jotted down how I didn't leave a pair of waterproof Velcro sandals in El Rancho for one of my hosts. They were my only shoes besides flip-flops. I wish I had left them. My descriptions detail if and when kids wore shoes [many spent their days barefoot] up through the marginalia in my fieldnotes in the United States about the brand-name sneakers worn by the children of the 1.5 insurgent generation.

Perhaps it's not surprising how often [the lack of] shoes come up and stand in for the bodily exhaustion of revolution—all that insurgent walking and carrying that characterized mobilization. Shoes become objects of war that mark personal sacrifice, and their traces illuminate the injustices of postwar. The thing about shoes is powerful. Not having shoes was debilitating, as Pacita's stories in the last chapter reflect. Another former insurgent Chalateca wanted me to imagine what it meant not to have shoes and to be part of a clandestine, insurgent army. She sketched a hypothetical situation born from lived experience: "Now let's say that the two of us are in the guerrilla and it's your turn for the *tarea*, then you would wear the shoes. If tomorrow it was your turn to rest and I had to go, then you wouldn't have shoes and I would put them on. And there I would go on *tarea*, and like that, we would take turns." My interlocutor felt that these earliest combatants, whose (shoeless) bodies had been relied on from the start, were abandoned by the FMLN. I heard this a lot in the mid-1990s, as *Everyday Revolutionaries* documents.

In fact, here's another example. Elsy's father was forgotten—not rewarded for his service and sacrifice, as the story goes—all because of the lack of a pair of shoes. According to Elsy, her father had attempted to demobilize as an FPL combatant, following the peace accord's guidelines. He had worked in logistics for many years throughout the 1980s. But when he arrived at the demobilization camp, his own shoes nearly destroyed, the FMLN was unable to find shoes that fit him. He had atypical, large feet, size 45, Elsy explained between laughs. And the shoes that were sent to the camp for demobilized combatants were all much smaller. She narrated, "Entonces, le dijeron, 'Ay pobrecito, Don Justo, mejor váyase para la casa.' Y por eso no se encuarteló—So they told him, 'Oh dear, Don Justo, you should just go home.' And that's why he didn't demobilize in the camp." In the interview transcript I appear confused, incredulous, and just not getting the connection between shoes and a denial of peace accords benefits. Like, really, no benefits because of a pair of shoes? After all that sacrifice? Repeatedly, Elsy explained to me (exasperated, I see now), "Pues sí. ¡Porque no hallaron zapatos que le quedaban buenos!" (Well yes, because they couldn't find any shoes that fit!)

From an urban middle-class home in San Salvador to the rural countryside of Chalatenango, affective stories emerge about the "afterlife of objects." And while Santos's objects of war were cemented into his home's wall, many objects travel, and with them, a sensorium of meanings. Mike Anastario's *Parcels: Memories of Salvadoran Migration* forwards an ethnographically rich analysis of *viajeros*, Salvadoran couriers (most officially registered) who transport goods across borders to and from El Salvador and the United States. Anastario focuses on the circulation of packages as "nonhuman actors through transnational space" as they relate to the practices of diasporic social memory.[33] These nonhuman actors include "food, medicine, plants, documents, photographs, clothes, hammocks, electronics, school supplies, [and] letters" that are packaged expertly by couriers and inspected by state agents before reaching their destination.[34] Striking in Anastario's work is the sheer quantity of stuff and, importantly, the ways that memories about them "can fuel diasporic economies."[35] These are economies predicated on "practices of nostalgia . . . that cultivate diasporic intimacy and stoke imaginaries of return," all that *pollo campero, quesillo, gallina india*, and *pupusas*. Anastario recognizes the affective work of this assemblage of human and nonhuman actors that takes shape through migration in the diaspora.[36] This is not a romantic depiction, for these economies are steeped in US–El Salvador power relationships that root impunity and systemic forgetting.[37] Let's see how some of this works out in El Rancho.

DOCUMENTATION OF DEPORTED LIFE

One summer in the mid to late 2010s, I returned to El Rancho and spent a bit of time with Rosibel, an everyday revolutionary woman whose adult children lived spread out across the United States. Whereas Santos had intentionally cemented in his war memorabilia, Rosibel had little by little created a photographic exhibit of loss and longing. I noted a new gallery of images, an array of framed photographs all along the walls of her home—a museum of sorts, a timeline of war to postwar, of gains and losses, of growth and mourning. As a visitor I moved through the geographies and memories, commemorations of those who were not there: photographs of Rosibel's young children right at the end of war and portraits of her eldest son in Los Angeles with his US-born daughter in a sparkly dress and a new baby in his arms—a timeline of photographs. I was taken by the accumulation of images, many sent from the United States and put on display alongside a huge print of Rosibel's former lover, an insurgent who died in the late 1980s. I had seen that photograph before, but this version was blown up and framed alongside a letter that had been signed by FMLN party representatives and included a recuperated item, a personal artifact of war—a small pocket mirror. I wondered how they could possibly know that it had been his. Where had it been archived all these years?[38] Through whose hands had it traveled back to Rosibel? What had her lover used that mirror for? To shave his beard? Reader, do you remember Nanita's story about the gender-bending thief and his trickery with a pocket mirror?

To note, Rosibel's renovated home used to be one of the largest built with remittance moneys, but with the passing of time it has become comparatively quite modest in size and architectural design. The 1.5 insurgent generation has started to build their own homes, some with two stories, sliding doors, balconies, two bathrooms, and kitchens with granite countertops. Rosibel was raising two grandchildren, one born in El Salvador and the other born in the United States. It was the first time I was meeting little Lupita, feisty and an apparent lover of sugar, evident by the state of her baby teeth and the loads of candies she sucked on. Lupita for sure represents what scholars such as Daniel Kanstroom describe as impacted by "de facto deportation."[39] Anthropologist Deborah Boehm summarizes: "As people are deported, many more depart. Departed US citizens experience what Kanstroom calls 'de facto deportation,' removals that are informal and undocumented."[40] And as Heidi Castañeda's work clearly documents, it is critical to account for the US-born children of unauthorized parents and explore how families mobilize with resiliency around their "mixed-status" lives, where "illegality" is "a sociopolitical condition, juridical status, and relationship to the state."[41] So many missing stories. So many injustices committed, arcs interrupted, and citizenship rights trampled.

That visit to El Rancho was also the first and only time that I would meet Lupita's mother, Nancy. Both mother and daughter were temporarily living with Rosibel. In this section, I'm interested in honoring and thinking through Nancy's multiple postwar displacements, her migrations and returns, and the things she carried. You may have followed stories of deportation like hers in the media, studied other similar cases, or have intimate experiences with deportation and strong feelings about it. We can take this with us as we reflect on Nancy's suitcase, her valise full of stuff and crammed with paper—documents full of numbers: dates of capture, dates for hearings, the date of her daughter's birth, the date of notice to appear. I ask that we consider the materiality of deportation, of documentation and documenting as noun and verb, of deported life as an *archive of the returned*. What happens if we take a look at the material culture, the objects, the stuff that people bring back to their land of origin as part of the deportation process? This is crucial, in part, because it already refutes the iconic, violent, hegemonic, one-dimensional images of Central American deportees arriving in their home countries, walking out of airplanes and stepping out of buses with few or no possessions—a small plastic bag, a stuffed animal, a knapsack, or nothing. Boehm reminds us of the multiple ways that the "chaos of deportation" constructs the "alien" via dehumanization.[42] What do these objects tell us about entanglements with borders and the state, with forms of violence, chronic lives, and aspirations—with the very documentation of the unauthorized? What if we read this as an archive of violence?[43]

Scholars of migration offer us ample frameworks to think about this materiality, with many focusing on the power of documents. In a recent volume titled *Paper Trails: Migrants, Documents, and Legal Insecurity*, Sarah Horton and Josiah Heyman focus on the imbrication of a range of identity documents with state bureaucracies in the making of "global apartheid," where liminal, temporary, or "illegal" migration has become the de facto modality because of "heightened immigration restrictions in more prosperous nations that increasingly deny foreigners the stability of permanent legal status in the receiving country."[44] Specifically, they develop the concept of "bureaucratic inscription" and the way that migrants resist being "inscribed into official bureaucratic systems at various scales of government."[45] In part, they are interested in exploring the tension that arises between legibility and insecurity.[46] These are urgent times, and documents hold power and vulnerability. Anthropologists Gray Albert Abarca and Susan Bibler Coutin also illuminate how in the US context, noncitizens are propelled into a furious collection and archiving of documents for potential future use. Everyday paperwork from bills, check stubs, or a child's school registration, for example, may "speak back to the state in its own language, thus exploiting opportunities to challenge illegalization."⁴⁷ This is a negotiation between an intimate record keeping and state surveillance that exposes the fault lines of the state's sovereignty.⁴⁸

Identifying documents are also key objects of El Salvador's diasporic postwar. In my trips to El Rancho and Las Vueltas in the late 2010s, women I had first met when we are all much younger and their children and kin had not yet migrated to primarily the United States spent a lot of time discussing coveted documents—mostly that elusive US visa. Some mentioned the need to show a bank account with over $10,000, while others discussed the strategy of traveling first to the capital of Chalatenango and hiring a lawyer (an additional fee) to help fill out the complicated form. A visa application costs $250. One woman, one of the few who had been successful in the past, reminded me that what people sometimes forgot was that of course you first needed a Salvadoran passport—an additional complicated step, an additional expense that often shut down dreams.

On one of my last evenings in El Rancho, amid all the talk about documents and migration, Nancy, although reserved, unexpectedly lugged into the *sala* a large shiny blue vinyl suitcase—*an archive of her migrant life*. As she unzipped it, I wasn't expecting all those papers. Some were a jumble, and others were in Ziploc bags or envelopes. Most were in English. Among other things, the suitcase was full of records of Nancy's prenatal visits, her health records, the first ultrasounds of her pregnancy, the imprint of Lupita's little feet at birth, and the first lock of her baby hair. Lupita's birth certificate, immunization records, record of her blood type and mandatory HIV screening, social security number, and US passport were all together in one Ziploc bag within a larger folder. All of this was cared for, protected, and separated from the loose messiness of the suitcase. Nancy shared the documents with me. It felt so intimate, tender, and uncomfortable—the indignities of it all, of a life laid bare through partial documents. Yet, the papers became prompts for narrative unfoldings.

Boehm too warns us about the problematics of documents—their deep partiality, how memories vary across kin in terms of the "*the facts* of deportation cases," and how trying to piece together the linearity of removal through a paper trail is problematic, as most deportees don't have these records. As a result, she instead focuses on "the words and life events of those affected by deportation."[49] Yet, there they were, all those documents.[50] Saved, collected, and valued records of US penetration into Nancy's life. They traveled with her; she had archived them. In a suitcase. Under the bed she shared with her daughter. What kind of archive was this? A personal archive? A portable archive? What about the aesthetics of this archive, blue under her bed? This archive of the returned, I suggest, is one crafted out of love and anxiety.[51] Following Rosibel's request that I "help Nancy," I kept trying to make a chronology of the suitcase. Put a little "order" to the documents.[52]

Not surprisingly, there are no records of some stories, like the twelve days that Nancy spent walking the desert years ago, separated from her coyote and from many of the 250 people with whom she had started the journey, what with all the helicopters overhead that dispersed them all. As she described it, "Al final del camino, como nos perdimos, como le dije, nos habíamos perdido en el desierto, pero llegamos a ▮▮▮▮▮, y llegamos caminando. Y de ahí me quedé trabajando." (At the end of the journey because we were lost, like I told you, we got lost in the desert, but we got to ▮▮▮▮▮, and we got there walking. And there I stayed working.) There is no documentation of Nancy's original "push factor," of why she fled El Salvador in the first place. She told me she'd never tell the story again. Today she would have been called an unaccompanied minor.

The documents also don't reflect the varied, cosmopolitan life that Nancy made for herself. She worked and traveled and gave birth in various countries and enjoyed much of her life. She was surprised I had never been to Miami or the part of Mexico she was familiar with. She remarked on the beauty of those beaches and on what a good life she had carved out for herself. In a photo album she kept the images of a family she had lived and worked with and explained how much she still missed the kids. I was struck by how young Nancy looked in the photographs. They could have all been siblings, but she was their domestic worker.

It was in Mexico that she gave birth to her first child. Then she traveled to Guatemala, where her own mother met her to take the child back home to El Salvador. Nothing of the documents even hint at this. The paper trail also doesn't explain the years living in Mexico and the difficulties getting out. Nancy's story was complicated, full of what folks taking a legal testimony might describe as inconsistencies. There are holes in her story—clandestine elisions. She was not from the municipality of Las Vueltas and had no history of mobilizing or participating in collective action like her neighbors, but she had returned because her daughter's father was from El Rancho. She was and wasn't a Chalateca *retornada*.

THE SUITCASE: AN ARCHIVE OF MIGRANT LIFE

The year 2▇▇ was an important one for Nancy.[53] She told me that's when her troubles began, when she returned home to visit her dying father and was subsequently caught at the US border upon her attempt to return. She explained, "De los únicos papeles que tengo donde salgo archivada es del 2▇▇." (From all the papers that I have, the only ones that I have where I'm archived/filed are from 2▇▇.) Reader, are you struck with how she frames her capture, from papers to her archived body? Nancy explained to me that she had no regrets because she was able to spend a last few precious days with her father before he died. Our conversation ebbed and flowed as we passed documents and objects back and forth from the suitcase. I felt overwhelmed by all the documents, the sensorium of holding Nancy's personal documents. Rosibel had suggested that I help Nancy organize all those documents that were in English because, in fact, Nancy wanted to go back to the United States.

The next morning, we tried to "organize" her documents while audiotaping an interview. In the transcript I include the rustle of papers as I explored the pages and pages of incomplete documents regarding Nancy's legal status: court summons, an expert affidavit, the date for a deportation hearing, removal orders, and an incomplete, rejected application for asylum. Our conversation was consumed with Nancy's chronology, with temporality, with dates, with order, and with stitching together partial documents. We could never find pages 9–13, as if that would do what, exactly? But Nancy wanted to organize her documents; she wanted to walk me through the stacks of paper so that they could tell a story. She preferred to focus on what a paper trail could claim.

Much of the suitcase's contents focused on documents related to Nancy's year in a detention facility in Texas, while Lupita was safe in El Rancho. We found papers with lists of social services providers, and I asked about them. She replied, "Pues, pero ellos no contestan. Eso se lo dan a uno no más por la ley, pero ninguna de esas personas contesta." (Well, they never answer. They just give you that information, because of the law, but none of those people ever answer.) Regarding detention, she explained that it was like a prison, "ahí es como una cárcel." When I first reflected on this exchange, I experienced it as a troubling ethnographic encounter. Now, I wonder if we can read it as an allied moment of connective care-work in solidarity, born from my protracted intimate arc of research. There was something about moving through all those items, placing them in as much order as I could with Nancy, for an imagined possibility of something, so that her return would not be, as Boehm cogently states, a "foreclosure" of a future imagined.[54] Still, the transcript shows the contradictions of this care-work. There were many silences as we rustled through the documents, times when I kept pressing for that linear story.

Suddenly, there came a shift. Nancy found a thick envelope full of her drawings of flowers, of hearts, of angels, of princesses. She had more than fifty illustrations, all made during the year she was held in a deportation center, which, recall, she described as a prison.[55] The images were beautiful, graceful, careful, and cared for. Did they retain what Edmund de Waal, reflecting on his own pottery making and his familial collection of miniature Japanese wood-and-ivory carvings, describes as the "pulse of their making"?[56] What does it mean that she carried these construction-paper crayon-and-colored-pencil drawings with her from Texas to her mother-in-law's home? What sun, dust, and sky clung to the art she had carried across nations?

A rooster crowed, and Nancy's young daughter came in and out as we looked at the drawings. Lupita wanted to finish her own colorings that were also stored in the suitcase: "Espérate mi amor. Estos no son los suyos." (Wait, my love. These aren't yours.) When I commented on a particularly compelling drawing, Nancy offered it to me. I declined. I asked, though, how the drawings came about, and Nancy responded that "las hermanas de la iglesia evangélica" had organized a series of arts and crafts activities including the drawings and that the drawings were "como un recuerdo" (like a souvenir), in fact, like letters. There was a lot of time to spare, she reminded me. Nancy explained that, along with the illustrations, "hacíamos cartas a las amigas. Como nos hacíamos amigas y a veces ellas salían bien rápido." (we made letters for our friends. Because we became friends, and sometimes, they would leave really fast.)

Nancy also learned a series of crafts in detention. She explained, "Ahí aprende uno todo. Aprendí hacer pulseras, hacer rosario de bolsa de basura. Nosotros rompíamos las bolsas de basura y hacíamos rosarios. Hacíamos muchas cosas." (You learn a lot there. I learned how to make bracelets, how to make rosaries from trash bags. We would break apart the trash bags and make rosaries. We would make a lot of things.) That is an image. It brings me back to the now defunct arts and crafts workshop in El Rancho in the 1990s. It brings me back to Rubén and his childhood poverty, to him making flowers out of newspapers to sell at the market. As Nancy reminisced about the drawings, I kept jostling back and forth between the drawings and migration papers. I poured over a long document from 2▇, frantically looking for the one missing sheet. Meanwhile, Nancy continued looking over her drawings of hearts and princesses, gendered images for sure: "Estos corazones lo recortábamos y solo lo pintábamos. . . . Con un pedacito de papel y ya quedaban los corazones. Ahí está mi princesa, aquí está otra." (We would cut out these hearts and then just paint them. . . . With a little bit of paper you could make the hearts. There is my princess; there's another one.) Nancy wanted to frame the illustrations. Remember, Rosibel had all those photographs and objects lining her living room wall. Then Nancy found one drawing that a friend had given her with the message "Que Dios la bendiga" (May God bless you) and another drawing that was exchanged on "Happy Friendship Day," as well as a series of Santa Clauses drawn for Christmas.

The transcript holds a series of long pauses and contextualization notes about how we spent time looking over all the drawings. One section is particularly powerful in its invocation of a future possibility, contesting the documents and what they foreclose. Delicately, observing one drawing with Lupita between us, Nancy commented, "Ahí voy a terminar de pintar. Despacio [to Lupita]. . . . Este es un [long pause], quise hacer como la cara de la niña y la mía." (I'm going to finish drawing this one. Careful [to Lupita]. . . . This one [long pause], I wanted to draw my daughter's face and mine.) These unanticipated objects of detention held meaning and value. This paper was carefully claimed within the "disorder" of the suitcase, and calling to mind anthropologist Angela Garcia's findings on the weight of prison letters, Nancy shifted the conversation from these drawings to letters, how desperate she felt, how alone she was, and her need to be remembered, particularly by one sibling in the United States. She told me, "Yo le mandaba bastante, yo siempre esperaba una carta de ella. Yo lloraba." (I would send her quite a lot [of letters], and I always hoped for a letter from her. I would cry.) When you're inside there, you really want your family to remember you; you hope to at least receive a phone call. But some people don't even get one call . . . , and that's really hard." As she looked over her drawings Nancy explained how on Tuesdays in the detention facility, they provided free stationery and envelopes. Revealing a creative arc of multipurposing and resignifying letters similar to that seen in Garcia's work on the "prison archive," Nancy added, "Las cartas las hacíamos en las hojas de ICE al revés." (We would write the letters on the other side of the ICE paper.) There is something powerful and potently collective and transgressive in this act of writing against the very paper of their captors. Right?

Still holding the pictures, Nancy explained that a year was a long time to be in detention. The context was brutal and violent, and she and other women were continually mistreated by guards. She shared the story of one woman who was dying, and in her final moments she was crying out for help: "Brincando, llorando, 'Ayúdame, ayúdame.'" (Jumping and crying, "Help me, help me.") She also shared how they all joined in screaming for help but to no avail. Still, Nancy was not done trying to return to the United States. Since her release and return to El Rancho, she had tried four other times. She was desperate to return so that her US-citizen daughter could return and study. The logic here underscores the violence of US immigration policy: it is Nancy's unauthorized clandestine return to the United States, her violent precarity, that could sustain and recuperate her daughter's legal rights in the United States. Pointedly, she explained, "Yo quiero un futuro para ella ya que yo nunca tuve un futuro." (I want a future for her, given that I've never had one.) The suitcase comes to carry the violence of Nancy's foreclosed future.

Very little of what Nancy narrated, of course, was in those papers. Not her pleading to God about why she had suffered so much when all that she had asked for was to bring her daughter back to the United States with her. Not the everyday indignities of the piece of nylon under which she froze during detention or the hardened, cold bread that was thrown at her for a meal. As we wrapped up our time together—the suitcase full of papers in paper-clipped stacks, in some sort of incomplete categorization and chronology, her documents separated out from her daughters' documents, her health records separated out from legal files, and the drawings smoothed out and placed back safe in their envelope—I stated, "Intenté poner un poquito de orden." (I tried to put things in a little bit of order.) She replied, "Sí, lo voy a guardar." (Yes, I'm going to keep it.)

ARCHIVES OF THE RETURNED

I'm very much interested in reading Nancy's suitcase as an example of what I term an "archive of the returned" built of love and anxiety—a counterarchive of sorts.[57] As David Zeitlyn reviews, "archives need not be official and institutional. Many individuals and families maintain smaller-scale archives, which provide important evidence for a wide range of topics."[58] Think here not only about Nancy's suitcase but also about the practices of love and terror that underscore Claribel and Santos's walls and the objects that they archived. Archives can be simultaneously hegemonic and subversive, as so well detailed in the works of Derrida[59] and Foucault.[60] Many anthropologists have built on Ann Stoler's work on colonial archives, and among the points that have informed my thinking is her focus on "archiving as a process rather than [on] archives as things."[61] What process is revealed in the making of Nancy's personal portable-suitcase archive? I'm not necessarily suggesting that Nancy's archive mines or excavates hidden voices or silences. I'm not even sure if I'm calling to read "along the grain" like Stoler[62] argues or to "read against" it, as anthropologists Jean Comaroff and John Comaroff[63] have long suggested, in order to unmask the "biases and preoccupations of the creators of archived documents."[64] Nancy's suitcase-archive holds traces of the official and yet is affectively outside of the official record.[65] It anchored or guarded her own and her daughter's entwined paths.

Were Nancy's archived objects—her drawings of flowers and hearts and princesses, Stoler's "gestures of refusals"[66] and a resistance to US border violence and to a totalizing narrative about the making of who she is—her subjectivity (for example, a deportee/*una retornada*)? Nancy's process of storing, of keeping, was also one that illuminates how objects in archives are by definition out of circulation.[67] Liam Buckley's work on the discourses circulating around the decaying colonial photographs housed in the National Archives of Gambia provides insight. He highlights the subversive power of "the right to allow for decay."[68] What power is there in Nancy's partial, disordered, and decaying suitcase-archive created by her imbrication with the Department of Homeland Security?

Reading Nancy's suitcase as an archive of return characterized by its very transit speaks directly to analyses of violence in a few ways. Were those decaying objects part of a political struggle that renders the suitcase a "terror archive" with shifting meanings?[69] Historian Kirsten Weld's analysis of the Guatemalan National Police Archives suggests that it is key to explore the making and shifting uses of archives, their "archival logics."[70] The suitcase and its contents hold multiple contesting logics of state and bureaucratic violence that can be recuperated and transformed into acts of repair.[71] So, could we ask if there are liberatory potentials in that suitcase? Perhaps. Deborah Thomas's work on violence in Jamaica argues for the importance of an "archive of affect"[72] to think through how political identities are lived and made.[73]

There was such love in the touching of those documents and of those drawings. As anthropologist Angela Garcia does in her work on what she terms a "prison archive," the collection of letters between three generations of female kin, I want us to take these objects seriously for the everyday history that they tell. As with the letters that Garcia analyzed, they too "work against historical erasure"[74] that illuminates a "tension between what is lost and what remains."[75] The exchange that Nancy created when she opened up her suitcase and together we touched the objects, moved them from one part to another, rearranged them, replaced them in new envelopes or Ziploc bags, and circulated them between us, her mother-in-law, and daughter created a powerful living archival moment open to affection, struggle, meaning, mourning, and persistence.

I never met with Nancy again. After that first and only meeting, she carefully placed the suitcase under her bed, and in her last words to me, she said that she prayed to God to let her cross successfully because she hadn't done anything wrong. The only thing she had ever done was be a good daughter and return for a final goodbye to her father. That was the root of her suffering. She couldn't understand why it should be so. I'm not quite sure what Nancy did with that suitcase. She moved out of Rosibel's house to form a new home in Las Vueltas with a new partner and their newborn baby. She left Lupita with Rosibel and a year or so later headed for at least Mexico, if not farther north. Her microentrepreneurial plans of starting a small business in Las Vueltas where she would resell inexpensive new clothes from San Salvador didn't pan out. What happened to that suitcase? Did I imagine that archive? Should we be thinking more about the intimate temporality of archives and how they are fleeting? Did her counterarchive disappear or leave a trace? I wonder about what else went into that suitcase, when, and what meanings were attached to the objects. Because along with some other items, I had bought a new pink towel for my fieldwork visit and left it with Rosibel, who then gifted it to Nancy because she had loved its softness. I wonder if it is now part of her suitcase, worn thin, with its own global flow.

When I last saw Lupita running through El Rancho, she had grown so much, and her first adult teeth were coming in. What a grin! And this time, no suitcase.

ACCUMULATION AND THE COUNTERARCHIVE

We're wrapping up this chapter on objects and archives. I hope you have felt the intimacy of these things of war and postwar and the stories they bring up for the Chalatecas and Chalatecos at the heart of this book. The chapter would be incomplete without mention of the generations of former insurgents from Chalatenango now living in the United States. We'll round out our exploration of the objects of the *longue durée* of postwar in Maryland, United States. I do so to further trouble our assumptions about objects, their meanings, itineraries, or circulations—and the lives of their owners.[76] Take Marleni. Her story is quite different from most of the Chalatecas and Chalatecos I have met with in the diaspora. Her trajectory is for sure marked by documentation, which in her case was made possible through kin ties. Marleni, too young to be recruited into the insurgency, lived through the war with hunger and suffering, as she and her mother recounted to me on multiple occasions. Marleni gave birth to her children early into postwar and left El Rancho for the United States years before many of her neighbors did. Her long history in the United States, her regularized immigration status, and her legal documents make her part of the 44% of "foreign-born Salvadorans [who] have been in the U.S. for over 20 years, and 33% of foreign-born Salvadorans [who] are U.S. citizens."[77] Marleni's creativity, entrepreneurship, and community solidarity define much of her postwar life.

Although we lost touch for many years, we had kept tabs on each other through Marleni's mother, still living in El Rancho. Our *reencuentro* was moving, at least for me. Marleni quickly updated me on key shifts in her life. She had become a masterful maker of things, particularly of haute couture gowns. Marleni had learned how to design clothes for her wealthy clientele in the United States, who were mostly elderly women attending professional functions and who could be described as having atypical bodies. Marleni had learned to accommodate size and shape—when to add extra cloth or straighten the line of the back with a little weight sewed into the dress—all of this altering of a gown to give the illusion of normative asymmetry, a shoulder pad here, a push of the bustline there. A continuity of that ethics of collective care open to the anomalous? Maybe. She had also learned how to drive, invested in real estate in both the United States and Chalatenango, and developed her artistry and skills to build a diasporic small business.

In fact, Marleni mobilized her accumulated wealth to build up El Rancho. She launched a construction company, trained a new generation of Chalatecos, and remodeled many homes throughout the municipality to meet the desires of the Salvadoran diaspora who sent their remittances back home to build dream homes. Regarding her business, she focused on Chalatenango's new desires, on how tastes, sensibilities, and the ability to consume new things (made possible by remittance moneys) had drastically altered people's relationship with their stuff in a way that would have had been impossible in the past, during the war and its before. She explained, "Because now, everyone wants modern things. No one wants anything old—*antiguo*. Everyone wants the most modern thing possible. That's more expensive, but you work harder to get it. We all want the same things."[78]

All this talk of things prompted me to ask Marleni about her own relationship to objects, to things, from before. I used the term *un recuerdo*. I was curious about flipping my interest in the archive of the returned on its head. I was thinking about Jason De León's analysis on the modifications that migrants make to their goods (water bottles, gauze, shoes, ritual objects) that illuminate the "body techniques" involved in clandestine, desert-specific migration and that create a "recalibration" of suffering, a tolerance for embodied suffering, a routinization of corporeal indecencies that diminishes people and their things.[79] My previous ethnographic interviews with Chalatecos and Chalatecas in the diaspora on this topic were telling in the absence of stuff. One young man said that he had arrived in the United States with nothing, and the minute he could throw out his one shirt, his ripped pants, and the shoes that destroyed his feet, he did. Another woman said she had carried nothing, only her child in utero.

Marleni jumped at the question about objects from her past. From a bookshelf in her bedroom, she brought down a handmade clay coin bank in the shape of a piggy bank that she had brought with her from Chalatenango. It was bulky and had been packed in a suitcase on her first flight to the United States. Marleni explained that it had accompanied her for twenty years. She had bought it from artisans in La Palma, Chalatenango, famous for their art.[80] She instructed me on how to photograph it "so that people can really see it." And Marleni had lots to say about the meaning, the significance around that piggy bank. She told me that it served as a constant reminder of just how much more she had achieved than she ever thought possible. She had imagined just filling up that piggy bank once, but, in fact, she had done so much more, had accumulated so much more. Importantly, she had given back so much to her community, both in the United States and in Chalatenango.

I end this chapter with Marleni for several reasons. First, because so many of the ethnographic exchanges between her and me focused on stuff, on her desire for and accumulation of stuff that started when she was a child, before and during the war. She described this as an "adrenaline" for stuff, for acquiring stuff, and, powerfully, for sharing this stuff, which is again related to my theory on the collective logics of care that contest the state's right to maim.[81] Second, Marleni for sure does not reflect the image of the Salvadoran migrant who has become iconic in a polarized political field that constructs its own media-saturated archive. This is important. Nancy's story and archive, though, we could say, does reflect that image. I am trying to open up these spaces and hold up these truths through objects and their meandering stories.

Still, Marleni juxtaposed her past, in which having stuff was no small feat. She was the daughter of insurgents, and her father was a platoon leader for the FPL, but in our interview, she denied all of this. She claimed that her family was never organized, that they were just desperately poor and easily swayed. Wait for it, Reader—they didn't even have shoes. But they had a clean life, making it through with just rice and beans and, occasionally, a ripe avocado. She explained, "El día que encontraba un aguacate que se cayó del árbol uno se sentía rey. Sentía que ese era un tesoro." (The day that you would find an avocado that had fallen from a tree, you felt like a king. That avocado felt like a treasure.) In the marginalia of my fieldnotes from 1997, I see that Marleni's mother often discussed her own early life as one of poverty—she had stopped going to school because of her rag of a dress and had grown up without a pair of shoes, buying her first pair for two centavos when she was twelve years old. She had sold some fruit to get the money. Marleni described how she still experienced that adrenaline, born from her ambition, born from all that she had accomplished and gained in the United States, and that she made sure to share back home—the professional iPads sent to her mother, the four television sets, the truck she bought her father, the homes she built for her siblings, and the land she purchased and donated to the community for future social-service projects. Among her last words during our interview, to encapsulate her success through the ownership of things, were these: "When I start thinking about it, I mean, I didn't have shoes. I didn't have clothes."

This chapter has moved across time and place as I've built an analysis out of an ethnographic archive and record of Chalateco stuff—lost, found, stored, shared, adored, and storied. Tim O'Brien's invocation of the things they carried propelled the chapter forward as we honored the stories of survival through the landscape of Chalatenango, through the stories of objects worn on bodies, and through the epistemic weight of war and postwar. We've spent some time thinking about the sequelae of war through the *longue durée* of its material culture, like the objects of war commemorated inside a home to Marleni's abundance of things. We've spent some time thinking about the personal, communal, and political archives of the returned—Nancy's blue suitcase as a powerful thing for her and for her daughter that speaks back to the violences made of migration and deportation. I was thinking about all of this on my last trip to El Salvador in 2019. It's perhaps cliché to write about the enormous bags of Pollo Campero that travelers take with them as they leave El Salvador. I spotted them everywhere at the San Salvador airport as people waited to board their planes. An entire industry around the packaging of these boxes has emerged, where impressive-sized shopping bags are stapled tight to keep the chicken and sides of *pancito* warm and fresh for connecting and direct flights to the United States. I could smell that chicken through much of my flight back home, that nostalgic memory work so eloquently described in Mike Anastario's work on *viajeros* and the affective relationships created through the circulation of goods. Along with that Pollo Campero bouquet was a long line of wheelchairs. I counted thirteen on my last flight, with their passengers ready to board. An old man with his crisp, striped dress shirt and woven cowboy hat. A beautiful elderly woman in a long skirt and thick sweater ready for the airplane's air conditioning. Those wheelchairs waiting to carry loved, cared-for, frail, tired, hopeful, revered bodies laden with histories, so many histories. So many stories. Reader, we've come full circle, from the things once carried, to the things that carry.

CHAPTER FIVE

AFTER

> The light is perfect. Fausto's youngest daughter, around age six, is wearing her breezy mint-green cotton dress with white trim. She has her high-tops on. One sock is up and the other down. Her hair is golden. She looks like a sunbeam. Her arms are outstretched as she hangs out by the church door watching a few older girls receive communion, bow their heads, and return to the long church bench. The church walls are up but the albañil (bricklayer) hasn't started work on the roof yet. Why didn't I bring my camera? Kids one afternoon.
>
> —FIELDNOTES, EL RANCHO, OCTOBER 1996

> The view is absolutely breathtaking. Marleni's modernist home is nearly finished, perched right on top of the hill. She sold her first plot of land years ago and secured this new spot by her parents' second-time-around renovated home. The architectural plans were all Marleni's, designed and sent from Maryland. I can see nearly all of El Rancho from here, the cracked road, long and curved below, winding down the valley, and a new locally owned cement factory. The mountain peaks are majestic. The land is verdant. Expansive. Spacious. It's the end of the rainy season and there is so much vegetation. It's not like the first time I visited El Salvador when the earth was patchy, bombed, brown. I am with Marleni's mother, and of course, with Elsy. We look at the view for a while and we're quiet.
>
> —FIELDNOTES, EL RANCHO, NOVEMBER 2018

DEAR READER, we're coming to the close of the book, and I'm having a hard time finding a way to wrap up the long arc of my love for a country and its people.¹ The excerpted fieldnote entries at the beginning of this chapter are from the archive of my ethnographic work and capture two moments that have served to frame this book—a before and an after. The first epigraph describes the 1.5 insurgent generation when they were young and postwar was so full of daily activity. New infrastructure projects were coming in, and new modes of organizing life were taking root. It captures a moment of everyday life in which children of war and postwar were making their way into peace on a quiet afternoon and engaging in the rituals of cultural and religious life. The rebuilding of a church destroyed during the war symbolized the possibilities for reintegrating into full civilian life. The second entry reflects a moment of pause, connection, and return and highlights how my questions shifted to diasporic ones around the trajectories of generations of former insurgents. Marleni could have been there with us, leaning against the railing of her balcony, because she is one of the very few Chalatecas that I know who has the legal ability to travel back and forth from the United States to El Salvador. But she wasn't there. She was in the United States working, which, of course, made the grandeur of that home and the care of her parents and extended family possible.

In moving from the early 1990s through decades into the twenty-first century, I have sought to weave together stories across the tropes of numbers, bodies, and things that I believe have come to stand in for and reduce the complexity of Salvadoran lives as violent, aberrant, unproductive, to be feared, and so on. This isn't to say that violence is not a problem or that the long battle to end impunity for past human rights abuses has been resolved.² But I've been hoping to show how we can take these categories (numbers, bodies, things) and leverage them to tell a different kind of (post)war story³ that recognizes both the sequelae of trauma and the legacies of collective action in unexpected places and ways.

Through an ethnographic method that I presented as protracted, intimate, and in *solidaridad*, we've traveled across countries and times. I have introduced you to small towns in the rural countryside of Chalatenango known for their collective strength born from insurgency. I have introduced you to the many stories of wartime loss and postwar gains shared with me by women and men when the aftermath of revolution was still fresh and clandestine identities were in transition. In those early years of my youthful fieldwork, Salvadorans I met would frequently interchange their given names with their nom de guerre. They had carried that identity, often for more than a decade. I've also introduced you to my thoughts on the children born and raised into this Chalateco collective radical project, where insurgency was framed as justice. In the 1990s, this generation was also socialized into postwar exhaustion and disillusionment. Years later, I have returned to the particular of their experiences and trajectories, sometimes excavating the archive of my ethnographic notes and other times meeting them once again in the United States or in El Salvador. I suggest that there is something instructive and powerful in the lives of the 1.5 insurgent generation. In this final chapter, I will continue to move through an ethnographic archive that asks us to consider diasporic 1.5 insurgents as key to the *longue durée* of El Salvador's postwar and as key to the making of a better world. They are, as I've been suggesting, a model for our global futures.[4]

While I'm wary of creating a romantic, sentimental, or utopic framing that puts a neat and tidy expectation and pressure on youth to save us all or as the "answer" to El Salvador, I want to call attention to the quieter afterstories and to the arcs of once insurgent communities that transcend easy categorization. In the end, what I argue is quite ordinary: the legacies of insurgency run deep in often unanticipated ways and across generations. I'm not arguing for a direct through-line of militancy or radicalism or resulting electoral politics. There's quite a bit of coverage out there and new research that analyzes the 2019 defeat of both historic political parties—the FMLN and ARENA—and of the rise of and support for President Bukele's authoritarian populism, including in former insurgent populations and increasingly by the young.[5] So much for those quotidian statements I collected in the early to mid-1990s across Chalatenango that circulated despite critiques of FMLN party politics and the mounting disillusionment in everyday postwar life: "Once FMLN, always FMLN" or "My blood runs red like the FMLN." Instead, I want to invoke that radical ethics of collective care, those eruptions of practices of forgiveness that rub up against all that still needs to be reckoned, and the weight, literal and figurative, of carrying (on) through the *longue durée* of postwar. That's why I turn to the 1.5 insurgent generation, who were socialized through this all and in different ways—sometimes through remittances, sometimes through supporting the memories of their elders—sustain a collective radical Chalateco project across borders.

Here's one thing we know (from the numbers): remittances sustain El Salvador. In 2017, El Salvador received $5 billion in remittances; in 2019, $5.7 billion;[6] and by 2020, according to data from the World Bank, remittances comprised 24.093 percent of El Salvador's GDP.[7] What if we think about the moral frameworks that tether this economic flow to a Chalateco revolutionary insistence of the right to a dignified life? What if we juxtapose the mostly clandestine Chalateca and Chalateco service-sector labor in the United States against the everydayness of rural El Rancho life that is still, decades later, punctuated by multigenerational calls for truth, justice, and reparations? Do remittances then bolster or become a political act? Does the 1.5 insurgent generation in the diaspora become the hidden, absent, indirect actor that creates multigenerational public and private spaces for the recuperation and retelling of wartime memories? Maybe. Because we also know that local activism across the repopulated communities in Chalatenango continues, evident in the ongoing demands for accountability for cases such as the 1980 Río Sumpul Massacre. Does this local Chalateco political project still predicated in a religious-cultural life provide affective sustenance back to diasporic kin—those who for the most part do not enact a radical politics in the United States? Most Chalatecas and Chalatecos that I know don't engage in immigrant activism or mobilize as "Dreamers" who courageously disclose their status and push for regularization and a pathway to citizenship. Theirs is a US political quiet. I'll be suggesting that these postwar arcs are entwined in a rewriting of the promises of a Chalateca and Chalateco guerrilla life.

The chapter is organized through a series of sections that represent a range of what I'm calling after-stories as I play with the idea of stories that come after, stories about an after, and what stories can be told in the after. First, I'll offer an example of the ongoing call for "youth as a vanguard of the revolution" to show that I'm tapping into a larger interest in the lives of youth in what Clara Guardado Torrez and Ellen Moodie describe as "post-postwar" El Salvador.[8] Second, we'll explore the after-stories of two migrants, Miguel and Marleni, whose experiences, in terms of structures of opportunity[9] and discourses about their insurgent pasts vary dramatically. Third, I tack back to solidarity, to love, to accompaniment, and to El Rancho—virtually. We will commemorate the fortieth anniversary of the Río Sumpul Massacre, where on May 14, 1980, approximately six hundred campesinos were killed by Salvadoran Armed Forces as they were corralled on the border by the Honduran military.[10] We'll do so to think through the generational calls to end impunity. And we'll end where it always starts for me, with Elsy and her generosity, with her friendship, and with her love for storytelling—just like her mother. These after-stories underscore the connections between the discursive mobilization of youth and the future enacted through youthful lives.

THE VANGUARD OF THE REVOLUTION

It is of course not a new refrain that youth are the vanguard of the revolution. The future in youth can be romantic, aspirational, protected, and sacrificial, and as childhood studies teaches us, "youth" is not a universal category or experience.[11] Scholars, policy makers, and development practitioners have all been interested in Salvadoran youth.[12] According to national census data, 33.9 percent of Salvadorans are aged 15 and under.[13] The World Bank estimates that El Salvador's demographic median age of 27.1 years creates an excellent opportunity to "promote human capital" and in which "investments in children will play an important role in ensuring the sustainable and equitable wealth of the population."[14] The World Bank also reports that Salvadorans between the ages of 25 and 54 comprise 40 percent of the population. Reader, central to the data, to the numbers, is the 1.5 insurgent generation.

Childhood health is also of deep importance. By 2018, El Salvador surpassed the Millennium Development Goals regarding child and maternal mortality, according to the World Bank: "The under-5 child mortality rate was 14 children per 1,000 live births, compared to the Sustainable Development Goal of 20 children."[15] The World Bank assessed El Salvador's success to be "directly linked to the expansion in health care coverage for mothers and children over the last decade."[16] Let's think about generational experiences. In 1980, when many periodize the war's "official" start, the under-5 child mortality rate was 107 per 1,000 live births. In 1983, during the height of the war and when many Chalatecas and Chalatecos were living under siege,

FIGURE 10. Community festival and postwar play, Chalatenango. Early 1990s. Photograph courtesy of the Sprenkels Melara family, © Ralph Sprenkels.

the rate was 90.39 per 1,000—a wartime dip that misses the "less visible and measurable health effects of war."[17] Still, by 1993, a year into the transition to democracy, the rate was 50.2.[18] In 1997, if we think about the lives of what I'm terming the 1.5 insurgent generation, the mortality rate for Salvadoran children between the ages of 5 and 14 was estimated at 4.23 per 1,000 children. In 2020 it was approximately 3.15.[19] When we reflect on these numbers, I want us to remember Pacita's teen story of wartime maternal loss, her dead baby loved in the crook of her arm. When we read these numbers on youth across historical contexts, I want us to pause and imagine Andresito, mentioned in chapter 3's epigraph, whom we weren't really able to meet. He died so young in postwar. What life could he have lived, and what "choices" did his mother make when she resold those donated vitamins intended for him and his siblings? And when we read these demographic numbers I also want us to hold space for the pain, beauty, and joy of Miguel's life, whose stories will be shared later, as he has led an exceptional and ordinary 1.5 insurgent life in El Salvador and in the United States.

Along with international development assessments of Salvadoran youth, in Chalatenango there is also an interest in teaching new generations about their insurgent heritage. My past research captured those everyday narratives that were mobilized to counter hegemonic stories of heroic sacrifice and triumph. While children weren't necessarily the intended audience, they were socialized through hearing stories about the war, refugee camps, and repatriation—and although young, many had lived through these phases of war. According to Adriana Alas's ethnography in a repopulated community she calls El Corralito, these everyday narratives about the war continue, with new generations laying claims to their truth-telling.[20] There are also more organized calls to document historical memory as survivors of the war are getting older. We see this in collaborative international projects such as "Surviving Memory in Postwar El Salvador"[21] and in faith-based humanitarian projects such as Caritas's historical memory project, which is recording survivors' testimonies.[22] In part, this work is framed as being in service to the generations to come so that they know their history. And there are also calls in Chalatenango that beckon youth to keep the struggle going, to be the new vanguard of the revolution.

Take, for example, a YouTube post from December 2016 from the town of Arcatao in Chalatenango. Arcatao is about an hour and a half drive from Las Vueltas and is also a region with its own militant history, famous wartime FMLN comandantes, and present-day politicians, such as María Chichilco.[23] To note, in 2021, the FMLN lost the mayoral elections in this historic revolutionary town to the Nuevas Ideas political party that has swept the Salvadoran nation.[24] In any event, the video captures a few minutes of an event by the humanitarian organization Asociación PRO-VIDA and a speech made by its then executive director, Graciela Colunga, someone with a long history in the region.[25] The event inaugurated a food security partnership between the town and various government and nongovernment organizations.[26] What I find compelling about this clip is the invocation of generations of youth, from the wartime incorporation of children as insurgents to the claim that youth today must keep up the struggle, must remain steadfast in their FMLN allegiance. Anthropologists Guardado Torrez and Moodie theorize this latter generation as the "post-post war generation," those with "little or no memory of the war" but who have been raised through postwar violence and through the leadership of ex-guerrillas who have "resisted opening to new generations and proved themselves as corrupt as their predecessors."[27] They argue that it is this generation (across rural and urban spaces) that is resisting FMLN and leftist, top-down party lines, "la línea."[28]

As Colunga reminds the audience and her fellow panelists about their militant dreams and how their inclusive future was born from the gendered sacrifice and blood of the past,[29] she states, "La juventud sigue siendo nuestra vanguardia." (The youth remains our vanguard.) It's been . . . nearly 42 years and those that vanguardized the movement were just young people. They were so young." (Eran jovencitos.) Panelists state their ages at their incorporation into the guerrilla: José answers thirteen, and the *doctora* answers thirteen, more or less. Colunga repeats the ages with a knowing awe, having perhaps been there. There is no hint of recognition or appeal to the human rights United Nations Convention on the Rights of the Child.[30] What is there, then? There is agency and power in this "thirteen." Colunga asks another panelist, "And you, Umberto?" Get ready for it, Reader. The response? "Ten years old." Among the last words of the clip are "bien, el hecho es que la juventud es la que genera los cambios" (okay, the point is that it is the youth that generates change). Guardado Torrez and Moodie would agree: "Dramatic political and social changes are pushing younger generations. And younger generations are pushing change, heaving against the substantial historical weight of their elders."[31]

I've sat with this clip and with the refrain of youth as the vanguard of the revolution for a while. In the past, I've paid attention to critiques by Chalatecas and Chalatecos of their long, hard struggle for change. People had started to mobilize when they were so young, and by the 1990s many were exhausted. They were already wondering who would take on the baton, although they weren't ready to cede leadership positions. I wonder if Colunga's phrase taps into a transnational, intergenerational breadth that creates a new "vanguard of the revolution," several generations deep and perhaps not exactly as expected, as new research on Salvadoran youth exposes.[32] The late, brilliant Ralph Sprenkels reminds us, through the long arc of his scholarly and activist work, that it is critical to think more deeply and amply about these postinsurgent social fields, the "afterlives" of revolution, and the categories we use to think through this terrain.[33] This chapter takes up the challenge of thinking through the afterlives of revolution across generations—from the sun beaming in through a half-built church and spotlighting 1.5 insurgents in their church best to the currency of transnational hope etched in the brick and mortar of a new modernist home.

AFTER-STORIES

I recognize that there is hubris in writing about afters; there are so many to honor that stretch and bend beyond this ethnography.[34] But I try nonetheless in an effort to place this research alongside work that holds us all to account in that search for justice and for truth, to mobilize memory for an end to impunity.[35] Recall that the language of "after" or "posts" emerged quite quickly in the El Salvador that I first visited in 1993—a year and a half after the United Nations–brokered peace accords. The language of *posguerra* was everywhere, and with it, new personal trajectories and collective projects were launched across national and local sectors, as much scholarship has shown. Some of these projects were insurgent and utopic; others were steeped in neoliberal policies that were launched during the war;[36] and others were in between.[37] Across these perspectives and policies, the early to late 1990s were inflected with a set of concerns surrounding the immediacy of rebuilding society, from repairing infrastructure after twelve years of armed conflict to engaging in land transfer programs, dismantling repressive policing, creating the National Civilian Police (PNC), and instituting the FMLN as a political party. More than forty years after the official start of the war, while "afters" look quite a bit different, with multiple democratic elections,[38] with multiple iterations of Iron Fist, or Mano Dura, anti-gang security policies,[39] with decades of outmigration, and with the rise of authoritarian populism,[40] the curated story remains one of violence, injustice, and impunity. Aftermaths, posts, posts-posts, and so on, remain organizing frames. And so, I ask, what about the afterlives or after-stories of all these posts? What of the imbrication of the sweet scent of Chalatenango and homemade pupusas in New Jersey? What about the 1.5 insurgent generation? What can a life like Miguel's tell us?

Miguel: A Chalateco Future in the Migrant After (Story 1)

In the early 1990s, when he was little, Miguel invented songs and dreamed expansive dreams about the future. The protracted, intimate ethnography in *solidaridad* that I have "conducted" with Miguel has evolved from those first years when he was a spry, exuberant boy, always delightfully underfoot as I tagged alongside Elsy, his mother. I learned something new every day because of Elsy's generosity. And my fieldwork felt lighter, more real, and more rounded because of my participant observation of family life. My fieldnote entries are full of sidenotes about Miguel's antics, lively family dinner conversations, the mischief he got into, and the joy he brought to his home. There is a long history here, uneven, unequal, but there, to be shared. Today, Miguel is a father, a partner, a homeowner with an extended family, and a young man ever expanding his education and ambitions. Our relationship has remained special, for lack of a better word. He has thanked me for writing my first book, for being a good person, for loving his family, for accompanying him through his adult life full of gains and losses, and for being what he calls his second mother here in the United States. This language of ritual motherhood has moored me to Chalatenango and El Salvador in intimate, felt ways. It is another iteration of Deborah Thomas's recognition of love.

Our first interview happened in 2007, when Miguel was just a young adult and had recently arrived in the United States. He spent quite a bit of time narrating his migration journey, including his push-and-pull factors. He was *humillado* (humiliated) by his peers in El Rancho who had more wealth than he did, and he was inspired by his siblings who had arrived in the United States safely and were earning more dollars than would ever be possible in Chalatenango. Miguel shared how the journey was hard, from raising the initial border-crossing money all alone to mortgaging his mother's home and the anxiety of what this meant if he were to get caught and be unable to pay the loan back. At the time, Miguel's moves had a logic and a worn path. He planned his journey to the United States to take place after his youngest sister's *quinceañera* in El Rancho that had cost his stepfather $3,000. He wanted to experience one last celebration. Amid videotaping it all—the DJ, dancing, tamales, and everything else—Miguel explained his sadness in anticipating *what would happen after*. He told me, "That was a tough night. . . . I had tears streaming down my face thinking about the children who would be muchachos and gone like me, here now, and the elderly who might be dead." A Chalateco future predicated on generational, community, landed life is foreclosed.

Miguel also shared the traumas of his migration—for example, being left behind at the Mexican border when no one called out the code word he was given and the days of eating nothing but guava. He summarized, "Aguantamos mucha hambre." (We endured a lot of hunger.) I hear echoes of the hunger of wartime *guindas* endured by adults and children. Many readers may be familiar with the iterations of Miguel's migration story. Miguel talked about the objects he was given to cross the desert:

> Nos dieron dos galones de agua cada uno, una mochila con jacket, guantes, todo preparado por el frío, gorro, y una mochila llena de comida, tuna, pan, todo eso, como dos días y dos noches—They gave us two gallons of water each, a backpack with a jacket, gloves, all prepared for the cold; a hat, and a backpack full of food, tuna, bread, all that, for like two days and two nights. By the second day of walking the whole night, my feet just couldn't take it anymore. I was in terrible pain in the soles of my feet; my shoes were horrible, I still have them over there. I got a lot of pebbles in my shoes. I was in so much pain. . . . There were 45 of us, all walking in one column; we looked like ants there in the desert (he laughs). . . . Thank God, I never crossed paths with anyone from Migración, we rested quietly, and no one bothered us.

After crossing the desert, Miguel traveled by vehicle, in the truck's cabin because of his height, his lighter skin, and his embodied grace—a palpable lightness in his step, a sparkle in his eyes, an open gesture. As the guide stated, "Vos tenés un poco más de facha de estar acá." (You look a bit more like you're from here.) Miguel could pass into a recognizable Latinx "belonging," while the rest of the group was locked in the truck, "bien chingados" (really screwed; a Mexican, not Salvadoran, expression). Once in the United States, after a terrifying experience of abandonment and waiting for kin, Miguel shared his first moment of awe—his first fast-food meal. He explained,

"Yo admirado que en una hamburguesa y algo le salieron ocho dólares, y yo admirado. 'Wow,' le dije a él." (I was amazed when I saw that he paid eight dollars for a hamburger meal. "Wow," I told him.) Little did I know that I would be spending like fifteen dollars for breakfast before heading out to work because I'm very good at eating. Sometimes I spend a lot of money on food. But back then, I was amazed at those eight dollars for a hamburger." Perhaps it's that anthropological intimacy of time and place that makes me really understand the importance of that meal and what it signals about migration for Miguel. Because in the early postwar period, in one of the befores of this account that I'm weaving, Miguel's life was also full of deprivation. He dreamed of the day he could afford *pupusas* from the Chalatenango city market and wept the one time his stepfather bought a small container of the coveted Pollo Campero meal for his one biological daughter.

An insurgent radical project also contextualized Miguel's migration. He described the integrity of one of his human smugglers who was "formal," honorable, and humble and who had been a former insurgent. He wore no gold chains. Miguel further explained his own militancy, stating, "En mi mente yo soy un luchador todavía, porque yo lucho todavía para mi país—In my mind I am a fighter, because I still struggle for my country. I keep pushing myself here for my family, and for my country . . . because the money I send they spend over there, it gets invested in El Salvador; the taxes go to the Salvadoran government." Juxtaposing wartime definitions of politicized, nation-building masculinity, he stated, "Because you don't need a gun to be fighter. . . . You know how else you can struggle for your country? By not getting involved in bad things [here he invokes the hegemonic circulation of young, transnationalized Salvadoran men as the embodiment of societal ills through their involvement in gangs], because if you do then your family suffers, the country suffers. . . . It's a dishonor for our country that [the United States] says that the Salvadorans are the mareros, and for those who are lucky enough to have TPS, it will be our fault if we mess things up, and they will lose it [TPS], and people will suffer because of our own doing." It's as if he presaged Donald Trump's racist invocation of El Salvador's worth.[41]

This is an important and I would say "recognizable" rendering that depicts the *longue durée* of postwar characterized by migration, an expected discourse around a radical political project in a new land, and perhaps even what Andrea Dyrness and Thea Renda Abu El-Haj claim about how transnational experiences can create "unique forms of critical consciousness, civic and political awareness, and commitment to democratic rights that are foundational for active democratic citizenship."[42] In the past I have focused on migration stories and the building of new transnational lives as the culminating arc of a Chalateco "after," what you have just read. This is an after full of possibility but also trauma if we note the three times that Miguel invokes the term "suffer."

But Reader, something unexpected happened when I returned to the interview transcript years later, thinking anew about the life experiences of the 1.5 insurgent generation members like Miguel. This time I was struck by Miguel's youthful dreams and his goals for the future that included owning his own cattle, having his own land, and buying a new car. His cross-border dreams commingled agricultural, rural lifeways, multispecies love, and urban labor. These aspirations of everyday life are the quiet spaces of youth, the after-stories of the vanguard of the revolution. Let's look at another excerpt from the transcript a bit more closely.

Multispecies Debility (Story 2)

Miguel started work young. In his words, "Yo en mi caso, empecé a trabajar a los ocho años. Mi vida, más que todo lo dediqué a animales, a reses." (In my case, I started working when I was eight years old. My life, I dedicated it towards taking care of animals, cows.) From my fieldnotes I have documented that in 1997, when he was even younger, Miguel had just started helping a few neighbors with their cattle. He sometimes skipped school to do so. By the age of ten, he was already getting up at four in the morning, eating a breakfast of warmed-up tortillas and beans from the night before, and then heading up to the *potrero*, to the pasture, where his job was to corral the cows and make sure they didn't escape. Remember that by the age of ten, Umberto, referenced earlier, had joined the revolution. Miguel worked for a *patrón* in Las Vueltas and soon developed a reputation for being a great worker. While the patron's own sons moved to the United States with visas, Miguel looked after the cattle as if they were his own. Miguel's family for sure did not have the means to invest in cattle and did not have the land for pasture—neither before nor after the war. Miguel's family at the time was also not thinking about migration as a postwar strategy—documented or otherwise.

It is an after-story of multispecies debility that I argue offers an untold story or legacy of the insurgent project, that extension of radical acts of collective care that contests debility and a "right to maim"[43] that I developed in chapter 3. Let's listen to Miguel's story of his love and care for a sick calf, a *débil*-made animal, because I do see this as an unanticipated through-line.

> Me pasó una experiencia con un animalito que nació enfermito. Yo lo cuidé como un bebé, y yo estaba pendiente de darle su leche, ni pacha agarraba—I had an experience with a calf that was born sickly. I took care of him like a baby, and I was attentive to him, to give him his milk. He wouldn't even take a bottle. I would open his mouth and give him droplets of milk. He wasn't able to grow much. . . . He couldn't really stand. . . . Unfortunately, we weren't able to rescue him. . . . Nació golpeado, nació débil—He was born damaged (injured, banged up); he was born feeble (weak).

Miguel showed deep compassion for the congenitally atypical calf. In fact, he mobilized his labor and care beyond the normative expectations of whole bodies and gendered norms. The feeding of drops of milk can be read as an irreverent act by a campesino boy to transgress and engage in culturally defined maternal acts of caretaking linked to gendered substances—to milk. Feeding an atypical calf becomes a queer act that contests the hegemony of normative masculinity.[44]

Miguel explained how his *patrón* admired him for the work he was doing on behalf of the vulnerable calf, a calf that was more than likely not going to make it. Miguel took great care in letting me know that once, without realizing it, the *patrón* had witnessed Miguel's recognition of the inherent worth and dignity of the calf (one could say). It was during a storm in the afternoon, and Miguel was in the *potrero* sitting beside the calf, who, remember, couldn't stand: "Yo, mi jacket [said in English] me la quité y se lo puse a él [chivito], y él se temblaba del frío. . . . Y me daba mucha lástima." (I took off my jacket and I put it on [the calf]; he was shivering from the cold. . . . I felt so sorry for him.) Recall here too my suggestion from chapter 3 of how in

Spanish, *debilidad* (feeling weak for another) creates affective strength against the normative and is part and parcel of that radical collective love and politics. We see it here in Miguel's 1.5 insurgent dreaming.

Of all the stories to share with me about his past and how his life had changed in the decade since I had last spent time with his family in El Rancho, Miguel's multispecies care reads powerfully to me as a legacy of a radical project that emerged out of rural places and ways of life. Miguel's narrative is full of a recognition for debility that is transhuman and antiableist. He described the fragile calf as born *golpeado*—injured, hurt, beaten, damaged, and ultimately an agent in choosing its own death. As he explained, "No le convenía la vida." (Life didn't suit him [the calf].) This too is another question to ponder, an insurgent radical philosophy of death. Miguel explained that he was always kind in his care of cattle, never having to raise his voice. His voice was tender and full of affective love when he told me, "Con los animales no necesitaba ni gritarles no más le silbaba. Yo tenía una clase de silbido para traerlos." (With the animals I never had to yell at them; I just had to whistle. I had a particular kind of whistle to bring them around.) Reader, Miguel had a special, gentle whistle. I wish I could have heard it in that open pasture and under the Chalateco sky.

A Backyard Hortaliza *(Story 3)*

Fast forward to another after—Miguel in 2020, a proud father sharing stories about his daughter, Kristy, whom he suggests should call me Abuelita.[45] After one of my visits, he sent me a video of his little one doing what she loved best, helping him in his *hortaliza*, his vegetable garden. The video begins with a pan of Miguel's backyard. He has tilled the land and made an impressive garden full of familiar vegetables that in the United States would be called squash, tomatoes, and beans. It reminded me of his family's *hortaliza* back in El Rancho. His mother and grandmother were always growing vegetables and adding flowers to their small plot of land adjacent to their home. In the video, Kristy is not yet two. She is wearing a sun hat. No baby I saw in El Rancho ever had a hat. Perhaps, if they were newborns (*tiernitos*), their mothers had a bit of *trapito* (cloth) to shield their heads while they were carried in arms. Kristy is also wearing hot-pink plastic rain boots—her work boots.

Also something the kids I knew in El Rancho didn't have. Remember how Miguel rarely wore shoes? Miguel had packed Kristy a satchel with a snack.

The first words of the video are Miguel asking his toddler, "¿Ya te dio hambre?" (You're already hungry?) Kristy sits in the middle of the field (I call it the field, thinking in the language of the campo), eating her banana, with a plastic water bottle by her feet. Two more things that Miguel never had. If he was lucky, when his mother sent him to the fields to help his grandfather, she would pack for him two tortillas, some beans from the night before, and when there was a bit of extra, a slice of *cuajada*, or farmer's cheese. Miguel narrates and code-switches throughout the video: "Ahorita Kristy está en lunch" (Now, Kristy is having lunch). She answers, "Sí" (Yes). Miguel responds, "Tome agüita pues" (Drink some water, then), and Kristy takes a sip. I made a note to myself to ask Miguel about the vegetables he had planted and how his agricultural practices had shifted outside of his rural lifeway. In the video Miguel hands Kristy a paper towel to wipe her face and hands. Again, something that was hard to find in El Rancho back in the day.

I share this video as a moment of everyday vulnerable beauty in the after and as an example of one unanticipated future of 1.5 insurgents and current world-makers. I bring these three ethnographic moments to the fore in order to contextualize and deepen the imaginings we may all carry about Salvadoran migrants, campesinos, and insurgents. It is important to honor these pasts, presents, and unfolding futures as we unpack the narratives of the flow of migrants, of the Salvadoran diaspora, and of the legacies of war and militancy and foreground future imaginaries, livelihoods, and hope—from the *potreros* of Chalatenango to the backyard *hortalizas* in Virginia. For a different perspective, we'll turn to what I have learned from Marleni and her kin.

BILATERAL DREAMING AND MILITANT REFUSAL

Marleni was already living in the United States in the mid-1990s. Her son, Sebastián, was being raised in El Rancho by his grandmother who was loving, strict, and attentive to rearing Sebastián "right." Sebastián was for sure not traipsing around with Miguel or skipping school, and he was never barefoot beyond his home. In 1997 he had whispered into his abuelita's ear that he wanted to stay in El Rancho with her rather than travel to the United

States to be with his parents. When we met again in the United States, after twenty-one years, I didn't recognize him. We had each brought photographs from 1997 and recontextualized them, snapping photos of the old prints onto our smartphones. I have many striking portraits in black and white in which Sebastián is beside his grandmother as they clean recently harvested beans. He shared a photo I must have given him in 1997. In the image, Sebastián is about six. He's dressed in pressed light-washed jeans with a white polo shirt tucked in. He is sitting on my lap, and we're both smiling and at ease. Sebastián is now financially well-off. He graduated high school in the United States and became a successful entrepreneur, now making a six-figure salary.[46] He is a married homeowner and travels extensively for work. He is also one of the very few people from El Rancho who has become a US citizen. His mother, Marleni, updated me on all of this before our *reencuentro*. She wanted me to soak in Sebastián's living of the American dream.[47] Sebastián fits squarely into what I am terming the 1.5 insurgent generation, but his mother was a child of early war and represents herself as always too young to be considered a protagonist in it.

Marleni could also be said to be living that hegemonically constructed, pull-yourself-up-by-your-bootstraps, very American success story. She has articulated it as such but always with a twist—deeply inflected by an ethic of collectivity and care—whether Salvadoran or not, and across borders. Marleni and Sebastián wanted me to understand just how successful they were. I include this framing explicitly for several reasons. In part, it pivots the hyperrepresentation of, fixation on, and essentializing of "the" Central American migrant and by extension Latinx poverty, suffering, pain, and oppression that many of my students find reductive and discursively violent and have asked me to push against. It also honors Marleni's insistence that she had "realized all her dreams" and that she lived by "paying it forward" through her transnational entrepreneurship.[48] Through our conversations, Marleni made it clear that realizing her dreams involved sharing both her knowledge and her wealth across her communities—in the United States and in Chalatenango—as had been modeled for her.[49]

But Marleni's reflections proffer a different reading of a Chalateca's diasporic tracks and reveal yet another unexpected arc—one born out of *militant refusal*. Although Marleni explained that she was "too young" to have participated in the war, she had suffered plenty and intended to make sure that her parents in El Rancho wanted for nothing. Marleni also explained that her past of suffering and poverty pushed her to become an entrepreneur—from financing food trucks to investing in construction companies. In 2019 she hoped to buy El Rancho's first excavator in order to level a country that was so uneven: "Para hacer terrenos parejos en un país que es tan desparejo." That sentence is so telling. I asked her whether she meant literally or metaphorically uneven. She just smiled as a response. The World Bank, USAID, and those who study home associations and philanthropy would find all this thrilling, because Marleni was really intentional about leveraging new urban-based skill sets gleaned from years of living in the United States back to El Salvador, particularly for her deported compatriots. Marleni felt that her gains, her wealth, and her creativity needed to be shared.

Her expansive, generative, collective thinking prompted me to ask Marleni about her philosophy of the collective good. I was expecting a narrative similar to the one given earlier by Miguel, about the long struggle and the multiple ways to struggle—with and without a gun. But instead, Marleni offered an ample radical critique of the FMLN. I wondered if her vision came from her experiences as a child in war. I used words like "insurgencia," "revolución," and "militante"—insurgency, revolution, and militant. Marleni didn't have many good words to say about the struggle, about what she termed the mistaken call for socialism. She had never understood how it was all going to work. If everyone was equal and had the same station in life, who, for example, would raise the chickens and then cook them? She reported that as a child, she had asked this exact question, and her curiosity was shot down with the phrase "Ay cállese, niña." (Oh shut up, girl.) From this came her gendered *rebeldía*, her rebelliousness, *not* her insurgent militancy. In fact, Marleni credited the war for making her a critical, disobedient thinker, even regarding the cause. She explained, "Yo he sido siempre muy rebelde. Analizo, veo, y saco mis propias conclusiones y sigo mi propio camino. Se supone que eso es rebeldía porque yo no hago lo que los demás dicen." (I've always been very rebellious. I analyze, I see, and I draw my own conclusions and go my own way. That's supposed to mean I'm rebellious because I don't do what others say.)

Through much of our exchange, Marleni disavowed the revolution and reframed her family's militant history through a discourse of what I term *militant refusal*. She disagreed with my past research, in a sense, when she unequivocally claimed that her family members really weren't insurgents. They were just poor, ambivalent, and misinformed. When I asked, "But wasn't your father jefe de pelotón, a platoon leader for the FPL?" She shook her head no. Then she qualified and clarified that, well, he may have had that role, but they were never militants. It was simply the extreme poverty that had generated people's misguided choices. She provided a series of examples of her community's abject poverty, including the dearth of her own childhood imagination. Marleni shared that at the age of seven her grandest dream was to eat thirty hardboiled eggs at one sitting—and how that desire seemed unreachable. In contrast, she said that she and many of her compatriots now living in the United States had surpassed nearly all their dreams through migration, what with their many cars and homes across borders. She reminded me how far they had all come in such a short time from those adobe homes without electricity.

Critically, Marleni's militant refusal emerged from what she described as the "traumas of war." As I've mentioned throughout the book, in the 1990s, most Chalatecas and Chalatecos I spent time with rarely deployed the term or the framing of "trauma" to describe the extreme suffering and loss of war.[50] A new generation of scholarship on the war and historical memory in El Salvador, however, is focusing precisely on how the now aging protagonists of insurgency and their descendants rescue the past and articulate it through the language of trauma.[51] Because before seeking refuge in the Mesa Grande camps in Honduras, Marleni had seen countless people killed during military bombings and army attacks. She described dead, scarred bodies and the times she survived:

> Una vez cayó una bomba en un árbol de zapote y ahí estaba el campamento de la guerrilla y mi mamá le dijo a uno de los muchachos que estaba abajo que me alcanzara y me jalara a mí para llevarme, meterme en un tatú. (Once a bomb fell on a zapote tree right by the guerrilla camp, and my mom told one of the boys [guerrillas] that was there to grab me and carry me to the tatú.)

But Marleni fainted amid all the bombing and from the shock of seeing a man's throat slit from a piece of shrapnel. She didn't make it to the safety of the young guerrilla's arms. When she came to, she tried to walk, but her legs wouldn't stop shaking from the "fear or something." She was surrounded by dead people. Her mother grabbed her and dragged her, and they finally made it to the shelter. This was just one of many narratives of survival that Marleni shared with me.

In another story, she told me about her near-death experience during the 1980 Río Sumpul Massacre, a story that her mother had never shared with me. Marleni said that story was a "trauma" and a "nightmare" that would forever haunt her: "Hasta hoy en día, aún no lo supero." (Till today, I still can't get over it.) She still carried with her the intense corporal feeling of hunger, surviving three days with just a little bit of sugar and drops of water. She still carried with her the memories of the soldiers' military operation, how they were going to "peinar" it all—literally comb the area—but she explained that this meant *disparar*, or "shoot everything in sight." She still carried with her the images of massacred women and children, their bodies bloated and floating down the river. She survived the massacre separated from the three hundred other people also fleeing. She survived with her father and uncle as they took cover in a small deserted hamlet, where they survived by fishing. Regarding the dead floating bodies on the Sumpul River, she explained how her uncle took a ring from a dead woman's finger: "Pasó una señora muerta ahí. Él se fue y le agarró y le sacó un anillo que llevaba." Objects, things of the dead.

This history made Marleni wonder why had her family and neighbors kept living in *el monte*, "in the mountains," given all the repression? She told me that she spent a lot of time contemplating this question. This pondering marked her very personal afterlife of war and postwar. Unlike the perspectives shared in chapter 1 of this book by Don Gilberto and Nelson and unlike the many narratives I have collected in the past about Chalatenango's military and paramilitary brutality, Marleni theorized that her community's decision making stemmed from their rural misinformation and from being "brainwashed" by the urban youth who had come to "conquistar a la gente" (conquer the people).[52] She submitted this perspective:

Si analizo eso, fue por una falta de información y por ignorancia—If I analyze that, it's because of a lack of information and from ignorance. If we had left for the capital, for civilization, absolutely nothing would have happened to us. At the start some people went to the capital and some went to the mountains. . . . No debíamos absolutamente nada. No le habíamos hecho nada, nada malo a nadie. Pero el momento que empezamos a huir y andar más gente en el monte entonces ya éramos delincuentes para ellos—We owed absolutely nothing. We hadn't done anything, nothing bad to anyone. But the moment we started running away and heading for the mountains, then we were already criminals to them.

Apart from an evolutionary model that equates the urban with modernity and "civilization," Marleni's critique troubles a long-standing discourse on the dearth of political neutrality during times of war, seen in her statement that innocent victims did not "owe" anything to anybody. This is an important framing that has been mobilized to seek justice for massacre victims in places such as El Mozote in the neighboring Department of Morazán and in other cases, including the Río Sumpul Massacre.[53] Here, though, Marleni places blame onto the victims themselves—their "running away" roots the state's "misreading" of their act as delinquency and subversion. In the 1990s repopulated communities, residents agreed that political neutrality had not been possible, but this recognition was harnessed, most often, as an argument for the righteous, legitimate, honorable, brave, defensive, radical, and ultimately armed insurrection. Can we read Marleni's militant refusal as another side of the same Chalateco coin that demands redress and recognition for past injuries and the pain of war? Is this militant refusal part of the vanguard of the revolution?

Marleni did not absolve the military when we spoke, although she reproduced another common state-sponsored official and Cold War discourse that blamed the guerrilla for inciting violence through their (communist) organizing. She also qualified the horrors of counterinsurgency operations through framing culpability in terms of soldiers' ignorance: "La Fuerza Armada era unos grandes asesinos que asesinaban gente sin necesidad.—The Armed Forces were assassins who killed people without need. . . . Those poor ignorant soldiers were just sent by others. . . . It was all just a political show." Marleni juxtaposed state-sponsored violence with stories about the excesses of insurgent violence and the reprisals that followed—the execution, or "adjustment," of a guerrilla soldier by the FPL for abuses.[54] As Marleni explained it, the insurgent had killed for pleasure. She admitted her fascination on the topic of the war. She had asked many former combatants living in the United States and back in El Rancho about their militancy. She claimed that nearly all of them, 95 percent, stated that if they had known then what they know now, they would never have joined the revolution. Her own brother, a former FPL special forces soldier (so, not a militant?), refused to talk about the war with her and said that they should all just forget about it as if it were a "nightmare."

During much of our interview, Marleni evacuated the insurgent cause and the intellectual decision-making of everyday rank-and-file ordinary revolutionaries who populated the guerrilla. Do you remember Don Gilberto's epoch-thinking framing—that *longue durée* of violence that entangled temporalities from the biblical flood to conquest to the Cold War? Marleni concluded that it was all a "cheap fraud." No one got that imagined socialist chicken from her youth. In fact, she reminded me that *the numbers* show that there is more violence now than ever before in El Salvador. So, she theorized, better had they all migrated to the United States and "progressed" and set aside the masculinist war effort that derailed people's human and economic development in the name of killing. She offered one last eyewitness account of insurgent abuse through the story of suicide bombing—an insurgent tactic that in my expansive ethnographic and bibliographic research I have yet to come across. When she told me the story, I admit that I was stunned into silence. I listened to the recording again and again as I transcribed it to make sure that I wasn't misunderstanding. Her story, told through the lens of a child eyewitness, is of course always already positioned and politicized. I'm not questioning its veracity, necessarily. But I wonder if it conflates past insurgent practices with the post-9/11 emblematic image of the terrorist, the suicide bomber. In Marleni's account, the Chalateco suicide bomber represents the idealized hypermasculine victim of youth betrayed and fits war and postwar tropes of martyred leaders. It underscores the profound and pained sacrifices of war. Again, I am and am not interested in the "truthfulness" of this account. I include the original Spanish for its force, poetry, and critique of insurgent rhetoric and practices, and I follow that with my translation into English. Marleni explained that

> Imagínese, imagínese cómo puede convencer un ser humano a otro. Y eso lo vi en carne propia. ¿Cómo va a creer que los convencían? Yo estaba ahí y no me lo contaron. Convencían a un muchacho tal vez joven, guapo con un futuro excelente hoy en día, o lo hubiera tenido. Le decían, "Tú vas a ser un héroe de la causa de la revolución." Y le escogían entre todos tal vez el más guapo el más fuerte, "Tú vas a ser nuestro héroe. Te vamos a adorar toda la vida. Vas a ser nuestro héroe. ¡Qué viva el compañero! no se que." Y le aplaudían . . . le hacían su gallina, todo. Le llenaban de minas en el cuerpo, y él, por voluntad propia, feliz: "Wow, yo voy a ser, en la historia, yo voy a ser uno de los héroes. Yo voy a dar mi vida para la revolución porque toda esta gente que está aquí, y la que no estoy viendo, estos van a vivir en un futuro, en un mundo soñado diferente—como dicen los evangélicos, en el paraíso." Um-hum. Se llenaba de minas todo el cuerpo y se iba a meter agachadito, como podía meterse infiltrado entre los soldados para que explotaran todititos, él y todos ellos. Que [pause] lavado de cerebro. ¿Y 'onde está su héroe? Los héroes están muertos, olvidados. [Pause] Entonces, ¿por qué el jefe no iba? Porque no quería morir. **Entonces, buscaban las mentes más débiles para usarlos.** Um-hum. Entonces, eso fue el uno y eso fue el otro. Los pobres soldaditos.

> Imagine, imagine how one human being can convince another. And I saw that in my own flesh and blood. How do you think they convinced them? I was there; they didn't tell me this. They convinced perhaps a handsome young youth who had an excellent future ahead of him, or he would have. They would tell him, "You, you're going to be our hero. We're going to worship you forever. You are going to be our hero. Long live our hero!" And they would applaud him. . . . They cooked him his hen, everything, and they put mines all over his body, and he of his own free will was happy: "Wow, I'm going to go down in history like a hero. I'm going to give my life for the revolution because all these people that are here, and all the others that I can't see are going to live a different future, a world imagined that is different—like the evangelicals tell us: paradise." Um-hum. He'd fill his whole body with

mines and then, crouched low, infiltrate the [army] soldiers to blow them all up, himself included, he and all of them. What [pause] brainwashing. And where is that hero? All the heroes are dead, forgotten. [Pause]. Why didn't the commander go? Because he didn't want to die. **So, they looked for the weakest most feeble [debilitated] minds, to use them.** Um-hum. So that was the one and that was the other. The poor little soldiers.

And here we are again, between heroic and debilitated, in the after.

AFTER-STORIES AND AFTER-ENDINGS— MEMORY ACROSS GENERATIONS

Marleni's transgressive political after-stories and Miguel's quotidian afterlives of war and postwar offer us particular paths for expanding the scope of postwar studies, for asking whose stories count and what we do with them. Though quite different, I believe they are part and parcel of a repertoire of Chalateco-insurgent multigenerational chronicles that honor the trauma of war, demand justice across sectors, and reframe a history of collective action. The values and moral frameworks that underscore this recognition can make for a better world for us all. I wonder if there is also a space for anthropological intimacies and responsibilities? Does all of this run parallel to the long arc of international solidarity, which is of course not unproblematic but rich with history and memory, still lived and unfolding locally and internationally?[55] Afters ask us to sit awhile, perhaps in a handwoven hammock, as we are invited back into one of El Rancho's homes or perhaps as we are welcomed and scooch in a booth in a bustling *pupusería* in Virginia. I'm not erasing the power of borders or systemic racism that dictates whether we've had the chance for both.

What I have tried to show is that across spaces and generations, memories keep spilling, leaking, blooming. Rubén, whom we met in chapter 3, had some specific things to say about these memories and tied them explicitly to the sacrifices of the 1.5 insurgent generation—although I didn't have the language for it back then. In 1997 he had shared with me that he "knew who he was." He hadn't been a "guerrillero," and those who really were—like his father, who had been in it ten years before the start and who came out of it unrecognizable, like a skeleton "era un esqueleto, no era mi papá"—were the ones least likely to talk about it. He told me back then in 1997, "Wait ten years, and then we can name my murdered grandfather and aunt. We can say their names. We can voice the pain." He theorized that the role of children of revolutionaries, like him, was to process the knowledge born from the sacrifices of their parents. I wasn't yet thinking about 1.5 insurgents. Rubén said to give it ten years. It's been decades, and only recently he shared that he was finally able to forgive his parents for abandoning him for the cause. He could, all these years after and deep into adulthood and fatherhood, understand it and "begin to awaken the memories" (empezar a despertar los recuerdos). In part he was prompted by a recognition that his own teen children "didn't know the smell of my past, from where I come from literally, from where I came" (no saben como huele mi pasado, de donde vengo literalmente, de donde salí). I appreciate Rubén's embodied, corporal call for memory, for wanting to pass on the already intergenerational sensorium (that smell of a Salvadoran past) of what Marianne Hirsch might analyze as postmemory.[56]

This brings me to examine more explicitly the multigenerational call for memory as a key part of the *longue durée* of El Salvador's postwar. For some, this is a call to recuperate and commemorate the victims and survivors of the war so that they are not forgotten, so that their deaths were not in vain, so that justice can finally be met. For others, particularly the generation of Chalatecos and Chalatecas born well into peace, the call for memory, as Adriana Alas's work so clearly shows, is one that seeks to uncover inconvenient stories that trouble the heroic narrative of the FMLN insurgency by asking, for example, about the lives of the *originarios*, or the original residents of repopulated communities who may not have shared a militant or revolutionary past. In everyday life, these stories don't quite "fit in" with insurgent narratives. This new generation is also asking about the hidden stories, including FMLN "excesses," or extremes of war. Or as Fernando Chacón Serrano documents for new generations of youth, the weight and wounds of war are never fully healed and live in dialectical relationship—theirs and not theirs—in the children of postwar.[57]

In recent years, what I find most interesting is how victimhood and suffering are leveraged to forge an alternate iteration of transitional justice in the ongoing call to end impunity. A new wave of academic interest on memory practices in El Salvador is pushing the conversation forward, evidenced in volumes produced across Central America and in El Salvador specifically, such as the edited volume *Revolución Revisitada*[58] and the 2019 special volume of the journal *Realidad* curated by anthropologist Benjamín Carlos Lara Martínez on historical memory. We see it also in the collaborative community, academic, and restorative justice projects that build memory sites and practices across El Salvador, such as the monument commemorating the massacre at El Mozote and its attendant "la ruta de la memoria" (the historical memory route).[59]

In Chalatenango, we see it in projects such as "Surviving Memory in Postwar El Salvador" that in part work toward the construction of the Sumpul Massacre Memorial Park at Las Aradas.[60] This massacre took place on May 14, 1980; approximately six hundred children, women, and men were brutally murdered in a military operation by the Salvadoran Armed Forces, the National Guard, the paramilitary group ORDEN, and the Honduran Army that cordoned off their border in one of the war's first emblematic cases of counterinsurgency extermination. The Río Sumpul Massacre was a key case investigated for the 1993 Truth Commission report, which found substantial evidence that the massacre was a violation of international humanitarian law and international human rights law and that there was a cover-up of the massacre by Salvadoran military command.[61] Marleni commented on living through that trauma, seeing floating bodies, and remembering how her uncle salvaged a ring. Was it gold or silver?

The Asociación Sumpul writes about their goals "that the present and future generations will know the truth about these events so that they do NOT happen AGAIN and we can finally solidify the foundations for true peace and justice."[62] Regarding why now is the time for their work, the association explains that survivors are aging, and knowledge of the past is weakening; that many of the recommendations articulated in the Truth Commission are still unmet; and that "those who survived the massacres and engaged in political struggle during the war feel obligated to share their experiences with the youth of El Salvador, not only to avoid repeating the traumas of the war but also to recognize the democratic rights they gained through organized

FIGURE 11. Commemoration of child martyrs, Chalatenango. Early 1990s. Photograph courtesy of the Sprenkels Melara family, © Ralph Sprenkels.

struggle." The call is a hegemonic insurgent one of mobilizing memories for the ongoing struggle to meet "core goals: justice, education, and dignity for the victims."[63]

This is a powerful statement. I recognize quite a few residents who are on the association's board of directors. Their collective discourse is historically contingent. For the most part, a language that incorporated trauma was not what I heard circulating at the start of postwar, when the protagonist generation was still riding the coattails of their own youth. Indeed, we'll see shortly the historical shifts and co-construction of social memory from one that underscored a hegemonic, heroic suffering through the category of guerrillero/a, compañero/a, or compatriot to one that decades later speaks to the sequelae of trauma, the injuries—corporal and psychic—of innocent victims. This is not to say that commemorations of wartime violence are new. The commemoration of the Río Sumpul Massacre has taken place for decades.

Although in the past, hundreds of local residents, human rights activists, government officials, NGO representatives, Catholic Church officials, and international delegations would make the walk through the mountains to the commemorative site at Las Aradas where a mass would be held, in 2020, because of the COVID-19 pandemic and Salvadoran quarantine orders, organizers shifted to a virtual event with various platforms dedicated to streaming a series of events.[64] And so, after many years, I also joined a virtual audience of listeners and accompanied the commemorations.[65] The discourse that surrounded the events moved through the past to the present to the future. The day's narratives evoked a sensorium of memories and included interviews with survivors who peopled the quantification of loss by telling stories about their murdered and innocent neighbors or kin; the reading of a press release by the president of the Coordinator of Communities in Development in Chalatenango (CCR), the long-standing grassroots organization that is part of the national historic human rights organization CRIPDES; the call to open military archives; and the naming of intellectual authors of the massacre read by the at-the-time child survivor: "Gral. José Guillermo García, Ministro de Defensa y miembro de la Junta Revolucionaria de Gobierno; Cnel. Eugenio Vides Casanova, director general de la Guardia Nacional; Cnel. Juan Rafael Bustillo, comandante de la Fuerza Aérea Salvadoreña; Cnel. Ricardo Augusto Peña Arbaiza, comandante del Destacamento Militar No 1 en Chalatenango; Cnel. Mario Adalberto Reyes Mena, de la Cuarta Brigada de Infantería El Paraíso, Chalatenango."[66]

Throughout I was struck by the intergenerational back and forth as community organizers applauded the work of a new group of activist youth such as the Misioneros de la memoria histórica, Chalatenango (the Missionaries of Historical Memory in Chalatenango),[67] young people who were rescuing the past, getting community stories down, so as not to forget—just as the earlier-mentioned Sumpul Association remarked. The categories of childhood and innocent victim were also repeatedly invoked as the day's events served as a history lesson, reminding listeners of the overarching repressive context of the 1980 massacre, how civilian organizing was met with blood and how today's gains stemmed from sacrifices made from this blood: "Nada ha sido regalado" (Nothing has been free). Repeated also was the refrain that memories, the right to memory, and the memories of martyrs were not in quarantine: "La memoria no está en cuarentena . . . , el derecho a la memoria . . . , la memoria de nuestros mártires no está en cuarentena." It was through the invocation of memories that a pathway for holding intellectual authors accountable for wartime crimes against humanity could be made possible so that reconciliation could finally be forged, so that as one survivor exclaimed, "Víctimas puedan perdonar sin el peso de la impunidad institucionalizada. Pero sólo puede haber perdón y reconciliación si se garantiza la verdad y la justicia." (Victims can pardon without the weight of institutionalized impunity. But there can only be forgiveness and reconciliation if truth and justice are guaranteed.)[68] Striking also is that forty years later, justice remains aspirational.

One of the opening speakers emphasized that the victims of the Río Sumpul Massacre were all civilians who had lined the community of Las Aradas, on the bank of the river, with white flags on trees only to be massacred in cold blood. He reminded the listeners that they were wrong to think that the Salvadoran government was going to have a "conscience" and respect their lives. They (community members) were wrong not to see, not to anticipate the "criminal alliance" between the Salvadoran and Honduran governments. But then, forty years later, the speaker, who had been a young child during the massacre, added that "también se equivocaron varios de nuestros dirigentes, quienes a pesar de que hubo varias advertencias incluso de soldados hondureños" (several of our leaders were also wrong, although there were several warnings even from Honduran soldiers). Honduran soldiers had warned groups of people washing by the river that an operation was forthcoming. But those FMLN dirigentes "se opusieron y impidieron a la gente que buscara vías de escapa. La consigna era 'vencer o morir.' Pero no podía vencer un pueblo indefenso y desarmado a un ejército con toda su artillería." (opposed and prevented people from seeking escape routes. The slogan was "win or die." But a defenseless and unarmed people could not defeat an army with all its artillery.)[69]

Reader, it was the first time that I had heard such a public critique of insurgent leadership during a commemorative event—although it aligns again with anthropologist Adriana Alas's ethnography of this commemoration and the reckoning that youth have asked of former insurgent leaders. Forty years later, this reckoning, this unpacking of memory and commemoration, is an after-story.[70] Missing though, were the Chalatecas and Chalatecos that didn't or couldn't accompany the day's events. They are no less part of the continuum. They were working in the diaspora—folding laundry in laundromats, working construction, cleaning offices, getting certified as electricians, raising their children, going to school, starting their own businesses, and so on. They constitute the less visible side of this labor that creates the space for the recuperation of memories that lie between victim and survivor in the renewed calls for truth, justice, and reparation. This ample call for a just future is made possible through an entwined 1.5 insurgent connection in which agentive moves for *verdad*, *justicia*, and *reparación* happen—yes, in commemorative acts but also in attending to Marleni's evacuation of insurgency and to Miguel's framing that there are many ways to be in the struggle. Entwined then is a radical ethics of collective care, open to possibilities of forgiveness through that carrying on in the search for postwar truths.

RECLAMO DEL PASADO—THE CLAIMS OF THE PAST
There is such conceit in endings, in making things appear neater than they are in that reinvocation of memory, testimony, and stories in the service of truth, justice, and reparation. Anthropological intimacies and responsibilities are also inflected in the after-stories I share that I hope will help us contest the elisions of the past and inform different kinds of narratives about El Salvador. Because I too have been held to account. I'll share an everyday example and end with Elsy, where so much of it all began for me. In 2020 she continued her community activism, her active grandmothering, and her love and care for her adult 1.5 insurgent children all living in the United States. Our relationship has ebbed and flowed. It has spanned decades, from letters that we exchanged starting in January 1994 for which I have a one-way record—an epistolary archive that I have not yet shared with anyone—to my return trips to El Rancho and my more frequent visits with her children and their kin across the United States. It was the latter, my easy reunions with Elsy's children and grandchildren that prompted Elsy to make claims on our shared past, to remind me of the always present potential of what is arguably anthropology's betrayal.

Here's one example. After sending Elsy huge congratulations on the birth of one of her grandchildren in the United States, a gorgeous baby that I was able to visit, *me reclamó*. I can really only think about the intimacy of the exchange in Spanish. Elsy held me to account. She checked my everyday privilege, the violence of US immigration policy, and my ontological complicity. Through text she told me that I simply had not done enough. I had not found a way to bring her to visit the United States to see her children, to hold her grandchildren. Anthropology's betrayal right there. My response failed. I apologized for the nation's racist and xenophobic immigration laws and explained that I would continue to do my best to "apoyar" and "acompañar," to support and accompany all her children. So much for the bags of baby clothes, feminist antiracist board books, and gender-neutral educational toys. That was all about me, right? Elsy thanked me for those. I sent her my love with an emoji heart. She responded cogently, politically, and beyond the personal, linking past and present, individual and collective with this: "Nosotros también te recordamos mucho. . . . Me regreso al tiempo pasado que fue tan difícil para nosotros." (We also remember you very much. . . . I think back to the past, the time that was so difficult for us.) Reader, Elsy's words push me to account, to examine the connections and shifts, to think about the unexpected possibilities and gains as well as the multiple interlocking injustices that remain. This too is an after-story of a Latina–South American gringa anthropologist studying El Salvador's postwar from US academic spaces.[71]

In this book I have tried to amplify what I have learned through listening to Chalatecas and Chalatecos's *reclamos* along with their analyses, interpretations, lived histories, and unfolding paths. I've done so by focusing on interrupting hegemonic tropes around violent numbers; troubled, unruly bodies; and the erasure of things. Throughout, I have foregrounded stories, individual and collective—some told in 1993, others in 1997, and still others in the 2000s, the 2010s, and the 2020s. I have discussed this methodology as based on a protracted and intimate arc that attends to shifts in solidarity—and to the need to step aside even as I write. My hope is that these stories of the particular, as Abu-Lughod so eloquently modeled for us all decades ago now, can speak to our ever-growing global challenges to think in new ways[72] in that search for a politics of love and recognition. My hope is that these stories also lead you, Reader, to the work of a generation of Central American and Central American–American authors whose critiques move from insurgency to migration and whom I have cited throughout this book. For now, I offer one last story, from Elsy. It's a good one.

AN INSURGENT PARROT

You may remember that this book opened up with Elsy's mother, Nanita, and her story about a gender-bending thief. I'm still not sure why she shared those folktales with me, but they are with us now. They are part of the Chalateca record to be honored. In 1996, when she shared them with me, the after of today was, of course, unimaginable. When Elsy and I returned to those stories, digitized via WhatsApp, she added after retelling several to me, "I have another story. It's about a parrot. I don't know if you want it. If you have the time, I'll tell it to you." Elsy actually asked if I had "the space" (si tenés lugar). I immediately said yes, because, well, at this point, Reader, you know it's all about the story for me.

> Había una vez una lora, ¿va? Una señora tenía una lora en la casa—Once upon a time there was a [female] parrot, right? A woman had a parrot in her home. And one time a group of guerrilleros went past the woman's house and they were chanting "FECCAS-UTC! FECCAS-UTC!" Lotti, have you ever heard that slogan? It was a slogan that the compas would chant when we were marching. That's what they said, "FECCAS-UTC! FECCAS-UTC! FECCAS-UTC!" It was when the war was just starting, when we were first the organization FECCAS-UTC. Era como una alianza—It was like an alliance.

Elsy was giving me a history lesson, all these decades later. It was 2020, and she related the story-joke in the present tense, reminding me of the early before of "official war" full of an imbrication of early clandestine organizing and state-sponsored repression. She continued,

> Entonces, como dice el chiste del cuento, dicen que pasaron los guerrilleros por esa casa que estaba la lora—So, as the joke of the story goes, the guerrillas passed by the parrot's house while they kept chanting, "FECCAS-UTC! FECCAS-UTC! FECCAS-UTC!" And the chant was engraved in the parrot's mind—A la lora, se le quedó grabado. So another day, the soldiers pass

by the woman's house, right? And when the parrot sees the soldiers passing by, she starts repeating, "FECCAS-UTC! FECCAS-UTC!" And the soldiers say, "Ahí están encerrados los guerrilleros en esa casa—There are the guerrilleros locked [with the implication of hiding out] in that house." And so the soldiers break into the house, but they didn't find not even one guerrillero, just the parrot. "Well," they say to the parrot, "Como no hemos hallado a los guerrilleros a vos te vamos a llevar—Since we haven't found the guerrillas, we're going to take you." And they put her hands behind her back and they took her.

Ethnographic-historical truths are in stark relief in this multispecies joke. Because indeed, listen to the negotiation, or is it conflation, of innocent civilian, citizen, insurgent, and victim. Elsy continued,

But because she was a parrot, they didn't take her to prison. Instead they took her to a chicken coop full of roosters and hens. And there a rooster tried to grab her, thinking that she was a hen, but she was a parrot. And they say that the parrot said, "Momento. A mí no me han traído por puta," le dijo. ["Wait a minute. They didn't bring me here because I'm a whore," she said.] "Si no por guerrillera," le dijo.—"Rather because I'm a guerrilla," she said.

In this section of the story, Elsy highlights the violent gendered and sexualized language of war, a language that perhaps in her reproduction of the joke or rather in my retelling of it is injurious, diminishing, demeaning, and violent such that it links up to larger gender-based violent tropes. But I include it because I believe it so eloquently combats ongoing assumptions about clear lines of resistance or victimization; of suffering, survival, and agency; and about what stories are told in the after. That parrot, first mistaken as a guerrilla, comes to own her insurgent identity through a radical claim to the security and ownership of her body. Elsy's multispecies agency is perhaps the catalyst to her son's logic of care, to his invocation of love and multispecies debility—that little calf who didn't make it despite his care, his feeding of droplets of milk. It also speaks to Donna J. Haraway's invocation of "staying with the trouble" where, in part, we must learn to live and die in "response-ability on a damaged earth."[73] To do so, Haraway argues there are no easy technofixes. Rather, we need a multispecies kinship of "oddkin" to contest the onslaught of violence from the Anthropocene, the Capitalocene[74] and to fight against the hopelessness that the "game is over" so that we can make a "resurgent world."[75] Resurgent insurgents as our future?

Elsy and I shared a little chuckle about her story. She wanted me to understand the boldness of the parrot, to make sure that I had gotten a key point about the bird's misrecognition: "Como a los guerrilleros los querían capturar, y no hallaron los guerrilleros sólo a ella [la lora] la capturaron." (As they wanted to capture the guerrillas but they didn't find them, they captured only her [the parrot].) The parrot comes to stand in for or to shape-shift and encompass the innocent (women) in their agentive and transformative move from civilian, bystander, listener, and repeater (meaning "to parrot") to insurgent. A former combatant, long dead, told her the story. Elsy told me, "Sí, nos reíamos nosotros cuando contaba ese cuento. Chistoso, ¿va? Está bonito." (Yes, we all laughed when he told us that story. Funny, right? It's a nice one.)

Reader, we've traveled through terrain and time and through analyses of numbers, bodies, things, and always stories. I end this book with Elsy as she tethers for us just one before with an ever-unfolding after-story. I end this book with deep thanks, to Elsy, to community members in the municipality of Las Vueltas and specifically in El Rancho, to their diasporic kin, and to so many Chalatecas and Chalatecos for finding time and space to speak truth to power and to leverage memories for recognition, truth, justice, repair, and accountability across our borders as we celebrate and honor diverse paths, lived experiences, and aspirations big and small. *Imagínese*—Imagine it.

ACKNOWLEDGMENTS

For a long time, I couldn't imagine this book. It exists in that anxious, tender space of transnational love, full of shared experiences and memories, of changing hopes and worries, of wanting to do right, and of wanting to do it right, from the sidelines, *con solidaridad, cariño, y un respeto inmenso* for the generations of Chalatecas and Chalatecos in repopulated communities and in the diaspora. As I use pseudonyms throughout the book, here I say to the *compañeras y compañeros* that I first met in extraordinary Chalatenango in 1993 and to the many whom I've had the privilege to learn from years along the way, thank you for everything, for showing us all what *compromiso* looks and feels like, for the *longue durée* of your *protagonismo*, for holding me to account, and for your generosity in keeping your doors open. I hope that in this ethnographic archive I do justice to your ancestors, to your stories, and to the arcs of your many futures that reckon with the past and present and that invite us all to work across borders for a just, inclusive, and righteous world. *Humildemente, esto es para ustedes.*

This book also exists through my complicated relationship to anthropological research and writing and to the everyday realities that entwine professional-personal life—the negotiation of teaching as a form of politics, the abundant administrative labor that sustains institutions and goes so often underrecognized, and the making of family. I thank the colleagues who supported my way back to this project as I brought in new interests in medical anthropology and disability studies. I thank Rachel Adams, who created an open space through Columbia University's the Future of Disability

Studies working group. I will forever be grateful to her for inviting me to join this group, which stretched me in life-changing ways. Thank you to Faye Ginsburg and Rayna Rapp, whose work and insights serve as a guide, and to Julia Rodas, who continues to generate some of the best conversations in critical disability studies around as we cochair the University Seminar in Disability, Culture, and Society at Columbia University.

An early presentation at the University of Pennsylvania's Program for Democracy, Citizenship, and Constitutionalism, where I was lucky enough to share the stage with Deborah Yashar, created a platform to think about the trauma of numbers. I thank colleagues Rogers M. Smith, Matthew Roth, Tulia Falleti, and Emilio Parrado for this invitation and for the subsequent writing and thinking. At Swarthmore College, Sa'ed Atshan gave me the opportunity to share my positioned work on bodies, injury, and debility. Many thanks to his students and his colleague Nanci Buiza in Peace and Conflict Studies.

Given the arc of the book and my return to ethnographic archives from the 1990s, I thank the institutions that made my original research possible. These include the Fulbright-Hays Doctoral Dissertation Fellowship, the Inter-American Foundation Fellowship, and the Organization of American States Dissertation Fellowship. Support from the City University of New York allowed me to develop the book. These include two PSC-CUNY Research Awards (60386-0048 and 62137-0050), a faculty fellowship at the Center for Place, Culture, and Politics, and a Mellon Mid-Career Fellowship at the Committee on Globalization and Social Change, both at the CUNY Graduate Center. I thank the colleagues who workshopped what would become elements of this book. Particular thanks to respective seminar leaders David Harvey, Ruth Wilson Gilmore, Sujatha Fernandes, and Gary Wilder and Susan Buck-Morss. Thinking through public scholarship and publication support for Ralph Sprenkels's photographs was made possible as a faculty mentor to Juliana Valente through the Andrew W. Mellon Foundation PublicsLab at the CUNY Graduate Center through the excellent leadership of Bianca Williams and Stacy Hartman. At my home campus of the City College of New York, the cogent critiques of anthropology and power and the calls for resistance by now generations of students has kept me going. So has thinking with colleagues about public scholarship, critical pedagogies, and the very work of the university. Thank you to Ramona Hernandez, Iris Lopez, Kathy McDonald, and Maritsa Poros—colleagues in allied departments whose gendered leadership is so appreciated. Thank you for the years of support to Juan Carlos Mercado, dean of CCNY's downtown campus for working adult students, where I had my start. I've been lucky to work alongside Asale Angel-Ajani, Sarah Muir, Matthew Reilly, Asha Samad-Matías, Arthur Spears, Stanley Thangaraj, and Diana Wall in a department that has long placed a commitment to antiracist pedagogy at the center of our everyday practices and community building with our students. Without the generosity and mentorship of Bob Melara from the Department of Psychology, who stepped in as department chair so that I could take a fellowship leave, I would not have had the time to write this book. I am indebted to Sarah Muir, who in solidarity took on the pivotal role of deputy chair with the brilliance that she brings to her scholarship, teaching, and leadership, so evident in how she carried the department forward during the emergence of the COVID-19 pandemic. Our work has been all the more possible through the remarkable leadership of Andy Rich, dean of the Colin Powell School at CCNY. Thank you.

I have leaned on cohorts of friends and colleagues, some for thirty years. Bambi Schieffelin's dedicated teaching, attention to method, unwavering support, and sage counsel serve as a guide for my own work with students. Deborah Thomas's expansive thinking, rooted in Caribbean history and everyday diasporic lives, has anchored this project, as has her feminist solidarity and the ways that she creates anticolonial professional practices of community building. My everyday is buoyed by my friendship with Ayala Fader and, amazingly, our decades-long conversations that get it all in, from how to hopefully craft a better ethical anthropology to motherhood and family. Thank you, Ayala, for being my go-to person for just about everything, for charting so much through your own work on religion and media, and for sharing your incisive and brilliant read through the years.

Three colleagues and friends read the entire manuscript. Thank you, Ethel Brooks, Mike Anastario, and Serena Cosgrove. It's difficult to find the words to express my gratitude for their critical yet kind reads that helped me move forward at different stages of writing and thinking. The years of nearly daily check-ins with Ethel about all things labor and life, big and small, mark the *longue durée* of a deep friendship that has seen it all and embraced the laughter and the tears. Her brilliance and building of a Critical Romani Studies charts a path for the work ahead for all of us. I thank her also for inspiring the title of the book. I am so lucky to count Mike Anastario as a friend and colleague. Part of a new generation of US scholars studying El Salvador through a commitment to participatory research, he has that rare and remarkable ability to bring quantitative expertise to bear upon ethnographic methodologies as he poses the most pressing of questions. I'm indebted to his read and to his hospitality in El Salvador. To Serena Cosgrove, *mil gracias por tu solidaridad, de verdad, tu compromiso político y académico, por tu cariño y por tu aporte a través años y redes*. Serena was the first to read the entire manuscript in its earliest form. Her line-by-line comments, questions, and edits, steeped in her decades of scholarship and accompaniment with colleagues and communities in Central America, supported me at the hardest of times. The faults in this book are my own.

It was through Serena that I met Padre José Alberto Idiáquez Guevara, S.J., president of the Universidad Centroamericana (UCA) in Managua, Nicaragua, whose leadership and university manifesto remind us that the *quehacer*, that the liberatory work of the university is to unmask systemic violence and to prepare students so that they can construct a more just and inclusive society. Thinking with him to illuminate the struggles of universities under fire in Nicaragua led to new forms of academic solidarity and to friendships across generations and topics. Thank you to Wendi Bellanger for her comparative work on academic capitalism at the intersection of state repression and neoliberalism and for the opportunity to work alongside her. And thank you to Andy Gorvetzian and Fiore Bran Aragón for sharing their projects that form part of the future of Central American studies.

The work of generations of Salvadoranists on postwar processes continues to ground my own. Thank you to Ellen Moodie for your scholarship and for your commitment to a new wave of Salvadoran scholars working across topics. It has been a privilege to be in conversation with Adriana Alas, Georgina Hernández, Hilary Goodfriend, Clara Guardado, Eduardo Maciel, Allan Martell, Ainhoa Montoya, Ninel Pleitez, and Elizabeth Velásquez Estrada, whose work on historical memory, postwar, and the politics of research are all a force. It is with tremendous sadness that I thank my dear late friend and colleague Ralph [Rafa] Sprenkels, a brilliant, generous, and prolific scholar, who pushed paradigms with his deep curiosity and his ability to ask important, difficult, poignant questions from a capacious space of humanity and solidarity. As I wrote these words, I held his own as a guide. We worked together as *peritos antropológicos* to submit expert dictamens on the *Caso Masacre El Mozote y Lugares Aledaños Causa Penal 238/1990*. The heft of his knowledge and activism carried us through. I thank him and his life partner, Michelle Melara, and their children Tamara and Simón for the use of his beautiful photographs that capture the complexity of Chalatenango's early transition to peace. I also thank Michelle and Darcy Alexandra for their solidarity and for inviting me to work more deeply with Ralph's photographic archive.

What a dream to have landed at Stanford University Press. Many thanks to Michelle Lipinski, who originally supported this project; to Kate Wahl, who so expertly took it on; and to Dylan Kyung-lim White, who so thoughtfully shepherded it through. I thank the two anonymous reviewers for the serious engagement with my work and their pointed feedback that I hope has made this book stronger. I also thank the amazing SUP editorial team, including Sunna Juhn, who kindly supported all the important steps to final product. Thanks to Gretchen Otto for overseeing with care the detailed work of copyediting. And thank you once again to Dave Luljak for the indexing expertise.

Mi gente. To friends and family not yet mentioned, thank you for following this arc and for your care. I'm grateful to Jenny Bayly, who has been a friend since we were eight years old and already on our way to becoming professionals in a dance studio. The life of a dancer is still in my body, and I thank Valerie Grace Vann-Oettl, Shawna Emerick, and Emma Poole for giving that breath, movement, and joy back. Ari Haberberg and Jordan Pavlin continue to be true sources of love and inspiration, and I thank Paula Grace, Horacio Sívori, Kety Fangmann, Alan Courtis, Federico Julián Gonzalez, and Cigal Tzohar for their ongoing friendship, and Patti DeMatteo for being a family friend when my kids and I needed it most.

The extended Rossi-Esmonde-Pimpinella-Silber-Amano-King-Iaconis families, with kin stretching across Argentina, Italy, Japan, the Dominican Republic, and the United States is now full of new generations of extraordinary young people who remind me to both step up and step aside. I thank them for giving me permission to share some of our own old-new stories. I hope this book honors the memory of Mario and Maria Rossi, who showed us all how to love deep and wide. Special thanks to my parents, Tomas and Rosita Silber, who were the first to teach me about the importance of *solidaridad*, always asked about and valued my work even when I didn't want the nudge, and continue to love and care in new ways for my no-longer-little children. Once again, my father read the entire manuscript, asked sharp questions, and reviewed my Spanish-English translations. While I was writing this book, he took on the translation of my grandfather's published poetry. Hans [Juan] Silber, exiled during the Holocaust to Buenos Aires, Argentina, and then to Montevideo, Uruguay, was a prolific writer. Among his poems a stanza from "Words Are Ways" speaks to the pull of the narratives that I highlight in the book: "Words are dreams in twilight / songs in the shimmering night / wisdom of the elders—boldness of the young / flying riotous and quiet thoughts."

I dedicate this book to my husband, Antonio Rossi, and to our two kids, Cenzo and Inés, who embody that arc from the wisdom of the elders to the boldness of the young, both quiet and riotous. The everyday of raising our family together over two decades in the hustle of New York City has been quite a partnership. Antonio has leveraged his own 1.5 immigrant trajectory to be our rock. His cinematographic lens and artistry for social, racial, and environmental justice documentaries have modeled for our family the importance of doing this collaborative essential work. *Para mis chicos ya no chiquitos*, I am moved daily by the spectacular young people you have become. Your moral compass, creativity, dedication, work ethic, critical perspective, kindness, and humor make me so proud and give me hope for imagining the future. Thank you for caring and for carrying this project with me. I have the decades-long birthday cards with words of encouragement and changing penmanship—from young to now college aged—to prove it. Our own epistolary archive. This is for you and because of you.

NOTES

PREFACE

1. The colón was the national currency until El Salvador's dollarization on January 1, 2001.

2. Bahareque is an indigenous and historically deep mode of housing construction that uses local resources such as wood, rocks, and mud. See, for example, Martínez et al. (2009).

3. See Thomas (2019) on witnessing and the politics of recognition.

4. See also Ralph (2020), who offers an anthropological method he terms "ethnographic lettering" (192). His text is comprised of a series of open letters written directly to his interlocutors. As he explains it, the letters are the "embodiments of exchange that place the onus of analysis on the ethnographer as well as research participants. In this book, this onus of analysis is imperative from the beginning to the end of my work with Chicago residents" (198). For Ralph, the ethnographic letter is "a mode of ethnographic writing and research methodology that sheds light on the perspectives of both the insider and the outsider" (198).

5. For a comprehensive analysis of what Ralph Sprenkels terms "political military organizations" (PMOs), see his book *After Insurgency* (2018). In it, Sprenkels walks readers through the historical and regional development of those clandestine organizations that would become the Frente Farabundo Martí para la Liberación Nacional, or FMLN. These PMOs include the FPL (Fuerzas Populares de Liberación/Popular Liberation Forces); ERP (Ejército Revolucionario del Pueblo/People's Revolutionary Army); FARN, or RN (Resistencia Nacional/Armed Forces of National Resistance); PRTC (Partido Revolucionario de los Trabajadores Centroamericanos/Central American Workers Revolutionary Party); and the historic PCS (Partido Comunista de El Salvador/Salvadoran Communist Party).

6. In this book, I continue to work with the grammatically gendered Spanish terms "Chalatecos" (masculine) and "Chalatecas" (feminine) because they are used by my interlocutors in everyday speech. Readers should note that there are substantial regional and

diasporic conversations regarding incorporating inclusive, gender-neutral language such as "x," "@," and "e," as in the possibility of writing "Chalateces."

7. Circa 1993–1994 in Chalatenango, mimeographed pamphlets often circulated across repopulated communities from grassroots organizations and from the former insurgent political and military forces and recently established political party—the FMLN. Pamphlets announced such things as political rallies and the importance of women's rights and provided analysis of the violence of neoliberalism. One pamphlet from the FMLN that I archived from this period reads as an introduction to the FMLN as a political party. The trifold document begins with an invitation to the reader, to an "amigo lector" (reader and friend) in the informal "you" (*tú*). I believe this invocation to the reader/listener reflects a larger narrative structure in regional storytelling practices. This book leans into this as a genre. I also point to Katherine McKittrick's *Dear Science and Other Stories* (2021), which provides a powerful model of Black studies and anticolonial praxis that takes the sharing of stories as method and as critical to invention, collaboration, wonder, resistance, and so on in the making of knowledge.

8. See, for example, Lara Martínez (2018), Martell (2020), Alas López (2021), Alas (2019), Cuéllar (2020), Osuna (2020), Hernández Rivas (2019), Maciel (2020), Velásquez Estrada (2015), and Guardado (2019).

9. There is an ample literature, some of which will be addressed more directly in the subsequent chapters. Readers may be interested in texts such as *Landscapes of Struggle* (2004), *Women and War* (2013), *Unraveling the Garment Industry* (2007), *Women's Leadership from the Margins* (2010), *Broadcasting the Civil War* (2010), *Aftermaths of Peace* (2010), *Fragmented Ties* (2000), *Parcels* (2019), and *After Insurgency* (2018). Readers could also turn to Burrell and Moodie's *Annual Review of Anthropology* piece on Central America (2015).

10. Abu-Lughod 2016, 275.

11. Abu-Lughod, 275.

12. Sociologist Rubén G. Rumbaut was among the first to coin the term. For an excellent text that addresses immigration and generation in the United States, see Portes and Rumbaut (2014). For El Salvador specifically, see the work of Suárez-Orozco and Suárez-Orozco (2001).

13. Sprenkels 2018.

14. Here and throughout the book, I am borrowing this historical term, *longue durée*, from Fernand Braudel and the Annales School because I want to make the claim that "postwar" in El Salvador has taken on this vast, multiscalar experience and knowing of time that stretches periodization and takes into account interconnected global processes. See Buchanan (2018), and Lee (2012) for a cogent analysis. Related to the Anthropocene, see Sawyer (2016). See also Enloe (2010).

15. Throughout the book I provide transcribed excerpts from audio recordings from interviews or events. At times I include the original Spanish followed by a translation into English. At other times I just provide the English translation. Unless otherwise indicated, these conversations occurred in Spanish. If code-switching into English took place, this is noted.

16. Here I am also thinking about Saidiya Hartman's *Wayward Lives, Beautiful Experiments*, which recuperates through an historical and archival method of "close narration" the "radical imagination" and agentive historical city-world making of "young black women" who have been erased from historical narratives but who were key, everyday figures (2019, xii–xv).

17. My first book explored gendered disillusionment in postwar El Salvador. Ellen Moodie's work has been foundational in the discussion of democratic disenchantment (2010). Critical research underway in El Salvador by Grazzia Grimaldi explores the current authoritarian turn in El Salvador through an ethnographic research project on the supporters of President Nayib Bukele. See Grimaldi (2021). For a comparative case that theorizes disillusion in the everyday narratives of crises, see Muir (2021).

18. This topic is gaining currency in anthropology and builds on the classic work of Karl Manneheim ([1928] 1952). For example, see "Generations and Change in Central America: An Introduction" in the *Journal of Latin American and Caribbean Anthropology*, edited by Jennifer Burrell and Ellen Moodie (2021), which addresses a range of issues around social movements, the politics of memory, and social change. Generation is also key to this volume's production of knowledge that seeks to decolonize the field via authorship and publishing. For example, each article is intentionally coauthored across generations and across the Global South and North. For other contemporary examples on generation, see Shalini Shankar's *Beeline: What Spelling Bees Reveal about Generation Z's New Path to Success* (2019).

19. Burrell and Moodie 2021. This scholarship includes Alas López (2021), Bellino (2017), Bran Aragón and Goett (2020), Burrell, El Kotni, and Calmo (2020), Frank-Vitale and Martínez d'Aubuisson (2020), Guardado Torrez and Moodie (2020), and Rayner and Morales Rivera (2020).

20. Zetino Duarte and Brioso (2012).

21. See, for instance, Alas López (2021), Bran Aragón and Goett (2020), and Guardado Torrez and Moodie (2020). For a comparative study on framings of violence, see González, Rodríguez, and Urrutia (2019).

22. Abrego 2014. See also Barrera (2013).

23. Author's translation from the original Spanish: "angustia existencial." This article also includes the finding that one in four Salvadoran youth desire to emigrate (Chacón Serrano, Gómez, and Alas 2013, 511, 512).

24. See also Steven Osuna's work on generation and his project on second-generation youth from multiple Latinx backgrounds and their "transnational obstinate memories" (2017, 78) and the ways that parental narratives around fleeing repression, for example, impact the second generation's political activism (2017, 89).

25. Cosgrove 2010; Cosgrove et al. 2021.

26. With this concept, I intentionally play with the Spanish words *cifra* (figure or number) and *cifrar* (code, encrypt, cipher). I add the preposition *en* to coin a new phrasing that aims to index processes of entanglement, embodiment, and time. This concept emerges from the particularities of my own bilingual/bicultural formation that involves

code-switching between Spanish and English and the fluidity of linguistic borders and creation of terms that can result.

27. Hartman writes, "Slavery had established a measure of man and a ranking of life and worth that has yet to be undone. If slavery persists as an issue in the political life of black America, it is not because of an antiquarian obsession with bygone days or the burden of a too-long memory, but because black lives are still imperiled and devalued by a racial calculus and a political arithmetic that were entrenched centuries ago. This is the afterlife of slavery—skewed life chances, limited access to health and education, premature death, incarceration, and impoverishment. I, too, am the afterlife of slavery" (2007, 6).

CHAPTER 1. BEFORE

1. In 2018 the Spanish-language edition, *Cotidianidad Revolucionaria*, was published by UCA Editores in El Salvador. I was able to present the book both at the Universidad Centroamericana José Simeon Cañas and in several repopulated communities. I gave many copies of the Spanish-language version (with a new preface) to various community members and local leaders in a few historic repopulated communities and to staff at the NGO CORDES, which had facilitated my entrance into the repopulated communities in 1993. I believe that having the book accessible in Spanish and circulating in El Salvador from Chalatenango to Salvadoran academic spaces is a form of public scholarship. That said, I make no claims on the impact of the text or its circulation.

2. Throughout this book I employ the anthropological convention of using pseudonyms because of ongoing concerns with people's everyday lives, now made more transparent via social media. Throughout the text I also alter biographical markers in order address issues of confidentiality and anonymity. Additionally, I play with the making of composites.

3. I was born in Argentina and raised in the United States. In the past I have described my positioning as a "South American gringa." To note here is that I grew up without extended kin (i.e., grandparents, uncles and aunts, cousins, etc.) and often entered into ritual kinship relationships. This does not erase the problematics of doing so in fieldwork contexts and the choices I would perhaps make now.

4. Larkin 2013.

5. Unless otherwise indicated, quoted speech is from the original Spanish. I have provided the translation into English. In many cases, I provide the reader with portions of the original Spanish to honor the words of my interlocutors. Sometimes the original Spanish will be at the beginning of the quote; sometimes in the middle, when a particular word or expression is of critical importance; or sometimes at the end, to emphasize a declarative statement. Interviews with the 1.5 insurgent generation in particular also reveal a play with language, and here too I aim to capture the code-switching that may happen during an exchange.

6. I thank Clara Guardado and Adriana Alas for their research support and expertise in discussing the writing of this word. It appears to be a regional expression of the word *fustán*. I also confirmed the regional spelling with one of my interlocutors in El Rancho.

7. I thank Inés Rossi for sharing with me her work on the trickster character for a paper she developed at Bard High School Early College Queens for the course "Mito prehispánico en literatura latinoamericana" taught by Graciela M. Báez. Texts included Paul Radin's *The Trickster* (1956).

8. There is significant testimonial literature across Central America, including texts such as *I, Rigoberta Menchú* (1984), *Hear My Testimony* (1994), and *They Won't Take Me Alive* (1987). By the 1990s there was also a significant scholarly focus on the role of the *testimonio*, including Beverley and Zimmerman (1990), Beverley (2004), and the Latina Feminist Group (2001). Ample scholarly debate on the veracity of the *testimonio* emerged around the work of David Stoll (1999). See, for example, Arias (2001). In *Everyday Revolutionaries* I sought to demonstrate the continuities and discontinuities with the *testimonio* in the transition to postwar where the *testimonio* as a genre, as an ideological tool, was less clear.

9. This contrasts quite dramatically with the recent surge of (re)interest in memory by a new generation of scholars, mostly from Central America. See, for example, Alas López (2021), Hernández Rivas (2019), and Martell Pereira (2020).

10. See, for example, Harrison (2010).

11. As a student of William Roseberry I was introduced early on to the work of Carlos Rafael Cabarrús (1983).

12. I follow established ethnographic conventions regarding naming locality. I use a pseudonym for El Rancho, a *cantón* in the municipality of Las Vueltas in the Department of Chalatenango. It was repopulated shortly after Las Vueltas, primarily from refugee camps in Honduras. See Silber (2011).

13. Unless otherwise indicated, I am translating oral or written speech or fieldnotes verbatim from the original Spanish into English.

14. I thank Ayala Fader for suggesting this term during one of our many conversations on the ethical issues of our different ethnographic research projects.

15. Durán Fernández's ethnography in Morazán explores gendered generational questions as well. She compares what she terms "adultas de la guerra" (so, what I call the protagonist generations) with their daughters, "las infantes de la guerra," who were born in the late 1970s through the mid-1980s (2020, 22–23). Specifically, she explores the different strategies deployed in everyday survival—from the new skills (such as embroidery) that daughters learned (83) to the peace felt in embodied labor such as the gathering of wood (105).

16. Geertz 1973.

17. Jackson 2013, 14.

18. Jackson 2013, 152. Jackson urges us to check ethnography's "call for ever more obsessively detailed and fine-grained renderings of one's observational prowess."

19. Here too we should note and question the ableist language (to see) inherent to the ethnographic enterprise.

20. Haraway 2016.

21. An interesting comparison could be made to Michelle Bellino's classroom ethnography in postwar Guatemala. She uncovers a key paradox in which youth are

simultaneously identified as victim and perpetrator rooted in a long history of colonialism and exploitation (2017). Youth here are the "inheritors" of so much—of failed dreams, of all the wartime silences, of the wartime fear, of the postwar uncertainty and anxiety (2017, 5). Like others, Bellino is specifically interested in how youth are always in transition and in waiting in postwar contexts and how they learn to think through the categories of peace, democracy, and transitional justice (2017, 6) She looks specifically at "postwar generation adolescents" (2017, 12) and how they learn to avoid risk, to wait rather than actively transform the future (2017, 12). Bellino defines this as "wait citizenship."

22. I thank an anonymous reviewer for suggesting this term.

23. As mentioned in the preface, the FMLN was comprised of five political and armed forces. Officially the FMLN became a political party with the peace accords. ARENA (National Republican Alliance) was the ruling party of the government of El Salvador during the negotiated peace, until March 2009.

24. Preliminary research first made possible by a Tinker Research Fellowship via New York University took place during the summer of 1993. Follow-up research occurred in the summer of 1994. Fourteen months of grant-funded research were conducted during 1996 and 1997 via fellowships from Fulbright-Hays, the Inter-American Foundation, and the Organization of American States.

25. Boellstorff et al. 2012.

26. Please see *Parcels* (2019) by sociologist Mike Anastario, in which he makes an argument for using the gender-inclusive term "lxs Chalatecxs." This is a powerful and important theoretical and representational move.

27. See *Oxford English Dictionary*, s.v. "protracted," accessed March 28, 2020, https://www-oed-com.ccny-proxy1.libr.ccny.cuny.edu/view/Entry/153343?rskey=OZW1Wv&result=1&isAdvanced=false#eid.

28. Asad 1995; Stocking 1993.

29. There is a tremendous literature to cite here beyond the scope of this book. Examples include Clifford (1988), Abu-Lughod (2016), and Marcus and Fischer (1986).

30. These works included texts by Faye Harrison (2010), Patricia Hill Collins (1990), and Kirin Narayan (1993). For an excellent analysis, see Jafari and Jobson (2016).

31. Haraway 1988.

32. Abu-Lughod 1993; Narayan 1993, 671–86.

33. Roseberry 1988, 161–85.

34. Nordstrom and Robben 1995.

35. Smith, Bayer, and Diskin 1988; Smith and Boyer 1987.

36. Cosgrove 2010; Silber 2011; Smith-Nonini 2010.

37. Sanford 2003.

38. Theidon 2012.

39. Brooks 2007.

40. Moodie 2010.

41. Peterson 2007, 59–77; Speed 2007.

42. Thomas 2007. Please note that this paragraph signaling example texts is not intended as a comprehensive review.

43. Borofsky and De Lauri 2019, 6.
44. Borofsky and De Lauri, 15.
45. In *Everyday Revolutionaries* I spend quite a bit of time theorizing about the role of NGOs and governmentality in postwar Chalatenango. Much of this explored the work of two organizations: CORDES and CCR (Coordinadora de Comunidades en Desarrollo Chalatenango/Coordinator of Communities in Development in Chalatenango).
46. For recent coverage, see Bonner (2019), and Malkin (2018). For ongoing coverage, see elfaro.net. To note is that this massacre takes place during a military operation known as "Operación Rescate" (Operation Rescue) in northern Morazán and pursued what is known as a scorched earth policy (Binford 2016, 18). Readers may note a variety of dates in December depending on when investigators periodize the beginning and end of the counterinsurgency operation.
47. See Amaya, Danner, and Consalvi (1996).
48. See Binford (2016). See also Danner (1994).
49. Evidence and sources include the United Nations Truth Commission report (1993), the human rights work of organizations such as Cristosal and Tutela Legal del Arzobispado de San Salvador (hereafter known as Tutela Legal), the analysis of exhumed skeletal remains by the Argentine Forensic Anthropology Team, which started the exhumation in 1992 (Binford 2016, 141), and the extraordinary in-court testimony of nearly forty victim survivors.
50. It is important for victim survivors to have their communities named. Besides El Mozote, the current court case names the following communities and geographic locations: La Joya, Ranchería, Los Toriles, Jocote Amarillo, Cerro Pando, and Cerro Ortiz. The work of Tutela Legal includes Arambala as well.
51. See Binford (2016), Danner (1994), and Tutela Legal (2008) for comprehensive accounts.
52. For example, the Argentine Forensic Anthropology Team testified in court regarding their forensic expert analysis. Other expert documents included a report by Stanford University distinguished professor Terry Lynn Karl and a technical military dictamen by Clever Alberto Pino Benamú, colonel of the Peruvian Army. The latter experts defended their testimony in televised court proceedings in Morazán in April 2021.
53. There is a growing literature on the role of the "cultural peritaje" in Latin America. See, for example, Loperena, Mora, and Hernández-Castillo (2020) on "cultural expertise" and the anthropologist as witness. See also Rodriguez (2021).
54. In the article "Disquieting Complicities: The Double Binds of Anthropology, Advocacy, and Activism," Elana Zilberg (2016) analyzes her work on immigration cases, such as her work in defense of a friend, a former Salvadoran gang member, and a key founder of a community organization called Homies Unidos. Like many scholars of Central America and its diaspora, Zilberg's work takes shape in an always eruptive frame of violence, fear, trauma, and emergency. She theorizes how her scholarship becomes "reductive" for the courts and her publications, perhaps compromising to her interlocuters, precisely because of all the complexities and entanglements that anthropology tends to offer.

55. For work on testimony and borderlands, see also Cervantes-Soon (2012, 373–91).

56. Stephen 2017, 85–86. See also Carolyn Forché's memoir *What You Have Heard Is True: A Memoir of Witness and Resistance* (2019).

57. Stephen 2017, 105.

58. See, for instance, Pleitez Quiñonez (2018), Sierra Becerra (2016), and Martell Pereira (2020).

59. Thomas 2019, 2.

60. Thomas, 3. Emphasis in original.

61. Angel-Ajani 2004, 135.

62. Angel-Ajani, 142. See also Angel-Ajani, Dean, and McLagan (2021).

63. Waterston and Rylko-Bauer 2006.

64. Waterston 2019. Waterston's (2014) method reminds me of Barbara Myerhoff's classic work on aging in a Florida community of Jewish Holocaust survivors and the power of storytelling. At the time Myerhoff offered a radical style of writing, what Victor Turner called "compassionate objectivity, or better yet, as realistic human kindness" (xiii) and what Myerhoff herself explained as conversations that "sometimes crossed the invisible line from informed disclosure to inadvertent confidence" (1978, 27).

65. I am referring here to how my Argentine whiteness (so, southern European and German Jewish heritage) factors into my lived experiences of "Latin Americanness" in El Salvador, and into my "Latinidad" in the United States with Salvadoran interlocuters, and more generally.

66. See, for example, C. Smith (1996).

67. Coutin 1993.

68. There is excellent literature on this movement. See, for example, Nepstad (2001), who writes about how the image of assassinated and martyred Archbishop Romero mobilized a transnational collectivity. See also Guardado (2021, 285–309) for a theological analysis of the role of sanctuary in the Church's accounting for the case of Central American asylum seekers.

69. Silber 2007, 163–83.

70. See, for example, the work of Christopher Loperena (2020). Additionally, in the United States during spring 2020, a powerful critique of performative allyship in antiracist work gained momentum in the public sphere through a generation of Black public intellectuals such as Rachel Elizabeth Cargle. See https://www.rachelcargle.com.

71. Cosgrove, forthcoming, 14.

72. Cosgrove, forthcoming, 9.

73. Cosgrove (forthcoming), for example, details what she terms "interuniversity solidarity" and offers multiple examples of university programming across her home institution of Seattle University and the Universidad Centroamericana (UCA) in Managua, Nicaragua.

74. Liu and Shange 190.

75. Cosgrove, forthcoming, 24.

76. Berry et al. 2017, 560.

77. Berry et al., 558. This is a politics of accountability across gendered, raced, classed, and sexed bodies and between interlocuters and anthropologists. It matches up with the paradigmatic work of *Decolonizing Ethnography: Undocumented Immigrants and new Directions in Social Science* (2019) by Carolina Alonso Bejarano and her colleagues. Their project is predicated on reciprocity and the making of "undocumented activist theory" (11). This is quite different than the testimonial genre. This is decolonial research, from project design to publication, enacted through horizontal collaboration between a team comprised of a full professor, a graduate student, and two undocumented activists. See also Hurtado Moreno (2021), where he theorizes the relationships of his own positioning along with his kin through the category of *testimonio*.

78. See Valencia (2018). He discusses how past secular solidarity spaces such as CISPES (Committee in Solidarity with the People of El Salvador) operated through the "making of the white middle-class radical," a whiteness that unraveled by the early 1990s.

79. Perla 2008.

80. Stuelke 2014, 768. As Stuelke further argues, the solidarity movement did not make the systemic or structural connections between US foreign and domestic policy and the violence of neoliberalism. Instead it operated through a mode of repair that "redeem[ed] the guilty US nation and its citizens, instantiating a reparative vision of the nation's future as a neoliberal multicultural family" (768).

81. Brooks 2007, 138.

82. Brooks 2007, 153.

83. Stuelke 2014, 786–87.

84. See Didier (2012).

85. See Abu-Lughod (1993).

86. The war is officially periodized as starting in 1980 with the insurgent "Final Offensive" (which was not final) and ending in 1992 with the signing of United Nations–brokered peace accords between the rightest Salvadoran ARENA government and the former FMLN insurgent forces. See Montgomery (1995).

87. Murray 1997, 15.

88. The United Nations Truth Commission report (1993) remains a critical text documenting the atrocities of war. Readers may also be interested in the work of the Asociación Pro-Búsqueda de Niñas y Niños Desaparecidos, at http://www.probusqueda.org.sv. See also Sprenkels (2001).

89. See Sprenkels and Melara Minero (2017, 126). Sprenkels and Melara Minero provide a periodization of the war, pointing to evidence from the Truth Commission report that 1980 was the most violent year. They offer the following chronology of phases of war: (1) 1970–1979: construction of clandestine structures and the increase in repression; (2) October 1979–1980: repressive escalation; (3) 1981–1983: offensive and counteroffensive; and (4) 1984–1991: low-intensity war (2017, 83). See the edited volume *Revolución Revisitada* (Menjívar Ochoa and Sprenkels 2017) for recent groundbreaking interdisciplinary scholarship on the war.

90. Karl 1992.

91. Hayner 2011. See also Popkin (2000).

92. Sprenkels offers a rigorous and comprehensive critique of DDR in *After Insurgency* (2018). Jenny Pearce, in conversation with Wolfgang Dietrich, makes the cogent point that along with DDR "the tragedy for Central America is precisely that these social energies were 'demobilized' after the war, as exhausted and traumatised people lost the possibility of agency in the peace" (2019, 270).

93. See Silber (2011), chap. 2, for further details.

94. United Nations 1993, 41–42. Ten percent of cases were attributed to unknown actors. See Sprenkels and Melara Minero where they discuss the FMLN's significantly less violent actions that were nonetheless factors in the conflict, "radicalizing" the political process on both sides. These tactics included kidnapping and executions of government officials and business elites and the forced recruitment of insurgents (2017, 126–27).

95. Moodie 2010.

96. Wade further explains that "drawing on Labonte's definition of *capture*, I use the term to describe the system by which elites controlled and manipulated institutions (whether formal or informal) and policy outcomes to preserve and advance their own interests" (2016, 10).

97. Wood 2000, 2003.

98. Binford 2016, 1998.

99. See, for example, Cosgrove (2010), Kampwirth (2002, 2004), Shayne (2004), Sierra Becerra (2017), Silber (2011), and Viterna (2013).

100. Segovia 2009, 8, 18.

101. Zilberg 2011.

102. Montoya 2018, 7.

103. Montoya, 241.

104. Pearce and Perea 2019, 251.

105. See the critique by Sprenkels in *After Insurgency* (2018).

106. *Guindas* is a local term used to describe the arduous en masse escapes on foot through the hills during a military bombardment and attack.

107. See Todd (2010). For classic writing on the region see the work of Pearce (1986) and books written within a solidarity movement such as Doljanin (1982), and Metzi (1988). Schrading (1991) documented the repatriation movement, and Classen (1992) writes from an explicitly faith-based solidarity.

108. Sprenkels 2018. For a comparative reading on repopulated communities, see, for example, Cagan and Cagan (1991), I. Cortez (2018), and MacDonald and Gatehouse (1995).

109. In 2019 Nayib Bukele won the Salvadoran presidency—upending the polarized ARENA/FMLN political field. Bukele, once FMLN mayor of San Salvador and then removed from the FMLN party, became president, representing the party he founded, Nuevas Ideas and GANA (Great National Alliance). Academics, journalists, and human rights actors are currently exploring and exposing corruption, repression, and authoritarian shifts with the presidency of Bukele, whose victory was forged through a populist

"anti-corruption" campaign. See Cuéllar (2020); and for consistent reporting, see the digital newspaper *El Faro* at https://www.elfaro.net.

110. Alas López 2021. Alas López distinguishes between three generations: *generación de la guerra*, *generación de hijos de la guerra*, and *generación de hijos de la posguerra*.

111. At the time, the Unidad de Salud provided me with a photocopy of the detailed report. It has become part of my ethnographic archival material like many pamphlets and mimeographed documents from the time.

112. UNDP 2005.

113. See http://www.censos.gob.sv/cpv/descargas/CPV_Resultados.pdf. Accessed April 17, 2020.

114. See Ministerio de Economía (2014).

115. Alas López 2013, 37. Here we could ask questions about return migration and also whether the outlining communities, rather than just the municipal seat, were included in the counting.

116. Cecilia Menjívar's foundational text *Fragmented Ties* (2000) details the history of Salvadoran migration to the United States. See also A. P. Rodríguez (2017).

117. Gammage 2006. See also Warnecke-Berger, where he argues that "the Salvadoran economy is part of a transnational economic space, but this space is perverse: Although the poor are nominally receiving more money, remittances cause them to be caught in a vicious cycle of economic instability. At the same time, the elites are able to access remittances indirectly by becoming a Keynesian oligarchy—an oligarchy that extracts wealth by controlling the demand structure of the economy instead of production" (2020, 1). Thus, remittances bolster neoliberalism and elites.

118. Noe-Bustamente, Flores, and Shah 2019.

119. See https://www.pewresearch.org/hispanic/fact-sheet/u-s-hispanics-facts-on-salvadoran-origin-latinos/#language.

120. This book builds on the critical literature on Salvadoran migration that contextualizes the history of US immigration laws (Coutin 2016). This work addresses questions such as belonging (Coutin 2007); fragmented communities (Menjívar 2000); remittances (Wiltberger 2014); the affective work that rubs up against structural forces in the making and sacrificing of transnational families (Abrego 2014); the state and migration (Baker-Cristales 2004); the hegemonic circulation of the Salvadoran as entrepreneur (Pederson 2013); the making of "U.S. Central Americans" (Alvarado, Estrada, and Hernández 2017) or "Central American Americans" (Cárdenas 2018); and much more. In El Salvador, the journals *Estudios Centroamericanos* and *Realidad* have dedicated significant attention to this topic. See, for example, Ares Mateos (2015) on the Salvadoran community in Boston, and Cartagena (2005) on the role of remittances in Chalatenango specifically.

121. Brooks 2013.

122. Here I'm also thinking of Saidiya Hartman's (2019) call for reading the "minor" actors of history, their "wayward" acts as central world-makers.

123. Marroquín Parducci 2014.

124. Marroquín Parducci 2019, 175.

125. Marroquín Parducci, 175 (author's translation of original Spanish). The extended quote is as follows: "Los migrantes son parte de un proyecto individual que deber ser leído como una resistencia colectiva contra los proyectos del capitalismo extractivista de América Latina. Los migrantes se mueven desplazados por la sequía, por las violencias, por la pobreza y el despojo al que muchas veces son sometidos en sus países de origen. Pero también, como diría Benjamin, es desde los más desesperanzados que podemos construir esperanza. Sus resistencias, su risa, sus canciones permiten soñar un mundo más humano, sin fronteras, un mundo sin campos de concentración, sin *centros de aseguramiento* en donde los niños son colocados en cárceles y separados de sus padres. La esperanza de los migrantes debe volver al centro del discurso, de la comunicación, de la vida."

126. Alvarado, Estrada, and Hernández 2017.

127. Cárdenas 2018.

128. Alvarado, Estrada, and Hernández 2017, ix.

129. Alvarado, Estrada, and Hernández, 5. Alvarado and colleagues develop the term "U.S. Central American" to highlight "shared histories, cultures, and struggles of Central American diasporic communities in the United States" (2017, 24). Scholars have of course explored the specificities of the Salvadoran diaspora such as Rodríguez and her concept of "Salvadoreñidades" (2005). Leisy Abrego in this volume also writes against stereotypes and tropes around Salvadoran migrant identities evidenced in the refrain "somos gente emprendedora" (we are enterprising, hardworking people) (2017, 60)—to show how this obfuscates the structural barriers that are invisibilized in this narrative construction. Cárdenas (2018) too argues for a (trans)regional identity, "Central American," and a (trans)national one, "Salvadoran" (2). She focuses on the particularity of a Central American identity in the United States. Rather than a Latinx identity, she is positing an "isthmus-based identity" (4). She is interested in "forms of effacement," "displacement," and "dislocation" of Central Americans (6).

130. See Anastario's excellent analysis on diasporic memories that illuminates how those tortillas, beans, and local cheese move from El Salvador to the United States in the making of transnational assemblages (2019).

131. Wood 2003, 235.

132. Scholars and immigrant rights activists have mobilized around regularizing liminal legal status in the United States for Salvadorans and other migrants. See Cohn, Passel, and Bialik (2019) for a recent summary. Briefly, key US immigration laws that impact Salvadoran migrants include the Immigration Reform and Control Act of 1986; the lawsuit by solidarity movement activists that highlights the discrimination against Salvadoran applicants for political asylum during the war period; the development of TPS, which has created ongoing and liminal legal status in the lives of eligible Salvadoran migrants since 2001 (implemented as earthquake relief) and was a key battle issue under the Trump Administration. As of this writing, TPS for El Salvador has been extended to December 31, 2022; and the Nicaraguan Adjustment and Central American Relief Act (NACARA) of 1997, created to address (adjust) the ways that US foreign policy dictated immigration laws during the Cold War. See Miyares et al. (2019) for an analysis of how

NOTES TO CHAPTER I

TPS constructs "truncated transnationalism" that creates deep lived anxiety and the duality of having to pursue two simultaneous paths: "investing in life in the United States; and saving for life at home" (3).

133. I wonder if Don Gilberto would have appreciated Beatriz Cortez's work on the relationship between the historic movement of seeds from Central America to the United States that exposes colonial violence and the making of white supremacy and the resistance to it. She writes, "Las plantas son sobrevivientes de represión, prohibiciones, colonización, esclavitud, capitalismo, imperialismo, eugenesia, experimentación genética, entre otros. Sin embargo, la naturaleza resiste los embates de los humanos." For Cortez, following these plants shows the futility of borders—they leave their traces, "van dejando evidencia de las migraciones," and are keepers of memory (2018, 123).

134. See, for example, Lovato (2020).

135. For further analysis, see Gould and Lauria-Santiago (2008).

136. On extractivism in Latin America, see Gómez-Barris (2017).

137. This language of giving to one side or the other is emblematic of wartime narratives. As occupying forces would come through communities, they would often demand sustenance, such as tortillas and beans, and a place to rest. Much has been written about the inability to be neutral during the war and how this was not a survival strategy. The emblematic case is the massacre at El Mozote and surrounding communities.

138. There is a growing archive of declassified documents made available at the National Security Archive, from which I was able to access documents. Other extraordinary declassification efforts include projects such as the University of Washington's Unfinished Sentences. Please see https://unfinishedsentences.org.

139. See Defense Intelligence Agency Assistant Directorate for JCS Support (1981, 101). This report provided information through September 30, 1980.

140. FBIS Chiva Chiva PM to FBIS Washington, DC, telegram, October 14, 1982.

141. Fuerzas Populares de Liberación (Popular Liberation Forces) was founded on April 1, 1970, and comprised one of the five branches of the FMLN's political military organizations (Sprenkels 2018, 276). Sprenkels summarizes the emergence of these organizations and how they were able to mobilize 2,000–3,000 peasants (43). The FPL was a key insurgent force in the repopulated areas.

142. UTC stands for Unión de Trabajadores del Campo (Rural Workers Union); FECCAS stands for Federación Cristiana de Campesinos Salvadoreños (Christian Federation of Salvadoran Peasants).

143. The BPR, like Nelson explained, was created by the FPL to bring together different popular FPL organizations. It was created in 1975 in response to the massacre of university students during a march (Sprenkels 2018, 46–47).

144. Romero was removed from office via a military coup in October 1979.

145. Defense Intelligence Agency Assistant Directorate for JCS Support 1981, 92–93. FAPL can be translated as Popular Armed Forces of Liberation.

146. For an excellent overview, see Sprenkels (2018, 54–58).

147. Defense Intelligence Agency Assistant Directorate for JCS Support 1981, 94.

148. Defense Intelligence Agency Assistant Directorate for JCS Support, 94.

149. Chávez 2017.

150. For attention to questions of memory see, for example, Lara Martínez (2018), Martell Pereira (2020), Alas (2019), Alas López (2021), Cuéllar (2020), Osuna (2020), and Hernández Rivas (2019). For a historical perspective on positioned perspectives from the Left, see López Bernal (2017). On how these memories are deployed, see López Bernal (2014), and Sprenkels (2011); on how reconciliation is emphasized over justice, see Sprenkels (2017); and on narrative typologies, see Ching (2016).

151. A census was not conducted during the war. The last census before the war was in 1971. In 1992, the V Censo de Población y IV de Vivienda was conducted. In 2007, the VII Censo de Población y VI de Vivienda were conducted.

152. Plan International explains that it has worked in El Salvador since 1976 and impacted over one million families. See https://plan-international.org/el-salvador.

153. See "Country Report: El Salvador" at https://www.paho.org/salud-en-las-americas-2017/?page_id=119.

154. For instance, Amelia Frank-Vitale and Juan José Martínez d'Aubuisson's ethnographic work with "youth" in post–coup d'état Honduras, including those moving through "migrant caravans," point to the socially constructed gendered-male and racialized category and bodies of youth as both vulnerability and risk (2020, 565). Jeremy Rayner and Valeria Morales Rivera (2020) track "the politics of emancipation and of age cohorts or generations" as they explore the "life cycle" and significance of generation in social movements in Costa Rica (569). In a comparative case for Guatemala, Jennifer Burrell, Mounia El Kotni, and Ramiro Fernando Calmo (2021) offer a critical reading of the anticorruption movements that have been at the center of activism and calls for justice. They show the weight of social relationships and practices of clientelism that come to define the contradictions and precarity of youth. This latter article is also methodologically significant in its use of virtual ethnography (i.e., Facebook) to analyze transnational (local) politics across generations.

155. Coutin 2016, 3.

156. Sprenkels 2001.

157. By October 2020 news started circulating in municipalities across the repopulated region about the remilitarization of the border between Honduras and Chalatenango. This militarization was on the order of President Bukele under the guise of a COVID-19 response. As communities contested this militarization, Bukele pushed back by accusing local mayors of association with narcotraffic, thus warranting the army presence. There are increasing reports of harassment of the community by the military (see https://www.elsalvadorsolidarity.org/militarization-chalatenango/).

158. Woodward 2009.

CHAPTER 2. NUMBERS

1. Please see note 26 in the preface, where I explain how I coined this term from a bicultural/bilingual play with Spanish and English.

NOTES TO CHAPTER 2

2. I mention this from the start because there is significant work that does precisely this—for instance, contextualizing when and why there was a decrease or increase in the homicide rate in El Salvador. For example, see Roberto Valencia's analyses, "Pequeñas batallas, grandes historias: Cinco Crónicas, cinco personajes, una búsqueda" (2016), and from Sala Negra de El Faro, *Crónicas Negras: Desde una región que no cuenta* (2013). See also the analysis by Elizabeth F. S. Roberts on "bioethnographic collaboration" in which she locates how ethnography can intersect with "number-based disciplines" to impact real-world change via "harness[ing] ethnographic excess for making better numbers and thus better knowledge" (2021, 355). See also Merry (2016), whose ethnographic work on the construction of global indicators of human rights issues explodes the ways in which they are produced, showing how they are partial, misleading, and anything but "objective" and how they are deployed to make global claims.

3. I thank an anonymous reviewer for pushing me to more explicitly articulate my thinking about the work of numbers and to clarify that there is significant and crucial work by scholars and reporters on the numbers that are indeed life-and-death matters. See, for example, the work by Pamela Ruiz, José Miguel Cruz, and Ellen Moodie cited throughout the chapter.

4. Semple 2014.

5. Stinchcomb and Hershberg 2014, 6.

6. Fassin 2012. Interdisciplinary literature has emerged that focuses specifically on unaccompanied youth, family migration, and deportation. See, for example, Terrio (2015), and Heidbrink (2014, 2020). See also Joanna Dreby's work that focuses on Mexican family separation (2010, 2015) and mixed-status families and how "illegality" is about the making of "social status" and a legal category (2015, 5) and how laws create injustice. See also the online platform Youth Circulations (http://www.youthcirculations.com; accessed July 15, 2020).

7. Documentary films, media reports, and academic texts have illuminated how Central American migrants make passage by jumping aboard Mexican freight trains known as *La Bestia*, or "The Beast." For a literary analysis, see Buiza (2018a).

8. Lopez and Krogstad 2014.

9. USCIS 2014. Updated figures indicate that nearly twenty-six thousand Salvadorans have DACA, 62 percent of those who are eligible (Menjívar and Gómez Cervantes 2018).

10. *Guardian* 2015b; Malkin 2015b; *Guardian* 2015a.

11. Watts 2015.

12. Fundaungo 2019, 2.

13. Valencia 2015. Investigative reporting by *El Faro* continues to expose the relationship between gangs and Salvadoran government administrations, this time illuminating negotiations that started in June 2019 between MS-13 (incarcerated leaders) and the Salvadoran administration of President Bukele. This reporting in the press indicates that negotiations were for a reduction in homicides and addressed prison privileges in exchange for electoral support of President Bukele's political party, Nuevas Ideas, in the

2021 congressional elections. This research explains that "thus far, 2020 is on track to unseat 2019 as the year with the fewest homicides since the 1992 peace accords. Between January and May of last year, El Salvador registered 1,345 homicides. Over the same span this year, there have been 519. The administration has publicized the reduction as one of its primary accomplishments." They juxtapose and contextualize these numbers with the 2012 truce: "In 2012, *El Faro* revealed how the Funes administration, of the FMLN party, likewise led different stages of covert negotiations, first for a fall in homicides and later for electoral support in the presidential elections of 2014. Those efforts led to a drastic reduction in homicides for two years. The rupture of that truce, however, made 2015 the most violent year on record, registering 103 homicides per 100,000 residents." (Martínez et al. 2020).

14. Dickey 2015.
15. Valencia, Martínez, and Valencia Caravantes 2015.
16. Alarcón 2015.
17. Kennedy 2014.
18. 2020, ix.
19. Fernandes 2017, 2–11. The book offers a multiplicity of examples of the deep reach of curated storytelling practices in which "histories, ambiguities, and political struggles are erased in an effort to create warm and relatable portraits of others who are 'just like us.'" (2). This is a mode that depoliticizes confrontational struggle.
20. Fernandes 2017, 4.
21. Thank you to Mike Anastario for his suggestion to think through Baudrillard's 1994 work on simulacra and sign value.
22. See Coutin (2007).
23. As mentioned previously, there is critical literature on migration and borders and the violence of US immigration policy that predates the Trump administration. Readers should also note that I'm not arguing that the violence of US immigration policy has ended with the change of administration. There is ample reporting on repression at the border as I write. A significant amount of research has also explored migration and youth and highlighted the paucity of information we have on the impact of their experiences with agents and agencies and structures of border control (i.e., Cardoso et al. 2019) and the psychological impact on children whose parents have liminal legal status (Rojas-Flores, Hwang Koo, and Vaughn 2019). Texts also include creative nonfiction (Luiselli 2017), fiction (Luiselli 2019), poetry (Zamora 2017), and photography (Bradley 2008).
24. Amelia Hoover Green explains another key point: "The need to address multiple aspects of civilian suffering creates, in turn, an intense need for sound approximations of patterns and trends in nonlethal violence. Yet this imperative too often devolves into a simple desire for numbers, any numbers" (2018, 23).
25. Nelson 2015, 9.
26. Nelson 2015, 9.
27. 2012, 480.
28. I am not making a larger claim about trying to get the numbers right or that these reports even got the numbers "wrong." I point here to the significant work by

scholars who are providing precisely this critical work, on gangs and extortion, for instance. See Ruiz (2020a, 2020b). Rather, I'm interested in the cultural production and consumption around the category of "the numbers."

29. Winifred Tate (2007) provides an excellent analysis of the production of statistics for deaths in Colombia, exploring, for example, how deaths are catalogued, commodified, and thus made legible in this way.

30. Pearce and Perea compare violences across war and peace and suggest key factors that generate violence, such as criminal economies across the region, but also mark the spaces to contest its reproduction, such as Indigenous movements (2019, 252). See also Kurtenbach (2019) for a strong analysis regarding ongoing structural problems that reproduce violence in Latin America and have opened spaces for the targeting and selective killing of human rights workers through increasing militarization of public security.

31. Perea 2019, 256. Across Latin America, the highest rates of "extreme violence" take shape outside the context of war, although we must note that peace is not defined as the absence of war (Perea 2019, 254; Moodie 2010). For example, in 2016, across Latin America "armed conflict was responsible for a tiny two percent of its total homicides" (Perea 2019, 255). Perea's definition of extreme violence is one about numbers: the rate of homicides is 25 or more per 100,000 inhabitants and persists for at least five years (257). Using this assessment, he concludes that "America is the most violent continent on the planet" (257). Central America has the highest homicide rate of the continent. From 2004–2016, the rate was 37 per 100,000. For scholars like Perea, the regional social reproduction of violence is predicated on structural inequalities that have allowed for the growth of "organized illegality" (crime and gangs), with its control of territory, and illicit markets (drug trade) that have penetrated into the social fabric (262–65).

32. Pearce and Perea offer that homicide rates do not address the significance of nonlethal violence, domestic violence, or the "cifra negra" (dark statistics)—the percentage of crimes that are not reported (2019, 249).

33. Nelson 2015, 9.

34. Nelson 2015, 83.

35. Pearce and Perea 2019, 248.

36. Kennedy and Parker 2020, 22.

37. Kennedy and Parker, 23. See Hoover Green and Ball (2019) where they review material and provide a statistical analysis that leads them to "estimate that there were about 71,629 (60,326, 83,775) civilian killings and disappearances during the conflict, or about 1–2% of El Salvador's prewar population" (781). They conclude that 1982 was the most violent year during the war, when 30% of the lethal wartime violence took place (807).

38. Nelson 2015, 29. Emphasis in original.

39. Nelson 2015, 4.

40. Readers may remember from chapter 1 the development workshop on safe water use in order to combat gastrointestinal diseases.

41. See also Nelson (2009).

42. LeMoyne 1985, 12.

43. Anastario 2019.

44. Rivas 2014, 5.

45. Van der Borgh provides a cogent summary of the role of the international community in peace building and how early on, policy makers linked security and development and structural reforms to successful peace building (2009, 303). Ultimately, this review critiques assumptions that underscore "liberal peace" models that are universalizing, decontextualizing, and Eurocentric. See also Sliwinski (2018).

46. That is, Hurricane Mitch (1998) and earthquakes (2001).

47. In doing so, residents of repopulated communities joined a longer and older wave of Salvadoran migrants in the United States as mentioned in previous notes. Readers may also be interested in Brigden's (2018) work on Central American migration, as she theorizes the violence and performativity of migration as "survival plays" (5) and the kinds of "improvisations" that mark encounters between strangers and the land as part of a "survival resource" (7).

48. The Pew Research Center cites the Census Bureau's 2011 American Community Survey, which places an estimated 2.3 million Salvadorans in the United States, the third-largest population of Hispanic origin and as of 2017, comprising 4% of the Hispanic population in the United States. https://www.pewresearch.org/hispanic/fact-sheet/u-s-hispanics-facts-on-salvadoran-origin-latinos/. Accessed July 10, 2020.

49. See https://www.pewresearch.org/hispanic/fact-sheet/u-s-hispanics-facts-on-salvadoran-origin-latinos/. Accessed July 10, 2020.

50. O'Connor, Batalova, and Bolter 2019.

51. Dominguez Villegas and Rietig 2015, 3.

52. Dominguez Villegas and Rietig, 6.

53. O'Connor, Batalova, and Bolter 2019. The Pew Research Center analyzes a spike in U.S-Mexico border "migrant encounters," meaning either apprehensions in which people are taken into custody in the United States or immediate expulsions of people. In July 2021 the monthly numbers reached 199,777, after a dramatic dip of 16,182 in April 2020 as a result of the COVID-19 pandemic. The July 2021 numbers were the highest since March 2000. Under the Trump administration most encounters led to expulsion and not apprehension through the use of Title 42 directly linked to the pandemic. Under the Biden administration expulsions decreased from 83% in January 2021 to 47% in July 2021, although Title 42 is still in use. The Pew Research Center also discusses a change in demographics since May 2019, with an increase of adult migrants and a decrease in family migration, although unaccompanied migration has remained the same at 9%. Their research also shows a further demographic shift regarding countries of origin, with an increase in migrants from Mexico and a decrease in migrants from the Northern Triangle. See Gramlich (2021).

54. O'Connor, Batalova, and Bolter 2019.

55. Kennedy and Parker 2020, 4. To address the migration of unaccompanied minors, US president Barack Obama urged for the creation in 2014 of the "Plan of the Alliance for Prosperity in the Northern Triangle: A Road Map" (at http://idbdocs.iadb

.org/wsdocs/getdocument.aspx?docnum=39224238). See the Migration Policy Institute's analysis of President Obama's record on deportation in Chishti, Pierce, and Bolter (2017).

56. See Silber (2019). The media reported President Trump's efforts to "bully Guatemala, Honduras, and El Salvador into serving as 'safe third countries'" through "cooperative asylum agreements" (Gonzales 2019). These agreements "disqualify individuals from requesting asylum in the United States if they have set foot in one of these countries and allow the United States to deport migrants to a 'safe' third country, ostensibly to request asylum" (Copeland 2020, 73). See also the press release available at https://sv.usembassy.gov/bilateral-agreement-security-migration/. Accessed July 14, 2020.

57. Agren 2020.

58. Flores, Noe-Bustamante, and Hugo Lopez 2019.

59. Kennedy and Parker 2020, 3; Menjívar and Gómez Cervantes 2018.

60. Menjívar and Gómez Cervantes 2018. See, for example, USCIS (https://www.uscis.gov/DACA), and American Friends Service Committee (https://www.afsc.org/blogs/news-and-commentary/4-things-you-should-know-about-changes-to-daca) for updates on DACA. Accessed January 11, 2022.

61. Ruwitch 2021. Although it is beyond the scope of this book, readers may be interested in following the ongoing enforcement of US border control covered in the media and that extends across various populations.

62. UNDP 2005, 222.

63. Moodie 2010.

64. See https://www.migrationpolicy.org/programs/data-hub/charts/total-remittance-inflows-and-outflows.

65. See https://www.migrationpolicy.org/programs/data-hub/charts/total-remittance-inflows-and-outflows. In 1980 El Salvador received $49 million in remittances. That number jumped to $366.8 million by 1990 and to $3 billion by 2005, more than a decade into postwar.

66. Gammage 2006.

67. Brooks 2013.

68. See Paarlberg (2021) for an analysis on the role of criminal violence in migration to the United States and the policy shifts implemented by the Biden administration, including reinstating fear of gang violence in political asylum claims. Paarlberg pushes for a more nuanced understanding of gang structures and activities in order to address the ongoing deportation regime and its unintended consequences that allow maras to thrive.

69. See, for example, the *Guardian*'s profile, "Detained: How the US Built the World's Largest Immigrant Detention System." https://www.theguardian.com/us-news/2019/sep/24/detained-us-largest-immigrant-detention-trump. Accessed July 10, 2020.

70. See https://www.amnestyusa.org/reports/usa-catastrophic-immigration-policies-resulted-in-more-family-separations-than-previously-disclosed/. Accessed July 9, 2020. For reporting on the unfolding violent legacies of these immigration policies, see https://www.nytimes.com/2020/10/21/us/migrant-children-separated.html. Accessed October 11, 2020.

71. See https://www.splcenter.org/news/2020/06/17/family-separation-under-trump-administration-timeline. Accessed July 9, 2020. Ample reporting continues regarding the Biden administration's attempt to address the "crises." See, for example, "Biden's Border Dilemma" at https://www.nytimes.com/2021/08/26/podcasts/the-daily/biden-immigration-policy-central-america.html. Accessed September 1, 2021.

72. See, for example, *El Faro*'s reporting on Salvadorans deported from Texas who tested positive for COVID-19. https://elfaro.net/es/202005/el_salvador/24467/Cuatro-deportados-por-Estados-Unidos-dieron-positivo-al-covid-19-en-El-Salvador.htm. Accessed July 13, 2020.

73. Deborah A. Boehm examines how deportations of foreign nationals, termed "removals" by the US DHS, erase and disappear: "Through removals, the state erases presence, undermines well-being, disrupts migration flows, unravels families across borders, upsets life trajectories, and undoes diverse forms of national membership" (2016, 3). As stated on the DHS website, "Removals are the compulsory and confirmed movement of an inadmissible or deportable alien out of the United States based on an order of removal. An alien who is removed has administrative or criminal consequences placed on subsequent reentry owing to the fact of the removal. Returns are the confirmed movement of an inadmissible or deportable alien out of the United States not based on an order of removal." https://www.dhs.gov/immigration-statistics/yearbook/2018/table39. Accessed May 14, 2020.

74. Author translation of original: "trabajar para que los retornados conozcan bien nuestro entorno económico y poderles facilitar su inserción, estamos en otro contexto muy diferente como el que tenía en Estados Unidos, ello nos exige una adaptación." By February 2017, in a new political climate in the United States, the Dirección General de Migración y Extranjería held a forum on the "protection of migrants and the reintegration of migrants" (foro para protección de migrantes y reinserción de retornados). https://www.migracion.gob.sv/noticias/realizan-foro-para-proteccion-de-migrantes-y-reinsercion-de-retornados/. Accessed October 23, 2017.

75. See Chacón Serrano, Gómez, and Alas for their analysis on the kinds of face-saving moves *retornados* make to resignify their return away from failure (2013, 514). For relationship to work in call centers, see Blitzer (2017), and Renteria Meza (2018).

76. ICE, *U.S. Immigration and Customs Enforcement Fiscal Year 2019 Enforcement and Removal Operations Report*, n.d, https://www.ice.gov/sites/default/files/documents/Document/2019/eroReportFY2019.pdf. Accessed January 10, 2022.

77. De Genova and Peutz 2010.

78. Castañeda 2019.

79. Roberts, Menjívar, and Rodríguez 2017, 13. See also Paarlberg (2021).

80. Roberts, Menjívar, and Rodríguez, 13. For El Salvador, specifically in 2014, there were nearly twenty-nine thousand Salvadorans deported from the United States alone (Goodfriend 2015, 50).

81. Kennedy and Parker 2020, 1.

82. See the Northern Triangle Migration Information Management Initiative of the International Organization for Migration. http://mic.iom.int/webntmi/descargas/sv/2018/12/ESdic2018mun.pdf. Accessed July 16, 2020.

83. See https://www.facebook.com/OIMElSalvador/posts/1065241950478367/. Accessed November 3, 2020.

84. Gutierrez 2017, 112. For example, "of the 21,877 deportations to El Salvador in 2013, 19,767 were male, while 2110 were female. Overall, Salvadoran males account for 90% of detainees and deportees to El Salvador" (Gutierrez 2017, 112). We'll return to these gendered numbers in a section below. See also Boehm and Terrio (2019).

85. Kennedy and Parker 2020, 3.

86. Kennedy and Parker, 3. The report also indicates that in the majority of cases, returned Salvadorans experienced the violence within the first year, and in many cases in the same month that they were deported (13).

87. Examples include "El Salvador es tu casa," or "El Salvador is your home." https://rree.gob.sv/elsalvadorestucasa/. Accessed July 13, 2020.

88. Author translation from the original Spanish.

89. See https://rree.gob.sv/salvadorenos-retornados-reciben-capital-semilla-para-emprender-sus-negocios/. Accessed July 13, 2020.

90. Literature on deportation and disappearances through the violence of the migration process has also been explored through what Allison Ramirez describes as the "new disappeared" (2017, 170) and the gendered activism that has emerged to contest this violence.

91. Segovia 2009, 7, 9.

92. Segovia writes about the demobilized from both the FMLN and FAES that a significant number "subsequently became part of the new National Civilian Police [Policía Nacional Civil] (PNC). In effect, the peace accords provided for their incorporation so long as demobilized individuals met the requirements for entrance to the National Public Security Academy (ANSP). . . . In subsequent agreements it was decided that each of the two demobilized forces could account for up to 20 percent of the members of the PNC" (2009, 9).

93. Hoover Green 2018, 5. She focuses on violence defined as "direct physical aggression, either against persons or against immediate necessities such as food or shelter; or specific threats of imminent, direct physical violence. Murder, sexual violence, arbitrary detention, torture, amputation, and other physical violence are included but so—for the purposes of this volume—are looting, livestock killings, and the burning of homes" (5–6).

94. Hoover Green 2018, 17. This is manifested when "commanders exercise consistent discipline *and* fighters internalize messages that valorize limited, controlled violence" (17; emphasis in original).

95. Hoover Green 2018, 20. She also points to a kind of fetishizing around numbers, arguing, for example, that the "rhetorical power of numerical evidence of human-rights

violations too often outstrips the quality of the evidence itself. The deep problems with statistics about even the most 'countable' human-rights violations raise questions about how numerical evidence came to have so much power in the human-rights community, and how the intractable measurement problems afflicting wartime human-rights violations can be dealt with in a way that simultaneously addresses immediate needs and opens the door to long-term accuracy and understanding" (23).

96. Sprenkels 2012, 77.

97. Key efforts included the October 25, 2012, judgment on the "Case of the Massacres of El Mozote and Nearby Places v. El Salvador" by the Inter-American Commission on Human Rights. The full text is available at http://www.corteidh.or.cr/docs/casos/articulos/seriec_252_ing1.pdf. Accessed July 13, 2020.

98. Over the last decade, the Spanish National Court has pursued justice in the Jesuit Massacre Case in which six Jesuit priests and university professors were assassinated along with two collaborators on November 16, 1989, by the Atlacatl Battalion of the Salvadoran army. See Whitfield (1994). In September 2020, the Spanish National Court found Colonel Inocente Orlando Montano guilty and sentenced him to 133 years in prison (Jones 2020). https://www.theguardian.com/world/2020/sep/11/ex-salvadoran-colonel-inocente-orlando-montano-jailed-for-1989-of-spanish-jesuits. Accessed October 28, 2020. See also https://www.guernicacentre.org/copy-of-trial-brief-9-1. Accessed January 12, 2022.

99. See Binford (1998) for an analysis of the massacre. See Rostica et al. (2020) for a recent analysis of the role and "responsibility" Argentina's military dictatorship had in the massacre.

100. As mentioned in the previous chapter, from February 2019, when I was sworn in as expert witness, until June 2019, when I submitted an official dictamen, I worked on this case as a *perita antropóloga*. As of the date of this writing, my court testimony remains pending.

101. ICTJ 2013.

102. See, for example, the statement by Fabian Salvioli, appointed by the United Nations Human Rights Council (2018) as the Special Rapporteur on the promotion of truth, justice, reparation, and guarantees of nonrecurrence. https://www.ohchr.org/EN/NewsEvents/Pages/DisplayNews.aspx?NewsID=24619&LangID=E. Accessed July 16, 2020. Reports covered President Bukele's veto of the passed law. See Alemán (2020). In August 2021, the Salvadoran Legislative Assembly passed additional laws that call for the dismissal of judges over sixty years of age. Human rights reporting makes a strong argument that this was aimed at separating judges from critical cases such as the El Mozote Massacre and is a danger to "judicial independence." https://www.hrw.org/news/2021/09/02/el-salvador-new-laws-threaten-judicial-independence#; https://elfaro.net/es/202109/el_salvador/25743/Juez-de-El-Mozote-Están-obligando-a-los-jueces-a-renunciar-bajo-un-chantaje.htm. Accessed September 26, 2021.

103. 2011.

104. Author translation of original: "Prevenir es siempre mejor que curar; cuando la enfermedad se encuentra presente—en este caso, la violencia—debe igualmente ser

abordada para permitir que las medidas preventivas puedan disminuir o eliminar el riesgo de aparecimiento de eventos de violencia." Instituto de Derechos Humanos of the Universidad Centroamericana, 2015.

105. Moodie 2006. On gender violence, see Hume (2009) and the work of organizations such as Las Dignas (https://www.lasdignas.org.sv) and their publications (2010).

106. Among this literature, see Holland (2013), and Wolf (2017). Iron-fist policies continue under President Bukele through what he calls the Territorial Control Plan. See Paalberg (2021).

107. This was a $2 billion plan under the Consejo Nacional de Seguridad Ciudadana y Convivencia, which was facilitated by the United Nations. See Silber (2018) for a brief summary of the plan. Analysts have compared it to former ARENA president Antonio Saca's "País Seguro" (Zablah 2015). Reporting by Parker Asmann (2018) questions the validity of the decrease in homicide rate during the plan. He quotes the expert opinion of Florida International University professor José Miguel Cruz, who "questioned whether the improvement was as significant as it appears on the surface. Cruz told *InSight Crime* that falling homicide and extortion rates may be more indicative of a growing sophistication among the country's gangs in response to extraordinary anti-gang measures, rather than a result of Plan Secure El Salvador." Fundaungo reports that in 2018 the rate was 50.4 homicides per 100,000 people (2019, 2).

108. See https://insightcrime.org/news/brief/el-salvador-extend-extraordinary-anti-gang-measures-2018/; and https://insightcrime.org/news/brief/390-years-for-barrio-18-members-who-took-part-in-el-salvador-massacre/. Accessed September 26, 2021.

109. Indeed, the push for this plan led to a constitutional crisis when on February 9, 2020, Bukele entered the Legislative Assembly with military officers and their automatic weapons as he called for the approval of an international loan of $109 million for the third phase of his security and anticrime plan. He had invoked Article 167 of the constitution in his take-over of the Legislative Assembly (Brigida 2020; WOLA 2020).

110. Seelke 2009, 10. There is an extensive literature on gangs in Central America, and in El Salvador more specifically. See texts such as Brenneman (2012), Cruz (2010), Martínez (2016), Martínez d'Aubuisson (2019), and van der Borgh and Savenije (2015). Elana Zilberg's work highlights the relationship between the history of US-supported counterinsurgency and new "transnational security agreements" in order to explode facile discussions on transnational gangs (2011, 2).

111. Seelke 2009, 9.

112. Defined as 10 homicides per 100,000 people.

113. Journalist Óscar Martínez frames these deaths comparatively, one could almost say, alluding to the violence of humanitarian inaction in two disparate cases. He remarks, "La epidemia de homicidios fue tan expandida en 2014 que quedamos a poco más de 1,000 cadáveres de alcanzar la epidemia de ébola del año pasado. Con un matiz: esa epidemia mató a unas 5,000 personas, pero en seis países africanos" (2015).

114. Osuna 2020, 4–5.

115. Colleagues in El Salvador suggested that I follow President Nayib Bukele on Twitter, for different political reasons, and take in his fascination with the epidemiological numbers. Some memes focused on Bukele's "geometry" or "algebra." See, for another example, this tweet from July 13, 2020, where Bukele announces that 2,496 COVID-19 tests were conducted, with 2,171 negative results and 325 positive cases. The tweet also breaks down cases by locality, starting with 31 in San Salvador. Bukele also retweets official statistics from the covid19.gov.sv website, which offers the daily and total counts of cases, tests, deaths, and whether cases were "local" or "imported." https://twitter.com/nayibbukele/status/1282947894450978818. Accessed July 14, 2020. I thank Mike Anastario for bringing this to my attention.

116. BBC 2020; Sheridan and Brigida 2020.

117. See Carlos Dada's (2020) poignant analysis in *El Faro*.

118. Osuna 2020, 5.

119. HRW 2020b.

120. Accuracy of the estimate implies that the value of the parameter that is the object of measurement is estimated with little error (Rothman, Greenland, and Lash 2008).

121. https://uca.edu.sv/postgrados/wp-content/uploads/2020/07/MAEST.pdf.

122. Mendoza Posada, Orellana Herrera, and Pocasangre Portillo 2016.

123. Here we can assume that these numbers reflect the full due diligence of the Salvadoran state in counting a homicide.

124. I thank Mike Anastario for alerting me to this work and to helping me think through the validity of the numbers. All faults in analysis are my own.

125. Córdova Macías, Cruz, and Seligson 2013.

126. These include Observatorio de Seguridad Ciudadana (2013), Fundaungo (2013), and Córdova Macías, Cruz, and Seligson (2013).

127. Córdova Macías, Cruz, and Seligson (2013, 113) compare data from 2004 through 2012 on the perception of insecurity that remains in the 40th percentile, from the lowest of 41.5 percent in 2008 to 49.7 percent in 2010.

128. This is a well-respected public policy organization founded in January 1992. They consistently produce critical public policy research aimed at promoting "development and democratic governance in El Salvador." http://www.fundaungo.org.sv/index.php?option=com_content&view=article&id=3&Itemid=8.

129. Observatorio de Seguridad Ciudadana 2013, 14–15.

130. Observatorio de Seguridad Ciudadana, 17–19.

131. Observatorio de Seguridad Ciudadana, 63.

132. Sources include La Fiscalía General de la Republica (FGR), Policía Nacional Civil, and Instituto de Medicina Legal.

133. Fundaungo 2013, 37. In a June 2019 publication, Fundaungo provided an update and overview through 2018. For example, they note that after the 2012 decline in homicides, the rate started increasing in 2014, with the highest rate in 2015, when there were 6,656 homicides (2019, 1). A decrease in homicides began again in 2016, with 3,346 homicides by 2018 (2019, 2). They summarize that from 2009 to 2018, there were 41,006 homicides in El Salvador (2019, 2).

134. Fundaungo 2019, 4. Fundaungo also compiled data for 2018 and offered slightly revised data: Across genders, youth ages 15–29 were the most vulnerable, with men 20–24 years old at highest risk (675 murders), followed by those ages 15–19 (469). Regarding women, they offer that the largest number of homicides occurred between ages 20–24 and 25–29 (51 murders) and 15–19 (50 murders) (2019, 5). Among their conclusions regarding the uneven phenomenon of violence, they write, "Otro dato a destacar es que la tasa de hombres jóvenes asesinados (159.4) triplica la tasa nacional (50.4); mientras que la tasa de homicidios de mujeres jóvenes (15.2) representa aproximadamente la tercera parte de la tasa nacional (50.4), pero es mayor que la tasa de homicidios de mujeres a nivel nacional (11.0)." This leads them to recommend that public policies need to focus more clearly on preventing "violencia juvenil." 2019, 14.

135. Fundaungo 2013, 33. There is significant literature on gendered violence in El Salvador (e.g., Hume 2009) and on feminicide (the murder of women because they are women) and much organizing by long-time feminist human rights organizing like Las Dignas. Recent numbers, for example, offer the following gendered breakdown for 2018: 87.9% of homicide victims were male, 11.5% were female, and in .6% of cases the biological sex of the victim was not identified (Fundaungo 2019, 3). See also Molina (2015) for an analysis of the invisibilization of violence against women.

136. Fundaungo 2013, 51.

137. Here I am making no claims that these are the "right" numbers or that other numbers for the region could be leveraged.

138. Garni and Weyher 2013, 641.

139. Garni and Weyher 2013, 624.

140. Fundaungo 2013, 59.

141. Fundaungo 2013, 85.

142. To note is that Fundaungo's 2019 fact sheet documents the recent decrease in lethal violence across municipalities, showing where it is above or below the national average (7) and suggesting that violence prevention strategies should include a focus on these territorial differences (14).

143. Fundaungo 2019, 11.

144. Fundaungo 2013, 101.

145. Fundaungo reports no deaths in Las Vueltas during 2018. They also report that forty-six municipalities did not register homicides during 2018. Seventeen of these were in Chalatenango (2019, 11).

146. See Ruiz (2020b). To be noted, a key policy recommendation is the need to improve data collection and analysis on extortion (VI). According to a recent InSight Crime (2021) report, "Between 2013 and 2017, Chalatenango recorded the lowest amount of extortion cases of any department in El Salvador. However, in recent years, members of MS13 have increasingly imposed extortion fees on merchants, especially those from El Paraíso and Tejutla. Extortion may consist of a weekly or monthly fee targeting transport operators." To note, this area does not comprise the repopulated communities.

147. During the COVID-19 pandemic the accusations around illicit movements of people and goods created a space for President Bukele to remilitarize the Honduran-Salvadoran

border across repopulated communities. Human rights organizations such as CRIPDES and the Chalatenango dioceses have called out against this militarization, which has impacted people's well-being and everyday lives and access to their lands. https://www.elsalvador.com/noticias/nacional/diocesis-chalatenango-militares-frontera-honduras-el-salvador-derechos-humanos/769015/2020/. Accessed November 1, 2020.

148. On gossip and rumors in El Salvador, see Dickson-Gómez (2002).
149. 2012, 500.
150. Moodie 2009, 2010.
151. Goldstein 2012, 4–5.
152. Goldstein 2012, 14.
153. Fanon (1963) 2004, 16–17.
154. See also Yashar (2013) for a discussion on the role of the "illicit" in the creation of new regimes of citizenship within neoliberal governments that propel citizens to take on new choices, such as unauthorized migration.
155. Tsing 2005.
156. Gay y Blasco and Hernández 2012.
157. Nelson 2015.
158. Velásquez Estrada 2015,70.
159. Velásquez Estrada, 79.
160. Silber 2011.
161. Stephen 2007.
162. Sprenkels 2011.
163. Velásquez Estrada 2015, 82.
164. One could also consider the sociomaterial aspect of *violencia encifrada* that could be amplified with access to technology and urban status. See Alarcón Medina's research on El Salvador and media technologies (2014, 2015).
165. Alas López 2021.
166. Petryna 2002.
167. Alas López 2021. For a comparative example of the making of disability claims on the state, see Kohrman (2005).
168. See, for example, Redfield (2013).
169. Bourgois and Schonberg 2009, 16.

CHAPTER 3. BODIES

1. See Scheper-Hughes (1993) for a powerful analysis of structural violence, cultural practices, and ideologies regarding maternal neglect and infant death in Brazil. In part, her political-economic analysis and narrative account is a critique of universalizing and reductive ascriptions of mother love.
2. This was an interesting shift, as nearly all residents in El Rancho raised chickens in their yards for fresh eggs and from time to time to slaughter for meat. The introduction of commercial chicken, already slaughtered, plucked, and cut into quarters, was something very new in the community. We could also analyze the language around "Indio" for this company.

3. In Chalatenango, maternal cultural practices include forty days of specialized rest and diet postpartum.

4. Sprenkels and Melara Minero 2017, 99–100.

5. Sprenkels and Melara Minero, 102.

6. Hoover Green and Ball 2019.

7. Please refer to chapter 1, which addresses the relationship between witnessing, listening, and intimate solidarity.

8. See https://www.asociacionsumpul.org/historical-background. Accessed July 30, 2020.

9. See http://www.probusqueda.org.sv/guinda-de-mayo-nunca-mas/. Accessed July 30, 2020.

10. And this included a systematic separation and forced disappearance of children. See Sprenkels (2001).

11. I am placing this description in quotes to call attention to an ableist slip. The father is walking, carrying his teen son who is disabled because of a bomb. Yet they are interdependently joined, the father walking for his son. See the work of Eva Kittay on interdependence and care (1999).

12. I call attention to the ample literature in childhood studies that argues that there is no universal category or experience of childhood and that, in fact, childhood is socially, culturally, and historically constructed, with shifting ideas around categories such as innocence, protection, and vulnerability (see Lancy [2015]). There is also ample literature on children and agency in contexts of war and violence (see Scheper-Hughes and Sargent [1998], and Stephens [1995]). Thus, my very affective response years later is framed by my cultural and intimate experiences of motherhood with an adolescent boy and is problematic.

13. *New York Times* 1985.

14. Bourgois 2001.

15. Biehl 2007.

16. Puar 2017.

17. See Chenhall and Senior (2018), where they use the idea of assemblage to think differently about the social determinants of health frameworks that allow for a more complex analysis of structural forces in particular contexts and on people's bodies.

18. Fernandes 2017.

19. Although for a very different context—unhoused substance users in California—I build from Bourgois and Schonberg's analysis and photographic images (2009).

20. Wool 2015.

21. Alas 2019; Sprenkels 2018.

22. De León 2015. For a review of the anthropology of death, see Engelke (2019). Groundbreaking work that must be taken into account to discuss spaces and bodies of death includes Katherine Verdery's *Political Lives of Dead Bodies* (1999) on the meanings and national narratives that emerge through reburial of leaders, "because the human community includes both the living and dead, any manipulation of the dead automatically affects relations with and among the living" (108). See also Achille Mbembe's

Necropolitics (2019), which builds in part on Michele Foucault's work on biopower and biopolitics.

23. Vogt 2018, 107.

24. Vogt, 109. Vogt's work helps us to rethink our definitions of borders through a reframing of what she terms the "arterial border" (8). She writes, "The arterial border is in constant flux, expanding and contracting as migrants, organized criminals, and local activists engage, evade, and contest the state along highways, train routes, and the network of shelters that traverse the country like arteries" (8). In part, she illuminates the lives that are mediated in transit and the economies of care that characterize them.

25. Friedner and Weingarten 2019. In this chapter I will not be attempting a survey or a review of an expansive interdisciplinary literature in disability studies, which has long critiqued a pathological and biomedical model of disability—a profound deficit-based paradigm that diminishes personhood and humanity. Readers may be interested in volumes such as *Manifestos for the Future of Disability Studies* (2019) by Katie Ellis and her colleagues and *Keywords for Disability Studies* (2015) by Rachel Adams, Benjamin Reiss, and David Serlin.

26. Ahmed 2006.

27. Friedner and Weingarten 2019, 487–88. Here they also build on the work of Julie Avril Minich (2016).

28. McRuer 2018, 23.

29. McRuer 2018, 24.

30. McRuer 2018, 23.

31. As mentioned in the previous chapter, I build on Bourgois and Schonberg (2009).

32. Livingston 2005; Puar 2017; Ralph 2020.

33. Narayan 1993. There is a tremendous literature and choice of intellectual or theoretical orientation that one could take to think through what I am offering on "the body" or "bodies." It is beyond the scope of this chapter or this book to map this all out. For sure, I could have followed a Foucauldian analysis to think through biopolitics and biopower. A feminist analysis that builds on the work of Emily Martin would also be fruitful ([1987] 2001), as would the classic analysis from medical anthropology on the individual body, the social body, and the body politic (Scheper-Hughes and Lock 1987). My thinking is also indebted to the work of scholars such as Thomas Csordas (1994), whose edited volume offered multiple entrances to the body as cultural and to theories of embodiment.

34. Scornaienchi 2003.

35. Bluebond-Langner 1978, 1996.

36. Kleinman 1988.

37. Charon 2006; Jurecic 2012.

38. I thank my family for allowing me to share aspects of their-our stories.

39. Landsman 2008.

40. There is an expansive, interdisciplinary literature on the disability rights movement in the United States. For a recent historical analysis, see Lennard Davis's *Enabling Acts* (2015).

41. The committee and convention can be found at https://www.ohchr.org/EN/HRBodies/CRPD/Pages/ConventionRightsPersonsWithDisabilities.aspx. It is beyond the scope of this book to explore the literature on the international convention. For an economic analysis on human development, health, and disability in international perspective, see Mitra (2018).

42. For an overview of this literature, see Rachel Adams, Benjamin Reiss, and David Serlin's *Keywords for Disability Studies* (2015), and Lennard J. Davis's *Disability Studies Reader* (2017).

43. For a helpful discussion on ableism, see Fiona Kumari Campbell's "Ability" (2015). Campbell writes, "Ableism denotes the ideology of a healthy body, a normal mind, appropriate speed of thought, and acceptable expressions of emotion. Key to a system of ableism are two elements: the concept of the normative (and the normal individual); and the enforcement of a divide between a 'perfected' or developed humanity and aberrant, unthinkable, underdeveloped, and therefore not really human" (13–14). See also Berger (2004) on trauma and disability.

44. Couser 2011, 28.

45. Brooks 2007.

46. Ginsburg and Rapp 2013, 54.

47. Ginsburg and Rapp, 54. See also Davis (1995) on the historical and sociocultural emergence of "normal."

48. Rapp and Ginsburg 2001, 537.

49. Rapp and Ginsburg, 538.

50. Kafer 2013, 6.

51. Kafer, 3.

52. Bourgois 2001, 12.

53. Child soldiers as a category have often been erased in the hegemonic Salvadoran war story.

54. In the article Bourgois also uses his fieldwork in East Harlem, New York, among crack cocaine users to problematize his previous writing on El Salvador. He states, "I labored under an unconscious Cold War imperative that led me to sanitize my depictions of political violence and repression among revolutionary peasants" (2001, 7). Juxtaposing both projects, he remarks, "In the revolutionary setting of El Salvador, I was eager to document the effective capacity of the dominated to resist state repression while, in the United States, I struggled to explain the politically demobilizing effect of interpersonal conflict and self-destruction that suffuses life in the inner city" (7).

55. See, for example, Alas López (2021), Hernández Rivas (2015), and Martell Pereira (2020).

56. Bourgois 2001, 15.

57. Consider Mitchell and Snyder's critique around the normative assumption that disability is always already equated as oppression. They describe this as a "foundational formula" that they seek to contest (2019, 191). To do so they focus on the experiences of those living with "low-level agency" (194). They write, "Low-level agency is therefore

often about the ways in which experiences of docility allow those who receive support to experience their own future expanding agency. This is the meaning of living with suffering—the paucity of language/narratives we have for describing what it brings into the world is due to the fact that liberalism does not seek to know about the experiential side of these embodied situations" (196).

58. For a different reading of Central American processes through a lens that takes on certain ideas regarding disabled bodies—the Mayan woman as missing, as the prosthetic upon which the Guatemalan nation "hobbles"—see Nelson (2001). See also Vrana (2021) for a historical analysis that centers disability in the making of the Guatemalan nation and citizenship.

59. Bourgois 2001, 17. Italics in original.

60. Bourgois 2001, 28.

61. Silber 2011.

62. See Pillen (2016) for a cogent review of work on trauma in anthropology. For a literary analysis on aesthetics and trauma in El Salvador, see Buiza (2018b).

63. See the *Latin American Perspectives* podcast "Resurgence of Collective Memory, Truth, and Justice Mobilizations in Latin America" at https://latinamericanperspectives.com/the-resurgence-of-collective-memory-truth-and-justice-mobilizations-in-latin-america/. Accessed July 27, 2020.

64. For an alternate reading, please see Carolyn Nordstrom's *A Different Kind of War Story* (1997).

65. See, for example, the extraordinary work of the Sumpul Association. https://www.asociacionsumpul.org/about-english. Accessed July 27, 2020.

66. See Janis H. Jenkins's (2015) work on Salvadoran cultural categories of illness such as "nervios" in the Salvadoran refugee population that comprised her study. She describes the "extraordinary conditions" that can emerge from violence and that "[refer] to conditions—illnesses, disorders, syndromes—that are culturally defined as mental illness. However, I also mean conditions—warfare and political violence, domestic violence and abuse, or scarcity and neglect of basic human needs—constituted by social situations and forces of adversity" (1). Specifically, Jenkins writes that the illness category nervios is about "distress of mind, body and emotion" and that for the Salvadorans she interviewed this was "embedded in conditions of chronic poverty and unrelenting exposure to violence" (153). She looks specifically at the somatic ways in which this was experienced, such as heat in the body (19). See also the classic work on social suffering by Kleinman, Das, and Lock (1997).

67. Quesada 1998.

68. Scheper-Hughes and Sargent 1998.

69. Courtney 2010.

70. McEvoy-Levy 2006. McEvoy-Levy's edited volume focuses on youth between the ages of 12 and 30 at the time of peace accords and the continuum of roles they can play, from militarized "criminal youths" to peace activists. Elsewhere, McEvoy-Levy (2012) focuses on Northern Ireland and discusses how "placemaking" by youth, such as creating rememoried "shared spaces," can be a key factor in peacebuilding.

71. For examples of foundational texts, see Garland Thomson (1997), Davis (1995), and Linton (1998). It is beyond the scope of this chapter to provide a review of disability theories.

72. Here, for example, see Shakespeare (2014), Adams, Reiss, and Serlin (2015), and Davis (2017).

73. Clare 2017, xvi. Italics in original.

74. A new wave of critical race and queer theory has pushed disability studies toward a critique of hegemonic whiteness and normativity. See, for example, Mobley and Bailey (2019), the special issue "Blackness and Disability" of the journal *African American Review* (2017), McRuer (2006), Pickens (2019), and Tyler (2022).

75. Puar 2017; Berlant 2007. Puar clearly works with Julie Livingston's project on debility and care in Botswana (2005, 2006). For example, in *Debility and the Moral Imagination in Botswana*, Livingston reframes conversations in disability studies through shifting to the expansive concept of debility as it operates in Botswana to make sense of the "frailties associated with chronic illness and aging and as the impairments underlying the word disability" (2005, 6). Through a historical study of health, bodies, and plural medical systems, she maps out the structures of caregiving and care work that are crafted over time.

76. Puar 2017, xvii.

77. Puar, xiv.

78. Puar, xvii.

79. Puar, 143.

80. Puar, 143.

81. See https://www.nytimes.com/2019/10/01/us/politics/trump-border-wars.html.

82. Wool 2015. Her recent work (2020) illuminates the violence of "veteran therapeutics" in soldiers' and veterans' lives.

83. See Anastario et al. (2020) for an excellent study that builds on Elizabeth Roberts's work on "bioethnography." Anastario and his colleagues explain that "we use an epistemologically pluralistic approach to examine shifts in slow-moving human/environment entanglements, particularly with agrichemicals, that implicate damage to human kidneys over time" (3). Orantes-Navarro and colleagues also document that in El Salvador, chronic kidney disease "is the second cause of death in men, the fifth in persons over 18 years old and the third cause of hospital deaths in the adult population" (2019, 29). See also Sarah B. Horton's focus on farmworkers in California who suffer heatstroke and chronic illness at alarming rates, a phenomenon that exposes the larger violent structural forces and state practices at the intersection of masculinity, migration, and disability (2016).

84. One could also turn to work such as Elaine Scarry's *The Body in Pain: The Making and Unmaking of the World* (1985) that opened up conversations on the foundational human processes and experiences of injury and pain in war making and the possible resistance to them in acts of enunciation.

85. Ralph 2014, 121.

86. Ralph 2014, 130.

87. Ralph 2014, 8.
88. Ralph 2014, 11.
89. Ralph 2014, 160.
90. Here I hold in tension Didier Fassin's timely critique about how "compassion" circulates in our contemporary period such that it mobilizes a humanitarian politics and masks deep inequalities (2012).
91. https://dle.rae.es/?id=BuAoNQi. Accessed October 22, 2019.
92. Kittay 1999. Readers may also be interested in anthropologist Ayala Fader's analysis of "life-changing doubt" in ultraorthodox Jewish communities (2020, 1), particularly her analysis around the ethical challenges and choices those living "double lives" make (chap. 7). Building on the work of Mara H. Benjamin (2018), Fader shifts the focus of ethics from individual virtue to affective obligation in families.
93. There is an ever-growing body of literature on care work, and I point to an important text on caregiving in Nicaragua. Yarris (2017) explores the critical work of intergenerational care that emerges in the context of migration, with all of its political and economic constraints and affective ties of solidarity. This is a crucial perspective on grandmothers that contests a deficit model of migration. As Yarris illuminates, "Grandmother care is thus a moral practice of *caring about* and *caring for*, over generations and across borders, that makes transnational family life possible" (xv). This is of course not a romantic story, as Yarris also points to the chronic and embodied anxiety over this transnational care work through the "idiom *pensando mucho* (thinking too much)," which is a register of complaint, a space to articulate their distress (29).
94. Her narrative also supports the chronology of armed organizing indicated by Don Gilberto and Nelson in chapter 1. She spent time discussing the shifts from weapons such as wood and nails to the development of special forces units.
95. Here I quote former President Barack Obama's eulogy for Congressman John Lewis when discussing the racist violence that Lewis organized against. https://www.nytimes.com/2020/07/30/us/obama-eulogy-john-lewis-full-transcript.html Accessed November 9, 2020.
96. This was more than likely the "Guinda de Octubre," which took place in 1981. See the work by Equipo Maíz (2008)—a map that documents the massacres across El Salvador.
97. See Livingston (2008) for an analysis of the negotiation of disgust and curiosity of impaired bodies in Botswana.
98. See Vázquez, Ibáñez, and Murguialday 1996.
99. Pickens 2019.
100. Fassin and Rechtman 2009.
101. Brave Heart et al. 2011.
102. Young 1997.
103. Interview with author, November 1997.
104. Ignacio Martín-Baró was born in Valladolid, Spain. He was a Jesuit, a social psychologist, and the vice rector of the UCA in San Salvador. On November 16, 1989, he, along with five of his Jesuit colleagues, a housekeeper, and her daughter, were assassinated

by a US-trained elite military battalion. In September 2020, in Spain's Audencia Nacional (its highest court), Inocente Orlando Montano was found guilty of these crimes and sentenced to 133 years in prison. https://www.theguardian.com/world/2020/sep/11/ex-salvadoran-colonel-inocente-orlando-montano-jailed-for-1989-of-spanish-jesuits. Accessed October 12, 2020. For a translation and compilation of his groundbreaking writing, including his foundational "Toward a Liberation Psychology," see Martín-Baró (1994b).

105. Martín-Baró 1988, 123. Author's translation.

106. Martín-Baró 1988, 123. Author's translation. The original states: "Esta situación de guerra produce un trauma psicosocial, es decir, la cristalización traumática en las personas y grupos de las relaciones sociales deshumanizadas. La polarización tiende a somatizarse, la mentira institucionalizada precipita graves problemas de identidad y la violencia aboca a una militarización de la misma mente. De ahí la urgencia de emprender una tarea psicosocial de despolarización, desideologización y desmilitarización del país."

107. Fassin and Rechtman 2009, 5.

108. James 2010.

109. Fassin and Rechtman 2009, 281.

110. Fassin and Rechtman, 262.

111. Jenkins 2015, 12. Jenkins builds on Judith Butler's theorizations around "precarity," extending the discussion to include mental illness.

112. Here, too, see Adriana Aleyda Alas López's work on the local discourse used to describe disability (2021).

113. Thomas 2019.

114. Kidron 2012, 723.

115. Hirsch 2012, 5.

116. Theidon 2012, 42–44.

117. Theidon explains how *curanderos* treat what are called "males de campo" as ways to diagnose and treat "social ills" (2012, 45). She explains that "*males de campo* refer to disordered social relations and to the spiritual and moral confusion that characterizes a postwar society." There is a surge of literature on the impact of war and terror on children. Further examples for Latin America include Cifuentes Patiño et al. (2011) for a review of the literature on children as former combatants and Cifuentes Patiño (2015) on children and youth as victims in Colombia and the challenges to social work.

118. Dickson-Gómez 2002.

119. Puar 2015, 152.

120. Puar, 152.

121. Puar, 152. She qualifies that this biopolitical tactic against resistance is a "fantasy."

CHAPTER 4. OBJECTS

1. Nguyen 2015, 394.
2. O'Brien 1990, 2.
3. O'Brien 1990, 14–15.

4. I don't intend to replace O'Brien's young American soldiers in the war's neocolonial, imperialist, gendered, raced, sexed, ethnic, and class distinctions with Salvadorans from Chalatenango who fought or stayed or fled during the war. That is a collapsing, a flattening, a commingling, and an erasure of Cold War geopolitical forces that is violent and wrong.

5. A few anthropological texts on ethnography and archives I'm thinking of here include Zeitlyn (2012), Thomas (2011), Otero (2018), and Hosemann (2019).

6. A new generation of scholarship explores historical memory etched in the land, memories infused by their territoriality as the cartographic work of Georgina Hernández Rivas makes clear (2019, 2015) and the analysis of forensic remains exhumed in the massacres of El Mozote also illuminates (Guardado 2019).

7. Appadurai 1986.

8. Bauer (2019) provides an excellent review of anthropological theories around objects. He reminds us that anthropologists have been interested in objects, their exchange, rituals around these exchanges and the relationships created across groups, and how meanings change over time. He reviews the critiques of the human-centered focus of this work (339) and illuminates the multiple theoretical frameworks we can use to think about "objects' complex entanglements" (336) and how objects have agency (339).

9. To learn more about this organization, see http://www.probusqueda.org.sv. Accessed January 20, 2020. Interdisciplinary scholars and practitioners have also studied the impact of this separation and return. See, for example, Barnert et al. (2019) and the processes of reunification.

10. I am intentionally temporally vague here.

11. De León 2015.

12. Thomas 2013. See also *Parcels* (2019) by Mike Anastario regarding the circulation of objects and memories.

13. Sprenkels 2015, 33. See the definition provided by Unfinished Sentences: "*tatú*—A hidden dugout used for shelter or storage. Translated as 'bunker' or 'bomb shelter.' A *tatú* created by an individual family would be dug by hand and used as a makeshift bomb shelter, hiding place, or storage for emergency food and supplies. *Tatús* maintained by guerrilla forces may have been reinforced or equipped for use as field hospitals or other purposes." https://unfinishedsentences.org/archive/glossary. Accessed March 8, 2021.

14. In Jason De León's *The Land of Open Graves* (2015), he develops Callon and Law's focus on "actants" as "sources of action that may be human or nonhuman" (De León 2015, 39) to underscore how US border policies, specifically "Detention Through Deterrence," mask the violence that roots this US law and erases US accountability by placing the blame on "nature," on the Sonoran Desert (38–44). As De León states, "People or objects don't act in isolation, but instead have complex relationships at different moments across time and space that sometimes create things or make things happen" (39). To understand migrant deaths in the Sonoran Desert, De León argues that we must take into account "all of the components—human, animal, mineral, weather pattern, and so forth—that make up a hybrid system." (40). Through this we gain a deep understanding of the "everyday terror of the desert" and how "hostile terrain" is deployed to mask US violence (44).

15. Sprenkels 2015, 35.
16. Sprenkels 2015, 36.
17. Sprenkels 2015, 36.
18. Sprenkels 2015, 36.
19. As elsewhere in the book, unless otherwise indicated, all names are pseudonyms.
20. For reasons of confidentiality and anonymity I am not naming this document.
21. Here I am also being intentionally vague and listing a composite of possible places of exile in people's trajectories at the time.
22. Sprenkels 2018. See esp. chap. 6.
23. Guidos 2021.
24. Here I also invoke my colleague Ralph (Rafa) Sprenkels and the many conversations we had about the responsibility of this work. I wonder how he would have methodologically approached these objects. He would more than likely push me to get the chronology of this object-driven analysis down. Push for the specifics, the empirical sequence of events, the positioned perspectives. Perhaps he would have me ask what really happened with the FMLN, what branch, at what time, in what location were Claribel and her children that they ended up in and out of the party? Where? When? How come? Why was there no money? Why were the parents separated? On what exact command post? What dates of transfer from being representative from here to there? And I wonder if Rafa would have named the locations.
25. See Ott (2015) for an excellent summary of prosthetics.
26. Levitt 2020.
27. For example, see Sanford (2003).
28. Alas López 2021.
29. There are local museums across Chalatenango. For example, in the repopulated community of Arcatao, there is the Museum of Historical Memory. See http://museohistoricodearcatao.blogspot.com. Accessed August 17, 2020. For additional museums, see https://chalatenango.sv/museos-en-chalatenango. Accessed August 17, 2020.
30. Otero 2018. Here too we could invoke Saidiya Hartman's (2019) historical method that also invokes an element of speculation.
31. Otero 2018, 3.
32. Otero, 6.
33. Anastario 2019, 2.
34. Anastario 2019, 2.
35. Anastario 2019, 2.
36. See also Dominique Raby's work in which she builds on Deleuze, exploring "domestic assemblages" in an "Indigenous Nahua context in Mexico" (2019, 529), and Pérez (2019) on memory and migration.
37. Anastario 2019, 95.
38. See Alas López (2021) for analysis of municipal commemorations of the repopulation of Las Vueltas in which individuals and community histories were recognized.
39. Kanstroom 2012.
40. Kanstroom (2012), in Boehm (2016, 46).

41. Castañeda 2019, 5. Castañeda writes about the 4.6 million mixed-status family households in the United States. She defines these households as families with members who have a variety of statuses, from that of US citizen or permanent legal resident to undocumented immigrant, which a majority of households have (9). Castañeda discusses the "de facto reduced citizenship" for approximately 6.6 million individuals and the missing conversation around the "450,000 foreign-born siblings of citizens, whose experiences have remained largely underinvestigated and unaddressed" (9). Scholars have also explored undocumented migration in terms of networks, labor, strategies for making a dignified life, the complex negotiations and processes of regularization in the immigration bureaucracy, and how these processes impact mixed-status families (Gomburg-Muñoz 2016, 2011). See also Gaborit, Orellana, and Orellana Sibrián (2014) for a social psychology perspective.

42. Boehm 2016, 23.

43. Thomas 2011.

44. Horton 2020, 1–2.

45. Horton 2020, 3.

46. Horton 2020, 6.

47. Abarca and Coutin 2018, 7.

48. Abarca and Coutin 2018, 17.

49. Boehm 2016, 22.

50. See also Marroquín Parducci for the ways that migration "en muchas ocasiones no deja registro alguno" (on many occasions leaves no record) (2014, 94). Translation by author.

51. Stoler 2010.

52. Boehm (2016) also critiques the expectation of putting things in order.

53. I am intentionally masking the date for reasons of anonymity and to call attention to the violence of numbers. I am also signaling the aesthetics and power of what is redacted in declassified documents.

54. Boehm 2016.

55. There is critical work on detention and deportation specifically in El Salvador. As a young Salvadoran deportee working in a call center corroborates in an interview with Hilary Goodfriend regarding detention centers and the injustice of prison for simply being an immigrant, "Te encierran en una cárcel federal de máxima seguridad con criminales, verdad, gente que ha hecho cosas malas, que fue condenada por delitos graves" (You're locked up in a maximum-security federal prison, with criminals, right, people who have done bad things, who were convicted of felonies) (2015, 53). Translation by author. See also Gutierrez (2017).

56. De Waal 2010, 16. De Waal discusses the sensorium produced by objects, how they feel held in a hand, how they are handled, and how they are passed on. He adds, "How objects are handed on is all about story-telling." (17).

57. See Stoler (2010).

58. Zeitlyn 2012, 462.

59. Derrida 1996.
60. Foucault 1982. For a cogent review, see Zeitlyn (2012).
61. Stoler 2002, 87.
62. Stoler 2002, 2010.
63. Comaroff and Comaroff 1992, 1991.
64. Zeitlyn 2012, 464. Stoler writes, "Reading only against the grain of the colonial archive bypasses the power in the production of the archive itself" (2002, 101). Regarding reading along the grain, Stoler explains that "colonial administrations were prolific producers of social categories" and that her "focus is less on taxonomy than on the unsure and hesitant sorts of documentation and sensibilities that gathered around them" (2010, 1).
65. Informative here is Salman Hussain's work on how family members contest state violence and the disappearance of their kin through the making of "dossiers of memory" (2019) that contain both official legal documents and "personal artifacts" (54). For Hussain, the dossiers "reveal the life of the file outside the courts, state office, and those who circulate them" (60) and can "unveil state violence" (64).
66. Stoler 2002, 99.
67. Buckley 2005, 215.
68. Buckley, 250.
69. Weld 2014.
70. In Kirsten Weld's work on the discovery of the Guatemalan National Police Archives, she analyzes the 80 million pages of decaying documents as "sites of contemporary political struggle" (2014, 3). She discusses the making of the "terror archive" and comes to this framing through her interest in "archival logics," because at first the police archives were created as surveillance, as part and parcel of the logics of state terror. It was later, when the documents were recovered by activists, that the archives' logics worked in the service of a powerful human rights call for truth, justice, and accountability (6).
71. Thomas 2019.
72. Thomas 2019, 6.
73. Readers may also be interested in Thomas's earlier work on "archive building and the problem of violence" (2013) that argues for looking beyond the national analytic in order to not lose the larger geopolitical structural and historical forces that shape our world, that shape the production of what some may call a counterarchive. Her case study is the production of an anthropological archive for the Caribbean, of the "archive of women's lives generated by feminist scholars" aimed at repairing hegemonic depictions of family dysfunction (35). Later, in her multimedia work on state terror and the 2010 incursion in Tivoli Gardens in Kingston, Jamaica, where between seventy-five and two hundred civilians were killed by agents of the state, Thomas pushes us to further unravel entangled histories of sovereignty and violence in order to ask questions about the making of political subjects. About an archive of affect, she writes, "We constitute ourselves through political activity in the everyday, both at the level of consciousness and at the level of embodiment. Assembling archives of affect thus should tell us something about how the sphere of

the political has been imagined and felt at various junctures and about the kinds of politics that are possible at these junctures" (2019, 7).

74. Garcia 2016, 573.

75. Garcia 2016, 578. In part, Garcia seeks to "underscore the materiality and meaning of the archive to illuminate writing as a site of intimacy and struggle, mourning and survival, both for the authors of the archived writing and for the anthropologist who engages it at a later moment" (2017, 30).

76. Bauer summarizes the concept of object itineraries from Rosemary A. Joyce, which actually speaks nicely to the work on El Salvador: "If things are mobile, moving across networks or along lines in meshworks of existence, as Ingold would have it, this mobility may be productively addressed by thinking of objects as having itineraries, which Joyce . . . defines as 'the routes by which things circulate in and out of places where they come to rest or are active.'" He contends that "itineraries are open-ended and multidirectional, and they include elements, fragments, transformations, and intersections with other itineraries and lines" (2019, 343).

77. See Noe-Bustamante, Flores, and Shah (2019).

78. As elsewhere in the book, verbatim language is translated from the original Spanish unless otherwise indicated. Thus, Marleni's (a pseudonym, as elsewhere in the book) comments are in Spanish, and the translation into English is by the author.

79. De León 2013, 321. For De León, reading artifacts and reading the traces of migrants' paths exposes the "sociotechnical system that is shaped by border enforcement, migrants and the human smuggling industry" (324). Through objects, he shows us the social processes that are part and parcel of a tolerance for suffering. He reminds us, urgently, that these objects tell of human suffering, often with no witnesses, and that "we diminish their voices when we reduce them to mere 'trash'" (341).

80. Salvadoran anthropologist Ramón D. Rivas explores the historical and cultural power of *artesanía*. He writes about the cultural patrimony, identity formation, knowledge production, and history making in the object—the cultural value of artisanal crafts. He shows *artesanía* is under threat from the loss of oral-tradition and knowledge production (2018, 83) and argues that *artesanía* is a testimony to our humanity (83).

81. Puar 2017.

CHAPTER 5. AFTER

1. See chapter 1 where I trouble this phrasing and build on the work of Deborah A. Thomas (2019).

2. See Bonner and Rauda (2021). The article documents President Nayib Bukele's attempts to end the El Mozote investigation in the courts and, at the time, under Judge Jorge Guzmán. The authors write, "On Aug. 31, the legislature, controlled by Bukele's party, fired every judge in the country older than 60. Guzmán is 61." And in documenting a consolidation of power, including the naming of loyalist judges for the Supreme Court, the article also summarizes the Supreme Court's ruling that allows Bukele to run for reelection (in 2024) despite the constitutional term limit as well as the highly

contested adoption of bitcoin as one of El Salvador's official currencies (the US dollar has been the official currency since 2001). Human rights organizations, activists, journalists, policy makers, and academics have all been reporting on and calling out the Bukele's administration authoritarian turn that impedes survivors' long struggle to combat impunity.

3. Nordstrom 1997.

4. My perspective on this hope is also informed by Julie Livingston's work on planetary parables that cautions against "self-devouring" capitalist growth (2019). It is also informed by work that explicitly addresses transnational youth and their politics, such as Dyrness and Abu El-Haj's work in which they focus on transnational youth's unique positioning and critical stance (2019, 5) and write against the stereotyped categories of violent, "alienated," "oppositional" youth, precisely because of their "critical awareness" and their "yearning for democratic citizenship" (2019, 10), full of "imaginative possibilities" to be tapped (11).

5. For example, see "At the Edge of Authoritarianism: Democratic Disenchantment and Radical Optimism in Postwar El Salvador," Grazzia Grimaldi's SSRC-supported dissertation project on the rise of populism through a study of President Nayib Bukele's everyday supporters. See also Sprenkels (2019). And see Guardado Torrez and Moodie (2020) for a prescient argument about the spaces of "post-post war" youth activism, from the FMLN youth meetings in Morazán to new middle-class activism that pushes us to think through what this political moment illuminates. Finally, the mass multisectorial organizing such as on September 15, 2021, to contest President Bukele's repressive regime is also being noted across the human rights community and received important press coverage. See Barrera (2021).

6. See https://www.migrationpolicy.org/programs/data-hub/charts/total-remittance-inflows-and-outflows. Accessed January 20, 2022.

7. See https://data.worldbank.org/indicator/BX.TRF.PWKR.DT.GD.ZS?locations=SV. Accessed January 20, 2022. See Cohen (2011) for an overview of the anthropological literature on remittances.

8. Guardado Torrez and Moodie 2020.

9. Menjívar 2000.

10. See https://www.asociacionsumpul.org/historical-background. Accessed November 30, 2020.

11. Much of this field has explored how infants, children, and adolescents are social and political actors in their own right. Significantly, much of this research pushes us to move beyond the problematic notion of "giving voice" to children (James 2007).

12. This also moves into the realm of the arts. In Chalatenango's repopulated communities, for example, Tiempos Nuevos Teatros (TNT), in San Antonio Los Ranchos, is a model of community theater and arts programming, facilitated by longtime activists and community collaboration that has historically focused on youth. http://www.tnt.org.sv/wp/. Accessed January 20, 2022. There are various partnerships and efforts, from governmental to university to nongovernmental. Consider, for example, the 2018

FMLN government commitment to "Jóvenes Con Todo" and "Salud Atiende" (https://www.salud.gob.sv/28-08-2018-gobierno-implementa-programas-jovenes-con-todo-y-salud-atiende/) or the UCA's concentrated work in Chalatenango via "Mesa de Articulación UCA-Territorio" (Maucat) that focuses in part on supporting the youth sector (https://noticias.uca.edu.sv/proyeccion-social/para-fortalecer-trabajo-territorial-uca-en-chalatenango). CORDES, a historic NGO, also highlights their work with youth, summarizing their workshops on identity and self-esteem aimed at economic empowerment (https://cordes.org.sv/taller-de-indentidad-y-autoestima-con-jovenes-de-iniciativas-economicas/; accessed June 20, 2020). See also Matza (2019) for a focus on children in development projects and concerns around accountability and evaluation. Studies have also focused on youth and health (Achalu et al. 2019) and on youth and the making of cultural politics (Samour 2013).

13. Gaborit, Orellana, and Orellana Sibrián 2014, 56.

14. The report explains that "El Salvador is still a country of young people and is approaching the stage of the demographic bonus with a median age of 27.1 years. About 20.2 percent of the population is aged between 15 and 24 years old and 40 percent is aged between 25 and 54 years old. . . . As a country of the young, El Salvador still has opportunities for growth and development, and therefore human capital investments in children will play an important role in ensuring the sustainable and equitable wealth of the population" (World Bank 2020, 8)

15. Maternal mortality was also significantly lower than regional statistics (46 deaths per 100,000 live births in comparison to 74) (World Bank 2020, 8).

16. World Bank 2020, 8. The report does indicate a rise in obesity (9). With the Bukele administration, the World Bank points to a new program to focus specifically on early childhood development, from birth to seven years of age, known as Crecer Juntos (10). See also http://www.isss.gob.sv/index.php?option=com_content&view=article&id=2102:seguro-social-se-suma-a-la-politica-nacional-de-primera-infancia-crecer-juntos&catid=1:noticias-ciudadano&Itemid=77. Accessed June 15, 2020.

17. Ugalde et al. 2010, 172.

18. See https://data.worldbank.org/indicator/SH.DYN.MORT?locations=SV. Accessed January 13, 2022.

19. See UN Inter-agency Group for Child Mortality Estimation at https://childmortality.org/data/El%20Salvador. Accessed January 13, 2022.

20. See Alas López (2021, chaps. 3–4).

21. https://www.elsalvadormemory.org/what-we-do. Accessed September 15, 2021.

22. Personal communication with Eduardo Maciel, coordinator for memory and pedagogy (Chalatenango) for Caritas.

23. https://www.youtube.com/watch?v=nphbhBZjYt8&t=8s. Accessed September 16, 2021.

24. See https://www.laprensagrafica.com/elsalvador/Elecciones-El-Salvador--Partidos-buscan-impugnar-resultados-municipales-20210303-0132.html. Accessed March 8, 2021.

25. The video includes all of these identifying markers and is a public video.

NOTES TO CHAPTER 5

26. See https://www.salud.gob.sv/05-12-2016-juramentacion-del-comusan-arcatao-por-ministra-de-salud/. Accessed June 11, 2020.

27. Guardado Torrez and Moodie 2020, 590. See Bran Aragón and Goett (2021) for a comparative analysis regarding the emergence of youth activism and subjectivity in Nicaragua's 2018 insurrection by a generation born after the end of the Sandinista revolution in 1990. They also provide a gendered reading as they focus on how some female university activists "reimagined the nation as a space of self- and mutual care rooted in feminist, ecological, and decolonial consciousness. This ethic of life critiques the heroic martyrdom of the revolutionary past and the militarism, extractivism, and heteropatriarchy of the contemporary state" (532).

28. Guardado Torrez and Moodie 2020, 603.

29. In the video, not all panelists are in view. She speaks to many colloquially and intimately, with their first names. On the dais there is also an officer from the Salvadoran army. He too claps during the event, but we don't know his story, his rank, his name, or where he served during the civil war. Was he trained, like so many others, in counterinsurgency at the School of the Americas (Gill 2004)?

30. El Salvador ratified this convention in 1990. See https://indicators.ohchr.org. Accessed June 12, 2020.

31. Guardado Torrez and Moodie 2020, 606.

32. Here again, see Guardado Torrez and Moodie's analysis of how the post-postwar generation "long recognized that publicly questioning political leadership is risky. Their desire to participate in decisions, to contribute beyond simply following the *la línea* (the party line), has been seen as impudence, even betrayal," and yet, they are following in their kin's footsteps and "demanding change" (2020, 592).

33. Sprenkels 2018. See also Sprenkels and Wiegink (2020) for their work on "war veteranship" that pushes us to think beyond the frame of "reintegration." In 2019, Ralph Sprenkels and I coorganized a special session on the "Afterlives of Revolution" in Central America for the LASA conference. We were just beginning to theorize the multiple meanings of this term.

34. For example, this text can only hint at the emergence of the political party Nuevas Ideas and how it won historic FMLN mayoral elections in 2021 in former war zones and staunchly FMLN towns such as Arcatao and Nueva Trinidad. The FMLN mayor was reelected in Las Vueltas, however. See https://www.laprensagrafica.com/elecciones-el-salvador-2021/alcaldias/municipio.html?id=35. Accessed March 8, 2021.

35. These are classics such as Maurice Halbwachs's *On Collective Memory* (1992), Paul Connerton's *How Societies Remember* (1989), Martha Minow's *Between Vengeance and Forgiveness* (1998), Victoria Sanford's *Buried Secrets* (2003), Thomas Abercombie's *Pathways of Memory and Power* (1998), and Dominick LaCapra's *History and Memory after Auschwitz* (1998). See Gellman (2017) for a comparative analysis about the mobilization of memory for cultural rights, and Ross and Sanchez (2018) on the ways that El Salvador is marked by "memory struggles" over the meanings of the war in a context of "low-intensity democracy" (41).

36. Brooks 2007; Moodie 2010.

37. Cosgrove 2010.

38. Tracking electoral politics is one powerful after-story, starting with the 1994 "elections of the century" with the FMLN participating for the first time as an official political party and making historic gains in the legislative assembly and in municipalities across the nation; decades of ARENA rule followed, however, that solidified elite power during the nation's transition to democracy (Wade 2016).

39. Also implemented by the FMLN governments. See Wolf (2017) for a comprehensive analysis.

40. During Latin America's "Left Turn" (Falleti and Parrado 2018) came the historic FMLN presidential victories of Mauricio Funes (2009–2014) and Salvador Sánchez Cerén (2014–2019) that were pushed back by the resounding victory of President Nayib Bukele (2019). Bukele's political party, Nuevas Ideas, took on both ARENA and FMLN power through a populist platform that rallied against violence and corruption, and his power was solidified via sweeping victories in municipal and legislative elections in February 2021. Readers can find excellent analysis and timely coverage on the presidency of Bukele at Elfaro.net. Regarding election coverage, see also https://www.nytimes.com/2021/03/01/world/americas/bukele-el-salvador-election.html. Accessed March 8, 2021.

41. Dawsey 2018.

42. Dyrness and Abu El-Haj 2019, 1.

43. Puar 2017.

44. I am indebted to Mike Anastario for pushing this point and for helping me with the language to make this claim.

45. In the context of the COVID-19 pandemic, many of our conversations focused on the health and economic crises in the United States and El Salvador and how our families were managing. Some of these conversations touched on the political response in both countries. For a critical reading of how Bukele has instituted and propagandized repression of gangs during the global pandemic, see Carlos Dada's incisive reporting: https://elfaro.net/en/202005/columnas/24457/Self-Portrait-with-Gang-Members----On-Bukele's-Prison-Crackdown.htm. Accessed June 23, 2020.

46. I am intentionally vague regarding his business for reasons of anonymity.

47. There is an ample literature that critiques this very framing. For El Salvador, see Mahler (1995). It is interesting, however, to note how Marleni deploys it.

48. See Abrego (2017) for a critique of the discourse around hardworking Salvadorans. See also Pederson (2013) regarding transnational entrepreneurism.

49. Attention to language and migration is also key. See, for example, the work of linguistic anthropologists of language justice, mobility, and migration Hilary Parsons Dick and Lynnette Arnold (2018) in which they explore the migration discourses by those who migrate and those who stay as well as how "North" (i.e., greed, imperialism) and "South" (i.e., family, dependency) get operationalized in a dialectical social field of understanding. Arnold also explores language making between migrant and nonmigrant kin, the making of subjectivities (2019), and how Salvadoran women narrate their unauthorized migration and the dissonance in being able to imagine the migrant life as "affective distress" (Dick and Arnold 2018, 24).

50. A recent study (Johnco et. al. 2020) notes the high incidence of traumatic events but finds that "less than 4% of children who experienced a trauma fulfilled PTSD criteria." They found that "parents preferred to handle their child's emotional problems themselves or seek help from nonpharmacological mental health services" (19).

51. See Alas (2019), Alas López (2021), Chacón Serrano (2019), DeLugan (2019), Durán Fernández (2020), Hernández Rivas (2019), Lara Martínez (2019), Martell Pereira (2020), and Sierra Becerra (2016). Take Durán Fernández's master's thesis in which she explores the wounds of trauma as "incrustado en los cuerpos y en la vida cotidiana de las mujeres de forma diferente con relación a las experiencias que cada persona ha vivido" (2020, 5). She focuses on the embodied pain born from the structural violence of postwar and the creative modalities of care and healing (17). See also Stephanie Huezo's analysis of the transmission of historical memory across generations through performance in repopulation reenactment celebrations that showcases lived experiences of war (2021) and Nilcer Melgar and Johana Mejía's work on the role of performance and community theater in the making of intergenerational memory (2021).

52. As indicated in chapter 1 and in my previous work on El Rancho's local history (Silber 2011), many residents reference a few youth from San Salvador and the university as arriving to organize the communities. There is also a significant literature on the relationship between urban and rural militants. Indeed, Chávez's groundbreaking historical work (2017) locates the critical role of peasant intellectuals in Chalatenango.

53. For a summary and updates on the prosecution of the case, visit Cristosal's website at https://www.cristosal.org/el-mozote. Online newspaper *El Faro* also has extensive coverage on the case, as do many human rights organizations and newspapers: https://mozote.elfaro.net/inicio. Accessed November 15, 2020.

54. In the later postwar, testimonials and research have documented the purges that took place within branches of the FMLN. For the FPL, Mayo Sibrián during the mid-1980s ordered what was called "ajustamientos" of supposed infiltrators. Sibrián was then executed by the FPL in 1991. See the powerful reporting by Claudia Palacios and Andrés Dimas in *El Faro* at https://elfaro.net/es/201912/el_salvador/23857/Los-exguerrilleros-que-acusan-al-FMLN-de-cr%C3%ADmenes-de-guerra.htm?st-full_text=all&tpl=11. Accessed December 6, 2020.

55. See Todd (2021).

56. 2012.

57. Chacón Serrano 2017, 2020. Diasporic, international human rights activism around discovering what happened to disappeared loved ones is seen in organizations such as Our Parents' Bones. https://ourparentsbones.com. Accessed September 27, 2021.

58. Menjívar Ochoa and Sprenkels 2017.

59. See http://www.cultura.gob.sv/inicia-instalacion-de-la-ruta-de-memoria-historica-en-el-mozote-y-lugares-aledanos/. Accessed September 14, 2020. See Paula Cuéllar (2014) on claiming justice in El Salvador.

60. See https://www.elsalvadormemory.org/commemoration. Accessed September 14, 2020.

61. United Nations 1993, 126–29.

62. See https://www.asociacionsumpul.org/message-from-the-board-of-directors. Accessed March 9, 2021.

63. See https://www.asociacionsumpul.org/historical-background. Accessed March 9, 2021.

64. The event was streamed on CRIPDES and CCR Facebook Live and on http://radiofarabundomarti.org (98.1 FM) and http://radiosumpul.org (92.1 FM). Accessed May 14, 2020. Much of the commemoration can be found curated by La Asociación de Radios y Programas Participativos de El Salvador (ARPAS). https://arpas.org.sv/2020/05/masacre-del-rio-sumpul-40-anos-sin-justicia-para-las-victimas/. Accessed December 8, 2020.

65. https://www.facebook.com/ccr.chalatenango.2017/videos/vb.100015226727765/878068962710653/?type=2&video_source=user_video_tab. Accessed May 16, 2020.

66. https://arpas.org.sv/2020/05/masacre-del-rio-sumpul-40-anos-sin-justicia-para-las-victimas/. Accessed December 8, 2020.

67. See https://www.facebook.com/Telenoticias29/videos/2889299824458339/UzpfSTEwMDAxNTIyNjcyNzc2NTo4NzkoNzAxODU5MDM4NjQ/. Accessed May 16, 2020. In a Telenoticias 29 newsclip, a young activist named Edith Cruz is interviewed about her work with the Missionaries of Historical Memory. Cruz articulates their positioning predicated on their youth and the connections to war stories. She is quoted as stating, "Como jóvenes nosotros queremos mantener viva la historia—As youth we want to maintain this history alive. That memory of all the survivors. We also want to work with the families of massacre survivors. Nosotros lo que compartimos como jóvenes es la historia que ellos, los sobrevivientes, nos comparten, ¿verdad? Desde esa historia nosotros partimos todo el trabajo que nosotros realizamos en las comunidades—What we want to share as youth is their history, that the survivors share with us, right? It's from that history that our community work takes off."

68. https://arpas.org.sv/2020/05/masacre-del-rio-sumpul-40-anos-sin-justicia-para-las-victimas/. Accessed December 8, 2020.

69. These quotes are from https://arpas.org.sv/2020/05/masacre-del-rio-sumpul-40-anos-sin-justicia-para-las-victimas/. Accessed May 16, 2020.

70. The words of various speakers were then recirculated via solidarity and activist sites and archived on Facebook. For example, see https://arpas.org.sv/2020/05/masacre-del-rio-sumpul-40-anos-sin-justicia-para-las-victimas. Accessed May 16, 2020.

71. See Victoria Sanford's comments regarding the history of US intervention in Guatemala and how as a result the United States should be held to account for reparations. https://azpbs.org/horizon/2021/09/guatemalan-war-deaths/. Accessed September 26, 2021.

72. Here I'm thinking about the grand narratives and theory building around the critique of international development by Julie Livingston in *Self-Devouring Growth* (2019) that focuses on the paradoxes of development. I'm also thinking about Donna Haraway's call for "tentacular thinking" (2016, 5).

73. Haraway 2016, 1–2.

74. Haraway spends considerable time in the text working with these categories and showing their intellectual lineage. For example, she shows how the term "Anthropocene" emerges through the work of Eugene Stoermer, who "introduced the term to refer to growing evidence for the transformative effects of human activities on the earth" (2016, 44). Similarly, regarding "Capitalocene," Haraway points to the multiple strands of thought (i.e., Marxist, too often Eurocentric) regarding the violence that such processes as capitalism and globalization inflict on humans, things, plants, and so on (47–51). Haraway spends the book introducing the reader to the Anthropocene, the Capitalocene, and the Chthulucene as "timescapes."

75. Haraway 2016, 3. She argues that "staying with the trouble requires making oddkin; that is, we require each other in unexpected collaborations and combinations, in hot compost piles. We become-with each other or not at all" (4). Here, too, readers should be interested in Deborah A. Thomas's thinking on repair rather than reparations: "Repair, like refusal, is practice-oriented and quotidian; it is non-eventful and deeply historical and relational. . . . Repair urges us to interrogate the multiple scales of entanglement that have led us to where we are now. But where reparation seeks justice through the naming of names, the exposure of public secrets, and the articulation of chains of causality, repair looks for something else. It demands an active listening, a mutual recognizing, an acknowledging of complicity at all levels—behavioral evidence of profound interior transformations that are ongoing" (2019, 212).

REFERENCES

Abarca, Gray Albert, and Susan Bibler Coutin. 2018. "Sovereign Intimacies: The Lives of Documents within US State-Noncitizen Relationships." *American Ethnologist* 45: 7–19.

Abercrombie, Thomas. 1998. *Pathways of Memory and Power: Ethnography and History among an Andean People*. Madison: University of Wisconsin Press.

Abrego, Leisy. 2014. *Sacrificing Families: Navigating Laws, Labor, and Love across Borders*. Stanford, CA: Stanford University Press.

———. 2017. "Hard Work Alone Is Not Enough: Blocked Mobility for Salvadoran Women in the United States." In *U.S. Central Americans: Reconstructing Memories, Struggles, and Communities of Resistance*, edited by Karina O. Alvarado, Alicia Ivonne Estrada, and Ester E. Hernández, 60–76. Tucson: University of Arizona Press.

Abu-Lughod, Lila. 1993. *Writing Women's Worlds: Bedouin Stories*. Berkeley: University of California Press.

———. 2016. *Veiled Sentiments: Honor and Poetry in a Bedouin Society*. Berkeley: University of California Press.

Achalu, P., N. Zahid, D. N. Sherry, A. Chang, and K. Sokal-Gutierrez. 2019. "A Qualitative Study of Child Nutrition and Oral Health in El Salvador." *International Journal of Environmental Research and Public Health* 16, no. 14: 2508. https://doi.org/10.3390/ijerph16142508.

Adams, Rachel, Benjamin Reiss, and David Serlin. 2015. *Keywords for Disability Studies*. New York: New York University Press.

Agren, David. 2020. "'Mexico Has Become Trump's Wall': How Amlo Became an Immigration Enforcer." *Guardian*, January 26, 2020. https://www.theguardian.com/world/2020/jan/26/mexico-immigration-amlo-enforcement-trump.

Ahmed, Sara. 2006. *Queer Phenomenology: Orientations, Objects, Others*. Durham, NC: Duke University Press.

Alarcón, Daniel. 2015. "The Executioners of El Salvador." *New Yorker*, August 4, 2015. http://www.newyorker.com/news/news-desk/the-executioners-of-el-salvador.

Alarcón Medina, Rafael. 2014. "Dreaming the Dream of a Dead Man: Memory, Media, and Youth in Postwar El Salvador." *Dialectical Anthropology* 38: 481–97.
———. 2015. "Peasant Warriors in an Electronic-Social Formation: From Rural Communities to Transnational Circuits of Dependence in Postwar El Salvador." *Convergence: The International Journal of Research into New Media Technologies* 21, no. 4: 474–95. https://doi.org/10.1177/1354856514544085.
Alas, Adriana. 2019. "Sensaciones a través del tiempo: El dolor en las negociaciones de posguerra de El Salvador." *Realidad: Revista De Ciencias Sociales y Humanidades* 153: 135–61.
Alas López, Adriana Aleyda. 2013. "La dinámica de los grupos domésticos en una repoblación al oriente de Chalatenango, municipio de Las Vueltas, cantón La Ceiba (2011–2013)." Licenciatura thesis, Universidad Nacional, San Salvador.
———. 2021. "El valor de las memorias: Tensiones intergeneracionales por las memorias en la posguerra salvadoreña." PhD diss., Colmich, MX.
Alegría, Claribel. 1987. *They Won't Take Me Alive: Salvadorean Women in the Struggle for National Liberation.* London: Women's Press.
Alemán, Marco. 2020. "El Salvador Reconciliation Law Vetoed over Impunity Fears." Associated Press. February 29, 2020. https://apnews.com/204c763e7750d0f10774fc649de4ac49.
Allen, Jafari Sinclaire, and Ryan Cecil Jobson. 2016. "The Decolonizing Generation: (Race and) Theory in Anthropology since the Eighties." *Current Anthropology* 57, no. 2: 129–48.
Alonso Bejarano, Carolina, Lucia López Juárez, Mirian A. Mijangos García, and Daniel M. Goldstein. 2019. *Decolonizing Ethnography: Undocumented Immigrants and New Directions in Social Science.* Durham, NC: Duke University Press.
Alvarado, Karina O., Alicia Ivonne Estrada, and Ester E. Hernández, eds. 2017. *U.S. Central Americans: Reconstructing Memories, Struggles, and Communities of Resistance.* Tucson: University of Arizona Press.
Amaya, Rufina, Mark Danner, and Carlos Henríquez Consalvi. 1996. *Luciérnagas en El Mozote.* San Salvador: Ediciones Museo de la Palabra y la Imagen.
Anastario, Mike. 2019. *Parcels: Memories of Salvadoran Migration.* New Brunswick, NJ: Rutgers University Press.
Anastario, Mike, Miguel Geovanny Arias Rodas, Milton Alexander Escobar Arteaga, Christian Villanueva, Fernando Chacón Serrano, and Hope Ferdowsian. 2020. "Genitourinary Systems Entangled with Shifting Environments in a Salvadoran Subsistence Farming Community." *MAQ* 35, no. 2: 246–65. https://doi.org/10.1111/maq.12616.
Angel-Ajani, Asale. 2004. "Expert Witness: Notes toward Revisiting the Politics of Listening." *Anthropology and Humanism* 29, no. 2: 133–44.
Angel-Ajani, Asale, Carolyn J. Dean, and Meg McLagan. 2021. "Witnessing: Virtual Conversations." *Cambridge Journal of Anthropology* 39, no. 1: 130–42.
Appadurai, Arjun, ed. 1986. *The Social Life of Things: Commodities in Cultural Perspective.* Cambridge, UK: Cambridge University Press.

Ares Mateos, Alberto S. J. 2015. "La comunidad salvadoreña en Boston." *ECA* 70, no. 743: 535–76.
Arias, Arturo, ed. 2001. *The Rigoberta Menchú Controversy*. Minneapolis: University of Minnesota Press.
Arnold, Lynnette. 2015. "The Reconceptualization of Agency through Ambiguity and Contradiction: Salvadoran Women Narrating Unauthorized Migration." *Women's Studies International Forum* 52: 10–19.
———. 2019. "Language Socialization across Borders: Producing Scalar Subjectivities through Material-Affective Semiosis." *Pragmatics* 29 no. 3: 332–56.
Asad, Talal, ed. 1995. *Anthropology and the Colonial Encounter*. New York: Rowman and Littlefield/Humanities.
Asmann, Parker. 2018. "El Salvador Citizen Security Plan Struggling to Reduce Insecurity." *InSight Crime*, July 16, 2018. https://www.insightcrime.org/news/analysis/el-salvador-citizen-security-plan-struggling-reduce-insecurity/.
Bailey, Moya, and Izetta Autumn Mobley. 2019. "Work in the Intersections: A Black Feminist Disability Framework." *Gender and Society* 33, no. 1: 19–40.
Baker-Cristales, Beth. 2004. *Salvadoran Migration to Southern California: Redefining el Hermano Lejano*. Gainesville: University Press of Florida.
Barnert, Elizabeth, Nathalie Lopez, Philippe Bourgois, Gery Ryan, Paul J. Chung, and Eric Stover. 2019. "My Child's Journey Home: Perspectives of Adult Family Members on the Separation and Reunification of the 'Disappeared' Children of El Salvador." *Human Rights Quarterly* 41: 91–114.
Barrera, Carlos. "La marcha grande contra Bukele." *El Faro*, September 15, 2021. https://elfaro.net/es/202109/ef_foto/25718/La-marcha-grande-contra-Bukele.htm. Accessed September 18, 2021.
Barrera, Juan Salinas. 2013. "La migración en jóvenes hijos de padres migrantes: Abordaje desde la comunicación." *Estudios Centroamericanos* 68, no. 735: 545–55. https://doi.org/10.51378/eca.v68i735.3320.
Baudrillard, Jean. 1994. *Simulacra and Simulation*. Ann Arbor: University of Michigan Press.
Bauer, Alexander A. 2019. "Itinerant Objects." *Annual Review of Anthropology* 48: 335–52.
BBC (British Broadcasting Corporation). 2020. "El Salvador: Gangs 'Taking Advantage of Pandemic.'" BBC, April 27, 2020. https://www.bbc.com/news/world-latin-america-52439856.
Bellino, Michelle. 2017. *Youth in Postwar Guatemala: Education and Civic Identity in Transition*. New Brunswick, NJ: Rutgers University Press.
Benjamin, Mara H. 2018. *The Obligated Self: Maternal Subjectivity and Jewish Thought*. Bloomington: Indiana University Press.
Berger, James. 2004. "Trauma without Disability, Disability without Trauma: A Disciplinary Divide." *JAC* 24, no. 3: 563–82.
Berlant, Lauren. 2007. "Slow Death (Sovereignty, Obesity, Lateral Agency)." *Critical Inquiry* 33, no. 4: 754–80.

Berry, Maya J., Claudia Chávez Argüelles, Shanya Cordis, Sarah Ihmoud, and Elizabeth Velásquez Estrada. 2017. "Toward a Fugitive Anthropology: Gender, Race, and Violence in the Field." *Cultural Anthropology* 32, no. 4: 537–65. https://doi.org/10.14506/ca32.4.05.

Beverley, John. 2004. *Testimonio: On the Politics of Truth*. Minneapolis: Minnesota University Press.

Beverley, John, and Marc Zimmerman. 1990. *Literature and Politics in the Central American Revolutions*. Austin: University of Texas Press.

Biehl, João. 2007. *Will to Live: AIDS Therapies and the Politics of Survival*. Princeton, NJ: Princeton University Press.

Binford, Leigh. 1998. "Hegemony in the Interior of the Salvadoran Revolution: The ERP in Northern Morazán." *Journal of Latin American Anthropology* 4, no. 1: 2–45.

———. 2016. *The El Mozote Massacre: Human Rights and Global Implications*, rev. and exp. ed. Tucson: Arizona University Press.

Blitzer, Jonathon. 2017. "Letter from El Salvador—The Deportees Taking Our Calls: How American Immigration Policy Has Fueled an Unlikely Industry in El Salvador." *New Yorker*, January 15, 2017. https://www.newyorker.com/magazine/2017/01/23/the-deportees-taking-our-calls.

Bluebond-Langner, Myra. 1978. *The Private Worlds of Dying Children*. Princeton, NJ: Princeton University Press.

———. 1996. *In the Shadow of Illness: Parents and Siblings of the Chronically Ill Child*. Princeton, NJ: Princeton University Press.

Boehm, Deborah A. 2016. *Returned: Going and Coming in an Age of Deportation*. Berkeley: University of California Press.

Boehm, Deborah A., and Susan J. Terrio, eds. 2019. *Illegal Encounters: The Effect of Detention and Deportation on Young People*. New York: New York University Press.

Boellstorff, Tom, Bonnie Nardi, Celia Pearce, and T. L. Taylor, eds. 2012. *Ethnography and Virtual Worlds: A Handbook of Method*. Princeton, NJ: Princeton University Press.

Bonner, Raymond. 2019. "El Salvador Mocks the Victims of El Mozote." *Atlantic*, May 23, 2019.

Bonner, Raymond, and Nelson Rauda. "Survivors of El Mozote Massacre See Justice Slip Away Again." *El Faro*, September 13, 2021.

Borofsky, Robert, and Antonio De Lauri. 2019. "Public Anthropology in Changing Times." *Public Anthropologist* 1, no. 1: 3–19. https://doi.org/10.1163/25891715-0020 1002.

Bourgois, Philippe. 2001. "The Power of Violence in War and Peace: Post–Cold War Lessons from El Salvador." *Ethnography* 2, no. 1: 5–34.

Bourgois, Philippe and Jeff Schonberg. 2009. *Righteous Dopefiend*. Berkeley: University of California Press.

Bradley, Heather. 2008. "Nosotros, los que quedamos atrás: Migración salvadoreña a través de la fotografía de niños y niñas en Arcatao y La Charca." *Revista Realidad* 118: 587–620.

Bran Aragón, Fiore Stella and Jennifer Goett. 2021. "¡Matria libre y vivir!: Youth Activism and Nicaragua's 2018 Insurrection." *Journal of Latin American and Caribbean Anthropology* 25, no. 4: 532–51.

Brave Heart, Maria Yellow Horse, Josephine Chase, Jennifer Elkins, and Deborah B. Altschul. 2011. "Historical Trauma among Indigenous Peoples of the Americas: Concepts, Research, and Clinical Considerations." *Journal of Psychoactive Drugs* 43, no. 4: 282–90.

Brenneman, Robert. 2012. *Homies and Hermanos: God and Gangs in Central America*. New York: Oxford University Press.

Brigden, Noelle Kateri. 2018. *The Migrant Passage: Clandestine Journeys from Central America*. Ithaca, NY: Cornell University Press.

Brigida, Anna-Cat. 2020. "Constitutional Crisis in El Salvador over Bukele's Security Plan." *Aljazeera*, February 10, 2020. https://www.aljazeera.com/news/2020/02/constitutional-crisis-el-salvador-bukele-security-plan-200210183636678.html.

Brooks, Ethel C. 2007. *Unraveling the Garment Industry: Transnational Organizing and Women's Work*. Minneapolis: University of Minnesota Press.

———. 2013. "Reclaiming: The Camp and the Avant-Garde." In *We Roma: A Critical Reader in Contemporary Art*, edited by Daniel Baker and Maria Hlavajova. BAK Critical Reader Series. Utrecht: Valiz/BAK.

Buchanan, Ian. 2018. *A Dictionary of Critical Theory*. 2nd ed. Oxford, UK: Oxford University Press.

Buckley, Liam. 2005. "Objects of Love and Decay: Colonial Photographs in a Postcolonial Archive." *Cultural Anthropology* 20, no. 2: 249–70. https://doi.org/10.1525/can.2005.20.2.249.

Buiza, Nanci. 2018a. "Crossing Mexico on *La Bestia*: The Central American Migrant Experience in the Documentary Films *Which Way Home* and *Who Is Dayani Cristal?*" *Hispanic Research Journal* 19, no. 4: 415–29.

———. 2018b. "On Aesthetic Experience and Trauma in Postwar Central America: The Case of Horacio Castellanos Moya's *El Asco* and Claudia Hernández's *De Fronteras*." *Hispanófila* 84: 99–115.

Burrell, Jennifer L., Mounia El Kotni, and Ramiro Fernando Calmo. 2021. "The Anti/Corruption Continuum: Generation, Politics and Grassroots Anti-Corruption Mobilization in Guatemala." *Journal of Latin American and Caribbean Anthropology* 25, no. 4: 610–30.

Burrell, Jennifer L., and Ellen Moodie. 2015. "The Post–Cold War Anthropology of Central America." *Annual Review of Anthropology* 44: 381–400.

———. 2021. "Generations and Change in Central America: An Introduction." *Journal of Latin American and Caribbean Anthropology* 25, no. 4: 522–31.

Cabarrús, Carlos Rafael. 1983. *Génesis de una revolución: Análisis del surgimiento y desarrollo de la organización campesina en El Salvador*. Mexico City: Ediciones de la Casa Chata.

Cagan, Beth, and Steve Cagan. 1991. *This Promised Land, El Salvador: The Refugee Community of Colomoncagua and Their Return to Morazán*. New Brunswick, NJ: Rutgers University Press.

Campbell, Fiona Kumari. 2015. "Ability." In *Keywords for Disability Studies*, edited by Rachel Adams, Benjamin Reiss, and David Serlin, 46–51. New York: New York University Press.

Cárdenas, Maritza E. 2018. *Constituting Central American–Americans: Transnational Identities and the Politics of Dislocation*. New Brunswick, NJ: Rutgers University Press.

Cardoso, Jodi Berger, Kalina Brabeck, Dennis Stinchcomb, Lauren Heidbrink, Olga Acosta Price, Óscar F. Gil-García, Thomas M. Crea, and Luis H. Zayas. 2019. "Integration of Unaccompanied Migrant Youth in the United States: A Call for Research." *Journal of Ethnic and Migration Studies* 45, no. 2: 273–92. https://doi.org/10.1080/1369183X.2017.1404261.

Cartagena, Edgar R. 2005. "Emigración y remesas—Un perfil para Chalatenango." *Realidad: Revista de Ciencias Sociales y Humanidades* 105: 399–425.

Castañeda, Heide. 2019. *Borders of Belonging: Struggle and Solidarity in Mixed-Status Immigrant Families*. Stanford, CA: Stanford University Press.

Cervantes-Soon, Claudia G. 2012. "*Testimonios* of Life and Learning in the Borderlands: Subaltern Juárez Girls Speak." *Equity and Excellence in Education* 45, no. 3: 373–91.

Chacón Serrano, Fernando Nelson. 2017. "Construcción de memorias sobre el conflicto armado de el salvador en jóvenes de una comunidad desplazada." Master's thesis, Universidad de Chile.

———. 2020. "Estamos en guerra": Memorias del conflicto armado salvadoreño y sus tramas narrativas en jóvenes de una comunicada desplazada." *ECA: Estudios Centroamericanos* 75, no. 763: 71–96.

Chacón Serrano, Fernando, Leslie Gómez, and Thelma Alas. 2013. "Configuración de imaginarios sociales sobre la migración irregular en jóvenes potenciales migrantes y retornados." *ECA: Estudios Centroamericanos* 68, no. 735: 511–43.

Charon, Rita. 2006. *Narrative Medicine: Honoring the Stories of Illness*. New York: Oxford University Press.

Chávez, Joaquín M. 2017. *Poets and Prophets of the Resistance: Intellectuals and the Origins of El Salvador's Civil War*. New York: Oxford University Press.

Chenhall, Richard, and Kate Senior. 2017. "Living the Social Determinants of Health: Assemblages in a Remote Aboriginal Community." *Medical Anthropology Quarterly* 32, no. 2: 177–95.

Ching, Erik. 2016. *Stories of Civil War in El Salvador: A Battle Over Memory*. Chapel Hill: University of North Carolina Press.

Chishti, Muzzafar, Sarah Pierce, and Jessica Bolter. 2017. "The Obama Record on Deportations: Deporter in Chief or Not?" Migration Policy Institute. https://www.migrationpolicy.org/article/obama-record-deportations-deporter-chief-or-not.

Cifuentes Patiño, María Rocío. 2015. "Niñez y juventud, víctimas del conflicto armado: Retos para el trabajo social." *Revista Tendencias and Retos* 20, no. 1: 161–77.

Cifuentes Patiño, María Rocío, Nathalia Aguirre Álvarez, and Nelvia Victoria Lugo Agudelo. 2011. "Niñas, niños y jóvenes excombatientes: revisión de tema." *Eleuthera* 5: 93–124. https://revistasojs.ucaldas.edu.co/index.php/eleuthera/article/view/5105.

REFERENCES

Clare, Eli. 2017. *Brilliant Imperfection: Grappling with Cure*. Durham, NC: Duke University Press.
Classen, Susan. 1992. *Vultures and Butterflies: Living the Contradictions*. Eugene, OR: Wipf and Stock.
Clavel, Tristan. 2017. "Barrio 18 Members Sentenced to 390 Years for El Salvador Massacre." *InSight Crime*, May 26, 2017. https://insightcrime.org/news/brief/390-years-for-barrio-18-members-who-took-part-in-el-salvador-massacre/.
Clifford, James. 1988. *The Predicament of Culture: Twentieth-Century Ethnography, Literature, and Art*. Cambridge, MA: Harvard University Press.
Cohen, Jeffrey H. 2011. "Migration, Remittances, and Household Strategies." *Annual Review of Anthropology* 40: 103–14.
Cohn, D'Vera, Jeffrey S. Passel, and Kristen Bialik. 2019. "Many Immigrants with Temporary Protected Status Face Uncertain Future in U.S." Pew Research Center. https://www.pewresearch.org/fact-tank/2019/11/27/immigrants-temporary-protected-status-in-us/.
Collins, Patricia Hill. 2000. *Black Feminist Thought: Knowledge, Consciousness and the Politics of Empowerment*. New York: Routledge.
Comaroff, Jean, and John Comaroff. 1991. *Of Revelation and Revolution, Volume 1: Christianity, Colonialism, and Consciousness in South Africa*. Chicago: University of Chicago Press.
Comaroff, John, and Jean Comaroff. 1992. *Ethnography and the Historical Imagination*. Boulder, CO: Westview Press.
Connerton, Paul. 1989. *How Societies Remember*. Cambridge, UK: Cambridge University Press.
Copeland, Nicholas. 2020. "A New Deal for Central America." *NACLA* 52, no. 1: 67–76. http://dx.doi.org/10.1080/10714839.2020.1733234.
Córdova Macías, Ricardo, José Miguel Cruz, and Mitchell A. Seligson. 2013. *Cultura política de la democracia en El Salvador y en las Américas, 2012: Hacia la igualdad de oportunidades*. Report prepared for the Latin American Public Opinion Project, Vanderbilt University, Nashville, TN.
Cortez, Beatriz. 2018. "La Memoria de las plantas: Sobre el devenir atmósfera. *Realidad: Revista de Ciencias Sociales y Humanidades* 152: 113–24.
Cortez, Israel. 2018. "Represión y refugio en tiempos de guerra: Las comunidades repobladas de El Salvador." *Identidades* 8, no. 12: 150–75.
Cosgrove, Serena. 2010. *Leadership from the Margins: Women and Civil Society Organizations in Argentina, Chile, and El Salvador*. New Brunswick, NJ: Rutgers University Press.
Cosgrove, Serena. Forthcoming. "Nicaraguan Solidarity 3.0: International University Partnerships and the New 'Normal' in Nicaragua." In *Higher Education at the Crossroads of State Repression and Neoliberal Reform in Nicaragua: Reflections from a University under Fire*, edited by Wendi Bellanger, Serena Cosgrove, and Irina Carlota Silber. London: Routledge.

Cosgrove, Serena, José Idiáquez, Leonard Joseph Bent, and Andrew Gorvetzian. 2021. *Surviving the Americas: Garifuna Persistence from Nicaragua to New York City*. Cincinnati: University of Cincinnati Press.

Courtney, Jocelyn. 2010. "The Civil War that Was Fought by Children: Understanding the Role of Child Combatants in El Salvador's Civil War, 1980–1992." *Journal of Military History* 74: 523–56.

Couser, G. Thomas. 2009. *Signifying Bodies: Disability in Contemporary Life Writing*. Ann Arbor: University of Michigan Press.

———. 2011. "What Disability Studies Has to Offer Medical Education." *Journal of Medical Humanities* 32: 21–30.

Coutin, Susan Bibler. 1993. *The Culture of Protest: Religious Activism and the U.S. Sanctuary Movement*. Boulder, CO: Westview Press.

———. 2007. *Nations of Emigrants: Shifting Boundaries of Citizenship in El Salvador and the United States*. Ithaca: Cornell University Press.

———. 2016. *Exiled Home: Salvadoran Transnational Youth in the Aftermath of Violence*. Durham, NC: Duke University Press.

Cruz, José Miguel. 2010. "Central American Maras: From Youth Street Gangs to Transnational Protection Rackets. *Global Crime* 11, no. 4: 379–98.

Csordas, Thomas J., ed. 1994. *Embodiment and Experience: The Existential Ground of Culture and Self*. New York: Cambridge University Press.

Cuéllar, Jorge E. 2020. "El Salvador's Hydrosocial Crisis." *NACLA Report on the Americas* 52, no. 3: 317–23. https://doi.org/10.1080/10714839.2020.1809101.

Cuéllar, Paula. 2014. "Obstáculos al ejercicio del derecho de acceso a la justicia por parte las víctimas del conflicto armado salvadoreño, y de sus familiares." *ECA: Estudios Centroamericanos* 69, no. 736: 119–41.

Dada, Carlos. 2020. "Self-Portrait with Gang Members—On Bukele's Prison Crackdown." *El Faro*, May 22, 2020. https://elfaro.net/en/202005/columnas/24457/Self-Portrait-with-Gang-Members----On-Bukele's-Prison-Crackdown.htm. Accessed July 13, 2020.

Danner, Mark. 1994. *The Massacre at El Mozote*. New York: Vintage.

Davis, Lennard J. 1995. *Enforcing Normalcy: Disability, Deafness, and the Body*. London: Verso.

———. 2015. *Enabling Acts: The Hidden Story of How the Americans with Disabilities Act Gave the Largest US Minority Its Rights*. Boston: Beacon Press.

———, ed. 2017. *The Disability Studies Reader*. 5th ed. New York: Routledge.

Dawsey, Josh. 2018. "Trump Derides Protections for Immigrants from 'Shithole' Countries." *Washington Post*. January 12, 2018. https://www.washingtonpost.com/politics/trump-attacks-protections-for-immigrants-from-shithole-countries-in-oval-office-meeting/2018/01/11/bfc0725c-f711-11e7-91af-31ac729add94_story.html.

De Genova, Nicholas, and Nathalie Peutz, eds. 2010. *The Deportation Regime: Sovereignty, Space, and the Freedom of Movement*. Durham, NC: Duke University Press.

De León, Jason. 2013. "Undocumented Migration, Use Wear, and the Materiality of Habitual Suffering in the Sonoran Desert." *Journal of Material Culture* 18, no. 4, 321–45. https://doi.org/10.1177/1359183513496489.

REFERENCES

———. 2015. *The Land of Open Graves: Living and Dying on the Migrant Trail.* Berkeley: University of California Press.
De Waal, Edmund. 2010. *The Hare with Amber Eyes: A Hidden Inheritance.* London: Vintage.
DeLugan, Robin Maria. 2019. "La guerra civil, la memoria social y la nación: Algunas consideraciones teóricas y éticas" *Realidad: Revista de Ciencias Sociales y Humanidades* 153: 9–21.
Defense Intelligence Agency Assistant Directorate for JCS Support. 1981. *International Terrorism: A Compendium Volume III—Latin America (U).* March. Digital National Security Archive.
Derrida, Jacques. 1996. *Archive Fever: A Freudian Impression.* Chicago: University of Chicago Press.
Dick, Hilary Parsons, and Lynnette Arnold. 2018. "From South to North and Back Again: Making and Blurring Boundaries in Conversations across Borders." *Language and Communication* 59: 17–27.
Dickey, Christopher. 2015. "Street Gangs More Vicious than ISIS." *Daily Beast*, July 31, 2015. http://www.thedailybeast.com/articles/2015/07/31/the-street-gangs-more-vicious-than-isis.html.
Dickson-Gómez, Julia. 2002. "The Sound of Barking Dogs: Violence and Terror among Salvadoran Families in the Postwar." *Medical Anthropology Quarterly* 16, no. 4: 415–38. https://doi.org/10.1525/maq.2002.16.4.415.
Doljanin, Nicolas. 1982. *Chalatenango la guerra descalza: Reportaje sobre El Salvador.* Mexico City: El Día.
Dominguez Villegas, Rodrigo, and Victoria Rietig. 2015. *Migrants Deported from the United States and Mexico to the Northern Triangle: A Statistical and Socioeconomic Profile.* Washington, DC: Migration Policy Institute.
Dreby, Joanna. 2010. *Divided by Borders: Mexican Migrants and Their Children.* Berkeley: University of California Press.
———. 2015. *Everyday Illegal: When Policies Undermine Immigrant Families.* Berkeley: University of California Press.
Dyrness, Andrea, and Thea Renda Abu El-Haj. 2019. "Reflections on the Field: The Democratic Citizenship Formation of Transnational Youth." *Anthropology and Education Quarterly* 51, no. 2: 1–13. https://doi.org/10.1111/aeq.12294.
Durán Fernández, Jacqueline Vanessa. 2020. "Memorias de violencia en El Salvador neoliberal: Mujeres de Yancolo y sus batallas por la vida entre el telar de las hamacas y la hornilla de leña." Master's thesis, Oaxaca, Centro de Investigaciones y estudios superiores en antropología social, Unidad Pacifico Sur.
Ellis, Katie, Rosemarie Garland-Thomson, Mike Kent, and Rachel Robertson, eds. 2019. *Manifestos for the Future of Critical Disability Studies: Volume 1.* New York: Routledge.
Engelke, Matthew. 2019. "The Anthropology of Death Revisited." *Annual Review of Anthropology* 48: 29–44.
Enloe, Cynthia. 2010. *Nimo's War, Emma's War: Making Feminist Sense of the Iraq War.* Berkeley: University of California Press.

Equipo Maíz. 2008. *Contra el olvido y la impunidad: Masacres cometidas por el Ejército, los Batallones de Reacción Inmediata (BIRI), la Guardia Nacional, la Policía Nacional, ORDEN, las Defensas Civiles y los Escuadrones de la Muerte (1974–1991)*. San Salvador: Equipo Maíz.

Fader, Ayala. 2020. *Hidden Heretics: Jewish Doubt in the Digital Age*. Princeton, NJ: Princeton University Press.

Falleti, Tulia G., and Emilio A. Parrado, eds. 2018. *Latin America since the Left Turn*. Philadelphia: University of Pennsylvania Press.

Fanon, Frantz. (1963) 2004. *The Wretched of the Earth*. New York: Grove Press.

Fassin, Didier. 2012. *Humanitarian Reason: A Moral History of the Present*. Berkeley: University of California Press.

Fassin, Didier, and Richard Rechtman. 2009. *The Empire of Trauma: An Inquiry into the Condition of Victimhood*. Princeton, NJ: Princeton University Press.

Fernandes, Sujatha. 2017. *Curated Stories: The Uses and Misuses of Storytelling*. New York: Oxford University Press.

Flores, Antonio, Luis Noe-Bustamante, and Mark Hugo Lopez. 2019. "Migrant Apprehensions and Deportations Increase in Mexico, but Remain Below Recent Highs." Pew Research Center. https://www.pewresearch.org/fact-tank/2019/06/12/migrant-apprehensions-and-deportations-increase-in-mexico-but-remain-below-recent-highs/.

Foucault, Michel. 1982. *The Archaeology of Knowledge and the Discourse on Language*. New York: Pantheon Books.

Forché, Carolyn. 2019. *What You Have Heard Is True: A Memoir of Witness and Resistance*. New York: Penguin Books.

Frank-Vitale, Amelia, and Juan José Martínez d'Aubuisson. 2020. "The Generation of the Coup: Honduran Youth at Risk and of Risk." *Journal of Latin American and Caribbean Anthropology* 25, no. 4: 552–68.

Friedner, Michele, and Karen Weingarten. 2019. "Introduction: Disorienting Disability." *South Atlantic Quarterly* 118, no. 3: 483–90.

Fundaungo. 2013. *Atlas de la violencia en El Salvador (2009–2012)*. San Salvador: Fundaungo.

———. 2019. "Evolución de los homicidios en el Salvador, enero 2009–diciembre 2018." *Aportes: Al Debate Sobre la Seguridad Ciudadana* 7: 1–15.

Gaborit, Mauricio, Carlos Iván Orellana, and Rafael Orellana Sibrián. 2014. "Migración infantil irregular salvadoreña: Reflexiones desde la psicología social." *ECA: Estudios Centroamericanos* 69, no. 736: 55–89.

Gammage, Sarah. 2006. "Exporting People and Recruiting Remittances: A Development Strategy for El Salvador?" *Latin American Perspectives* 33, no. 6: 75–100.

Garcia, Angela. 2016. "The Blue Years: An Ethnography of a Prison Archive." *Cultural Anthropology* 31, no. 4: 571–94.

———. 2017. "The Ambivalent Archive." In *Crumpled Paper Boat: Experiments in Ethnographic Writing*, edited by Anand Pandian and Stuart J. McLean, 29–44. Durham, NC: Duke University Press.

Garland Thomson, Rosemarie. 1997. *Extraordinary Bodies: Figuring Physical Disability in American Culture and Literature.* New York: Columbia University Press.

Garni, Alisa, and L. Frank Weyher. 2013. "Neoliberal Mystification: Crime and Estrangement in El Salvador." *Sociological Perspectives* 56, no. 4: 623–45.

Gay y Blasco, Paloma, and Liria de la Cruz Hernández. 2012. "Friendship, Anthropology." *Anthropology and Humanism* 37, no. 1: 1–14.

Geertz, Clifford. 1973. *The Interpretation of Cultures.* New York: Basic Books.

Gellman, Mneesha. 2017. *Democratization and Memories of Violence: Ethnic Minority Rights Movements in Mexico, Turkey, and El Salvador.* New York: Routledge.

Gill, Lesley. 2004. *The School of the Americas: Military Training and Political Violence in the Americas.* Durham, NC: Duke University Press.

Ginsburg, Faye, and Rayna Rapp. 2013. "Disability Worlds." *Annual Review of Anthropology* 42: 53–68.

Goi, Leonardo. 2017. "El Salvador to Extend 'Extraordinary' Anti-Gang Measures Until 2018." *InSight Crime*, February 8, 2017. https://insightcrime.org/news/brief/el-sal vador-extend-extraordinary-anti-gang-measures-2018/.

Goldstein, Daniel. 2010. "Toward a Critical Anthropology of Security." *Current Anthropology* 51, no. 4: 487–517.

———. 2012. *Outlawed: Between Security and Rights in a Bolivian City.* Durham, NC: Duke University Press.

Gómez-Barris, Macarena. 2017. *The Extractive Zone: Social Ecologies and Decolonial Perspectives.* Durham, NC: Duke University Press.

Gomburg-Muñoz, Ruth. 2011. *Labor and Legality: An Ethnography of a Mexican Immigrant Network.* New York: Oxford University Press.

———. 2016. *Becoming Legal: Immigration Law and Mixed Status Families.* New York: Oxford University Press.

Gonzales, Richard. 2019. "U.S., El Salvador Sign New Asylum Deal to Stem Tide of Migrants." NPR, September 20, 2019. https://www.npr.org/2019/09/20/762948556/u-s -el-salvador-sign-new-asylum-deal-to-stem-tide-of-migrants.

González, René, Silvia Rodríguez, and Xochilt Urrutia. 2019. "Representaciones sociales de la violencia directa de jóvenes descendientes y no descendenites de excombatientes de la guerilla salvadoreña." *ECA: Estudios centroamericanos* 74, no. 756: 37–71.

Gonzalez-Barrera, Ana, and Jens M. Krogstad. 2014. "U.S. Deportations of Immigrants Reach Record High in 2013." Pew Research Center. https://www.pewresearch.org /fact-tank/2014/10/02/u-s-deportations-of-immigrants-reach-record-high-in-2013/.

Goodfriend, Hilary. 2015. "'De donde soy ahora': Deportación y salvación en el call center salvadoreño." *Revista Realidad*, nos. 145–46: 47–60.

Gould, Jeffrey L., and Aldo Lauria-Santiago. 2008. *To Rise in Darkness: Revolution, Repression, and Memory in El Salvador, 1920–1932.* Durham, NC: Duke University Press.

Green, Linda. 1999. *Fear as a Way of Life: Mayan Widows in Rural Guatemala.* New York: Columbia University Press.

Gramlich, John. 2020. "How Border Apprehensions, ICE Arrests and Deportations Have Changed under Trump." Pew Research Center. https://www.pewresearch.org

/fact-tank/2020/03/02/how-border-apprehensions-ice-arrests-and-deportations-have-changed-under-trump/.

———. 2021. "Migrant Encounters at U.S.-Mexico Border Are at a 21-Year High." Pew Research Center. https://www.pewresearch.org/fact-tank/2021/08/13/migrant-encounters-at-u-s-mexico-border-are-at-a-21-year-high/.

Grimaldi, Grazzia. 2021. "At the Edge of Authoritarianism: Democratic Disenchantment and Radical Optimism in Postwar El Salvador." https://www.ssrc.org/grantees/at-the-edge-of-authoritarianism-democratic-disenchantment-and-radical-optimism-in-postwar-el-salvador/.

Guardado, Clara. 2019. "El Mozote nunca más: Debate sobre la contribución de los hallazgos forenses y el acceso a la justicia en El Salvador posconflicto." *Realidad: Revista de Ciencias Sociales y Humanidades* 153: 163–91.

Guardado, Leo. 2021. "Sanctuary for Asylum Seekers: Revisiting the Religious Principle and Practice of Refuge in the Church." *Theological Studies* 82, no. 2: 285–309.

Guardado Torrez, Clara, and Ellen Moodie. 2020. "La línea, los Indignados, and the Post-Postwar Generation in El Salvador." *Journal of Latin American and Caribbean Anthropology* 25, no. 4: 590–609.

Guardian. 2015a. "El Salvador Gang Violence Pushes Murder Rate to Postwar Record." https://www.theguardian.com/world/2015/sep/02/el-salvador-gang-violence-murder-rate-record.

———. 2015b. "El Salvador's 'Most Violent Month': Homicide Rate Hits Record High in May." https://www.theguardian.com/world/2015/jun/03/el-salvador-homicide-killings-gangs.

Guidos, Rhina. 2021. "El Salvador Sets Beatification Date for Jesuit Martyr Rutilio Grande." *America: Jesuit Review*, August 30, 2021. https://www.americamagazine.org/faith/2021/08/30/beatification-rutilio-grande-el-salvador-241304.

Gutierrez, Miguel, Jr. 2017. "Fragmented Identities: Contention of Space and Identity among Salvadoran Deportees." In *Deportation and Return in a Border-Restricted World: Experiences in Mexico, El Salvador, Guatemala, and Honduras*, edited by Bryan Roberts, Cecilia Menjívar, and Nestor Rodríguez, 111-30. Cham, CH: Springer.

Halbwachs, Maurice. 1992. *On Collective Memory*. Chicago: University of Chicago Press.

Haraway, Donna J. 1988. "Situated Knowledges: The Science Question in Feminism and the Privilege of Partial Perspective." *Feminist Studies* 14, no. 3: 575–99.

———. 2016. *Staying with the Trouble: Making Kin in the Chthulucene*. Durham, NC: Duke University Press.

Harrison, Faye, ed. 2010. *Decolonizing Anthropology: Moving Further toward an Anthropology for Liberation*. 3rd ed. Arlington, VA: American Anthropological Association.

Hartman, Saidiya. 2007. *Lose Your Mother: A Journey along the Atlantic Slave Route*. New York: Farrar, Straus, and Giroux.

———. 2019. *Wayward Lives, Beautiful Experiments: Intimate Histories of Riotous Black Girls, Troublesome Women, and Queer Radicals*. New York: Norton.

Hayner, Priscilla. 2011. *Unspeakable Truths: Transitional Justice and the Challenge of Truth Commissions*. 2nd ed. New York: Routledge.

Heidbrink, Lauren. 2014. *Migrant Youth, Transnational Families, and the State: Care and Contested Interests*. Philadelphia: University of Pennsylvania Press.

———. 2020. *Migranthood: Youth in a New Era of Deportation*. Berkeley: University of California Press.

Henríquez Consalvi, Carlos. 2010. *Broadcasting the Civil War in El Salvador*. Austin: University of Texas Press.

Hernández, Ester E. 2017. "Remembering through Cultural Interventions: Mapping Central Americans in L.A. Public Spaces." In *U.S. Central Americans: Reconstructing Memories, Struggles, and Communities of Resistance*, edited by Karina O. Alvarado, Alicia Ivonne Estrada, and Ester E. Hernández, 144–65. Tucson: University of Arizona Press.

Hernández Rivas, Georgina. 2015. "Cartografía de la memoria: Actores, lugares y prácticas en El Salvador de posguerra (1992–2015). Doctoral thesis, Madrid, Universidad Autónoma de Madrid.

———. 2019. "Experiencia cartográfica sobre relatos de éxodo, refugio y repoblación en comunidades rurales en El Salvador de posguerra: El rol de los cartógrafos sociales de la memoria." *Realidad: Revista de Ciencias Sociales y Humanidades* 153: 49–64.

Hirsch, Marianne. 2012. *The Generation of Postmemory: Writing and Visual Culture After the Holocaust*. New York: Columbia University Press.

Holland, Alisha C. 2013. "Right on Crime?: Conservative Party Politics and Mano Dura Policies in El Salvador." *Latin American Research Review* 48, no. 1: 44–67.

Hoover Green, Amelia. 2018. *The Commander's Dilemma: Violence and Restraint in Wartime*. Ithaca, NY: Cornell University Press.

Hoover Green, Amelia, and Patrick Ball. 2019. "Civilian Killings and Disappearances during Civil War in El Salvador (1980–1992)." *Demographic Research* 41, no. 27: 781–814. https://doi.org/10.4054/DemRes.2019.41.27.

Horton, Sarah B. 2016. *They Leave Their Kidneys in the Fields: Illness, Injury, and Illegality among U.S. Farmworkers*. Berkeley: University of California Press.

———. 2020. "Introduction. Paper Trails: Migrants, Bureaucratic Inscription, and Legal Recognition. In *Paper Trails: Migrants, Documents, and Legal Insecurity*, edited by Sarah B. Horton and Josiah Heyman, 1–26. Durham, NC: Duke University Press.

Horton, Sarah B., and Josiah Heyman, eds. 2020. *Paper Trails: Migrants, Documents, and Legal Insecurity*. Durham, NC: Duke University Press.

Hosemann, Aimee J. 2019. "Constructing a Decentered Archival Method: AILLA Recordings and Wanano/Kotiria Kaya Basa 'Sad Songs.'" *Journal of Linguistic Anthropology* 29, no. 2: 188–94.

HRW (Human Rights Watch). 2020a. "El Salvador: Police Abuses in Covid-19 Response: Arbitrary Detention, Hazardous Conditions in Detention, Quarantine." April 15, 2020. https://www.hrw.org/news/2020/04/16/el-salvador-police-abuses-covid-19-response#.

———. 2020b. "El Salvador: Inhumane Prison Lockdown Treatment: President's Call for Lethal Force Ignores Basic International Standards." April 29, 2020. https://www.hrw.org/news/2020/04/29/el-salvador-inhumane-prison-lockdown-treatment#.

Huezo, Stephanie M. 2021. "Remembering the Return from Exodus: An Analysis of a Salvadoran Community's Local History Reenactment." *Journal of Latino/Latin American Studies* 11, no. 1: 56–74.

Hume, Mo. 2009. *The Politics of Violence: Gender, Conflict and Community in El Salvador.* Malden, MA: Wiley-Blackwell.

Hurtado Moreno, Argenis. 2021. "An Anthropology about Us, for Us, by Us." American Ethnologist, May 12, 2021. https://americanethnologist.org/features/reflections/an-anthropology-about-us-for-us-by-us.

Hussain, Salman. 2019. "Violence, Law, and the Archive: How Dossiers of Memory Challenge Enforced Disappearances in the War on Terror in Pakistan." *PoLAR* 42, no. 1: 53–67.

ICTJ (International Center for Transitional Justice). 2013. "Twenty Years Later, A Chance for Accountability in El Salvador." www.ictj.org/news/twenty-years-later-chance-accountability-el-salvador.

Instituto de Derechos Humanos of the Universidad Centroamericana (IDHUCA). 2015. *Elementos para una política de prevención de violencia.* San Salvador: UCA.

InSight Crime. 2021. "Chalatenango, El Salvador: Geographic Profiles." March 22, 2021. https://insightcrime.org/el-salvador-organized-crime-news/chalatenango-el-salvador/.

Jackson, John L., Jr., 2012. "Ethnography Is, Ethnography Ain't." *Cultural Anthropology* 27, no. 3: 480–97.

———. 2013. *Thin Description: Ethnography and the African Hebrew Israelites of Jerusalem.* Cambridge, MA: Harvard University Press.

James, Allison. 2007. "Giving Voice to Children's Voices: Practices and Problems, Pitfalls and Potentials." *American Anthropologist* 109, no. 2: 261–72.

James, Erica Caple. 2010. *Democratic Insecurities: Violence, Trauma, and Intervention in Haiti.* Berkeley: University of California Press.

Jenkins, Janis H. 2015. *Extraordinary Conditions: Culture and Experience in Mental Illness.* Berkeley: University of California Press.

Johnco, C., A. Salloum, N. M. McBride, S. Cepeda, D. Guttfreund, J. C. Novoa, and E. A. Storch. 2020. "Child Trauma Exposure and Subsequent Emotional Functioning in El Salvador." *Traumatology* 26, no. 1, 19–28. https://doi.org/10.1037/trm0000193.

Jones, Sam. 2020. "Ex-Salvadoran Colonel Jailed for 1989 Murder of Spanish Jesuits." *Guardian*, September 11, 2020.

Jurado, Vanessa. 2020. "Diócesis de Chalatenango pide a unidades militares en la frontera que se respeten los derechos de los pobladores." *elsalvador.com*. October 27, 2020.

Jurecic, Ann. 2012. *Illness as Narrative.* Pittsburgh: Pittsburgh University Press.

Kafer, Alison. 2013. *Feminist, Queer, Crip.* Bloomington: Indiana University Press.

Kampwirth, Karen. 2002. *Women and Guerrilla Movements: Nicaragua, El Salvador, Chiapas, Cuba.* University Park: Pennsylvania State University Press.

———. 2004. *Feminisms and the Legacy of Revolution: Nicaragua, El Salvador, Chiapas.* Athens: Ohio University Press.

Kanstroom, Daniel. 2012. *Aftermath: Deportation Law and the New American Diaspora.* New York: Oxford University Press.

Karl, Terry L. 1992. "El Salvador's Negotiated Revolution." *Foreign Affairs* 71, no. 2: 147–64.
Kassie, Emily. 2019. "Detained: How the US Built the World's Largest Immigrant Detention System." *Guardian*, September 24, 2019. https://www.theguardian.com/us-news/2019/sep/24/detained-us-largest-immigrant-detention-trump.
Kennedy, Elizabeth. 2014. *No Childhood Here: Why Central American Children Are Fleeing Their Homes*. Washington, DC: American Immigration Council.
Kennedy, Elizabeth G., and Alison Parker. 2020. *Deported to Danger: United States Deportation Policies Expose Salvadorans to Death and Abuse*. New York: Human Rights Watch.
Kidron, Carol A. 2012. "Alterity and the Particular Limits of Universalism: Comparing Jewish-Israeli Holocaust and Canadian-Cambodian Genocide Legacies." *Current Anthropology* 53, no. 6: 723–53.
Kittay, Eva Feder. 1999. *Love's Labor: Essays on Women, Equality, and Dependency*. London: Routledge.
Kleinman, Arthur. 1988. *The Illness Narratives: Suffering, Healing, and the Human Condition*. New York: Basic Books.
Kleinman, Arthur, Veena Das, and Margaret Lock. 1997. *Social Suffering*. Berkeley: University of California Press.
Kohrman, Matthew. 2005. *Bodies of Difference: Experiences of Disability and Institutional Advocacy in the Making of Modern China*. Berkeley: University of California Press.
Kurtenbach, Sabine. 2019. "The Limits of Peace in Latin America." *Peacebuilding* 7, no. 3: 283–96.
LaCapra, Dominick. 1998. *History and Memory after Auschwitz*. Ithaca, NY: Cornell University Press.
Lancy, David F. 2015. *The Anthropology of Childhood: Cherubs, Chattel, Changelings*. 2nd ed. Cambridge, UK: Cambridge University Press.
Landsman, Gail. 2009. *Reconstructing Motherhood and Disability in the Age of "Perfect" Babies*. New York: Routledge.
Larkin, Brian. 2013. "The Politics and Poetics of Infrastructure." *Annual Review of Anthropology* 42: 327–43.
Lara Martínez, Carlos B. 2018. *Memoria histórica del movimiento campesino de Chalatenango*. San Salvador: UCA Editores.
———. 2019. "Presentación de Dossier: Memoria histórica del conflicto político-militar de El Salvador." *Realidad: Revista de Ciencias Sociales y Humanidades* 153: 5–8.
Las Dignas. 2010. *La Violencia contra la mujer*. San Salvador: Las Dignas.
Latina Feminist Group. 2001. *Telling to Live: Latina Feminist Testimonios*. Durham, NC: Duke University Press.
Lee, Richard E. 2012. "Introduction: Fernand Braudel, the Longue Durée and World-Systems Analysis." In *The Longue Durée and World-Systems Analysis*, edited by Richard E. Lee. Albany: SUNY Press.
LeMoyne, James. 1985. "How Rebels Rule in Their Corner of El Salvador." *New York Times*, December 26, 1985.

Levitt, Laura. 2020. *The Objects That Remain*. University Park: Pennsylvania State University Press.

Linton, Simi. 1998. *Claiming Disability: Knowledge and Identity*. New York: NYU Press.

Liu, Roseann, and Savannah Shange. 2018. "Toward Thick Solidarity: Theorizing Empathy in Social Justice Movements." *Radical History Review* 131: 189–98. https://doi.org/10.1215/01636545-4355341.

Livingston, Julie. 2005. *Debility and the Moral Imagination in Botswana*. Bloomington: Indiana University Press.

———. 2006. "Insights from an African History of Disability." *Radical History Review* 94: 111–26.

———. 2008. "Disgust, Bodily Aesthetics and the Ethic of Being Human in Botswana." *Africa* 78, no. 2: 288–307.

———. 2019. *Self-Devouring Growth: A Planetary Parable Told from Southern Africa*. Durham, NC: Duke University Press.

Loperena, Christopher A. 2020. "Adjudicating Indigeneity: Anthropological Testimony in the Inter-American Court of Human Rights." *American Anthropologist* 122, no. 3: 595–605.

Loperena, Christopher A., Mariana Mora, and R. Aída Hernández-Castillo. 2020. "Cultural Expertise? Anthropologist as Witness in Defense of Indigenous and Afro-Descendant Rights." *American Anthropologist* 122, no. 3: 588–94.

Lopez, Mark Hugo, and Jens Manuel Krogstad. 2014. "5 Facts about the Deferred Action for Childhood Arrivals Program." Pew Research Center. http://www.pewresearch.org/fact-tank/2014/08/15/5-facts-about-the-deferred-action-for-childhood-arrivals-program/.

Lopez, Oscar. 2021. "After El Salvador Election, Bukele Is on Verge of Near-Total Control." *New York Times*, March 21, 2021.

López Bernal, Carlos Gregorio. 2014. "Historia y memoria: Los usos políticos del pasado." *Revista Humanidades* (El Salvador) 5, no. 3: 13–19.

———. 2017. "El FMLN y las memorias de la Guerra civil salvadoreña." *Revista de Historia* 76: 47–71. http://dx.doi.org/10.15359/rh.76.2.

Lovato, Roberto. 2020. *Unforgetting: A Memoir of Family, Migration, Gangs, and Revolution in the Americas*. New York: HarperCollins.

Luan, Livia. 2018. "Profiting from Enforcement: The Role of Private Prisons in U.S. Immigration Detention." MPI. https://www.migrationpolicy.org/article/profiting-enforcement-role-private-prisons-us-immigration-detention.

Luiselli, Valeria. 2017. *Tell Me How It Ends: An Essay in Forty Questions*. Minneapolis: Coffee House Press.

———. 2019. *The Lost Children Archive*. New York: Vintage Books.

MacDonald, M., and M. Gatehouse. 1995. *In the Mountains of Morazán: Portrait of a Returned Refugee Community in El Salvador*. New York: Monthly Review Press.

Maciel, Eduardo. 2020. "Recordando desde enero o mayo. Memoria y olvido en El Salvador a partir del estudio estético de dos monumentos de la posguerra." *Realidad: Revista De Ciencias Sociales Y Humanidades* 156: 5–33.

Mahler, Sarah J. 1995. *American Dreaming: Immigrant Life on the Margins*. Princeton, NJ: Princeton University Press.

Malkin, Elisabeth. 2015. "El Salvador Cracks Down on Crime, but Gangs Remain Unbowed." *New York Times*, August 11, 2015. www.nytimes.com/2015/08/12/world/americas/el-salvador-cracks-down-on-crime-but-gangs-remain-unbowed.html.

———. 2018. "Survivors of Massacre Ask: 'Why Did They Have to Kill Those Children?,'" *New York Times*, May 26, 2018.

Manneheim, Karl. (1928) 1952. "The Problem of Generations." In *Karl Manneheim: Essays*, edited by Paul Kecskemeti, 276–322. London: Routledge.

Marcus, George E., and M. J. Fischer. 1986. *Anthropology as Cultural Critique: An Experimental Moment in the Human Sciences*. Chicago: University of Chicago Press.

Marroquín Parducci, Amparo. 2014. "La Migración Centroamericana: Apuntes para un mapa provisional." *ECA* 69, no. 736: 91–103.

———. 2019. "Comunicación y migración: Pedagogías lingüísticas y resistencias." *Chasqui: Revista Latinoamericana de Comunicación* 141: 161–76.

Martell Pereira, Allan Antonio. 2020. "Postmemorial Exhibitions: A Design Approach to Negotiate Cultural Trauma among Children and Grandchildren of Former War Refugees and Guerrilla Supporters." PhD diss., University of Michigan.

Martin, Emily. (1987) 2001. *The Woman in the Body: A Cultural Analysis of Reproduction*. Boston: Beacon Press.

Martín-Baró, Ignacio. 1988. "La violencia politica y la guerra como causas del trauma psicosocial en el salvador." *Revista de Psicología de El Salvador* VII, no. 2: 123–41.

———. 1994a. "War and Psychological Trauma of Salvadoran Children." In *Writings for a Liberation Psychology*, edited by A. Aron and S. Corne, 122–35. Cambridge, MA: Harvard University Press.

———. 1994b. *Writings for a Liberation Psychology*. Cambridge, MA: Harvard University Press.

Martínez, Carlos, Óscar Martínez, Sergio Arauz, and Efren Lemus. 2020. "Bukele Has Been Negotiating with MS-13 for a Reduction in Homicides and Electoral Support." *El Faro*, September 6, 2020. https://elfaro.net/en/202009/el_salvador/24785/Bukele-Spent-A-Year-Negotiating-with-MS-13-for-a-Reduction-in-Homicides-and-Electoral-Support.htm.

Martínez, Grande, Ángel Guadalupe Manzano Mejía, Jorge Luis Portillo García, and José Transito. 2009. *Trabajo de graduación: Investigación de procesos constructivos y diseño para vivienda con el sistema alternativo de Bahareque*. San Miguel, SV: Universidad de El Salvador.

Martínez, Óscar. 2015. "Palabra de pandillero: '24 muertos o más.'" *El Faro*, January 15, 2015. http://www.salanegra.elfaro.net/es/201501/bitacora/16479/Palabra-de-pandillero-24-muertos-o-más.htm.

———. 2016: *A History of Violence: Living and Dying in Central America*. London: Verso.

Martínez, Óscar, and Juan José Martínez. 2019. *The Hollywood Kid: The Violent Life and Violent Death of an MS-13 Hitman*. Translated by Daniela Maria Ugaz and John Washington. London: Verso.

Martínez d'Aubuisson, Juan José. 2019. *A Year Inside MS-13: See, Hear, and Shut Up*. New York: OR Books.

Matza, Tomas. 2019. "Global Ambitions: Evidence, Scale, and Child Well-Being in El Salvador." *Medical Anthropology Quarterly* 33, no. 3: 364–85.

Mbembe, Achille. 2019. *Necropolitics*. Durham, NC: Duke University Press.

McEvoy-Levy, Siobhán, ed. 2006. *Troublemakers or Peacemakers?: Youth and Post-accord Peace Building*. Notre Dame, IN: University of Notre Dame Press.

———. 2012. "Youth Spaces in Haunted Places: Placemaking for Peacebuilding in Theory and Practice." *International Journal of Peace Studies* 17, no. 2: 1–32.

McKittrick, Katherine. 2021. *Dear Science and Other Stories*. Durham, NC: Duke University Press.

McRuer, Robert. 2006. *Crip Theory: Cultural Signs of Queerness and Disability*. New York: New York University Press.

———. 2018. *Crip Times: Disability, Globalization, and Resistance*. New York: New York University Press.

Melgar, Nilcer, and Johana Mejía. 2021. "Performativa teatral como vínculo de la reparación social y dignificación desde el rescate de la memoria histórica intergeneracional." *ECA* 76, no. 765: 241–266.

Menchú, Rigoberta, and Elisabeth Burgos-Debray. 1984. *I, Rigoberta Menchú: An Indian Woman in Guatemala*. London: Verso.

Mendoza Posada, J. A., L. B. Orellana Herrera, and G. S. Pocasangre Portillo. 2016. "Modelado multivariable de homicidios y hurtos en el departamento de San Salvador." Tesis preparada para la facultad de postgrados, la maestría en estadística aplicada a la investigación. Universidad Centroamericana José Simeón Cañas, Antiguo Cuscatlán, SV.

Menjívar, Cecilia. 2000. *Fragmented Ties: Salvadoran Immigrant Networks in America*. Berkeley: University of California Press.

Menjívar, Cecilia, and Andrea Gómez Cervantes. 2018. "El Salvador: Civil War, Natural Disasters, and Gang Violence Drive Migration." MPI. August 29. https://www.migrationpolicy.org/article/el-salvador-civil-war-natural-disasters-and-gang-violence-drive-migration.

Menjívar Ochoa, Mauricio, and Ralph Sprenkels, eds. 2017. *La revolución revisitada: Nuevas perspectivas sobre la insurrección y la guerra en El Salvador*. San Salvador: UCA Editores.

Merry, Sally Engle. 2016. *The Seductions of Quantification: Measuring Human Rights, Gender Violence, and Sex Trafficking*. Chicago: University of Chicago Press.

Metzi, Francisco. 1988. *Por los caminos de Chalatenango: Con la salud en la mochila*. San Salvador: UCA Editores.

Minich, Julie Avril. 2016. "Enabling Whom? Critical Disability Studies Now." *Lateral* 5, no. 1. csalateral.org/issue/5-1/forum-alt-humanities-critical-disability-studies-now-minich/.

Ministerio de Economía. 2014. "El Salvador: Estimaciones y proyecciones de población municipal 2005–2025 (Revisión 2014)." Ministerio de Economía. Dirección General de Estadística y Censos-DIGESTYC. Fondo de Población de las Naciones Unidas-UNFPA. Centro Latinoamericano y Caribeño de Demografía-CELADE. División de Población de CEPAL.

Minow, Martha. 1998. *Between Vengeance and Forgiveness: South Africa's Truth and Reconciliation Commission*. Boston: Beacon Press.

Miroff, Nick. 2020. "'Kids in Cages': It's True that Obama Built the Cages at the Border. But Trump's 'Zero Tolerance' Immigration Policy Had No Precedent." *Washington Post*, October 23, 2020. https://www.washingtonpost.com/immigration/kids-in-cages-debate-trump-obama/2020/10/23/8ff96f3c-1532-11eb-82af-864652063d61_story.html.

Mitchell, David T., and Sharon L. Snyder. 2019. "Low-Level Agency: Disability, Oppression and Alternative Genres of the Human." In *Manifestos for the Future of Critical Disability Studies: Volume 1*, edited by Katie Ellis, Rosemarie Garland-Thomson, Mike Kent, and Rachel Robertson, 189–98. London: Routledge.

Mitra, Sophie. 2018. *Disability, Health and Human Development*. New York: Palgrave McMillan.

Miyares, Ines, Richard A. Wright, Alison Mountz, and Adrian John Bailey. 2019. "Truncated Transnationalism, the Tenuousness of Temporary Protected Status, and Trump." *Journal of Latin American Geography* 18, no. 1: 210–16.

Molina, Noemy. 2015. "Ni paz ni tregua para las mujeres en El Salvador: Un estudio sobre el significado de la violencia doméstica desde la perspectiva de las mujeres, en una de las muchas comunidades invisibles de San Salvador." *ECA* 70, no. 741: 223–48.

Montgomery, Tommie Sue. 1995. *Revolution in El Salvador: From Civil Strife to Civil Peace*. Boulder, CO: Westview Press.

Montoya, Ainhoa. 2018. *The Violence of Democracy: Political Life in Postwar El Salvador*. New York: Palgrave Macmillan.

Moodie, Ellen. 2006. "Microbus Crashes and Coca-Cola Cash: The Value of Death in 'Free-Market' El Salvador." *American Ethnologist* 33, no. 1: 63–80.

———. 2009. "Seventeen Years, Seventeen Murders: Biospectacularity and the Production of Post–Cold War Knowledge in El Salvador." *Social Text* 27 (2): 77–103.

———. 2010. *El Salvador in the Aftermath of Peace: Crime, Uncertainty, and the Transition to Democracy*. Philadelphia: University of Pennsylvania Press.

Muir, Sarah. 2021. *Routine Crisis: An Ethnography of Disillusion*, Chicago: University of Chicago Press.

Murray, Kevin. 1997. *El Salvador: Peace on Trial*. London: Oxfam UK and Ireland.

Myerhoff, Barbara. 1978. *Number Our Days: A Triumph of Continuity and Culture among Jewish Old People in an Urban Ghetto*. New York: Dutton.

Narayan, Kirin. 1993. "How Native Is a 'Native' Anthropologist?" *American Anthropologist* 95, no. 3: 671–86.

Nelson, Diane M. 2001. "Stumped Identities: Body Image, Bodies Politics, and the *Mujer Maya* as Prosthetic." *Cultural Anthropology* 16, no. 3: 314–53.

———. 2009. *Reckoning: The Ends of War in Guatemala*. Durham, NC: Duke University Press.

———. 2015. *Who Counts: The Mathematics of Death and Life after Genocide*. Durham, NC: Duke University Press.

Nepstad, Sharon. 2001. "Creating Transnational Solidarity: The Use of Narrative in the U.S.–Central America Peace Movement." *Mobilization: An International Quarterly* 6, no. 1: 21–36.

New York Times. 1985. "A Secret Radio and Doctors Keep Moving." December 26, 1985.

Nguyen, Viet Thanh. 2015. *The Sympathizer*. New York: Grove Press.

Noe-Bustamante, Luis, Antonio Flores, and Sono Shah. 2019. "Facts on Hispanics of Salvadoran Origin in the United States, 2017." Pew Research Center: Hispanic Trends. https://www.pewresearch.org/hispanic/fact-sheet/u-s-hispanics-facts-on-salvadoran-origin-latinos/#language.

Nordstrom, Carolyn. 1997. *A Different Kind of War Story*. Philadelphia: University of Pennsylvania Press.

Nordstrom, Carolyn, and Antonious C. G. M. Robben. 1995. *Fieldwork under Fire: Contemporary Studies of Violence and Survival*. Berkeley: University of California Press.

O'Brien, Tim. 1990. *The Things They Carried*. New York: Houghton Mifflin.

O'Connor, Allison, Jeanne Batalova, and Jessica Bolter. 2019. "Central American Immigrants in the United States." Migration Policy Institute. https://www.migrationpolicy.org/article/central-american-immigrants-united-states.

Observatorio de Seguridad Ciudadana. 2013. *Percepción de inseguridad y victimización por crimen en El Salvador 2012*. San Salvador: FUNDAUNGO, FLACSO Programa El Salvador y UTEC.

Orantes-Navarro, C. M., M. M. Almaguer-López, P. Alonso-Galbán, M. Díaz-Amaya, S. Hernández, R. Herrera-Valdés, and L. C. Silva-Aycaguer. 2019. "The Chronic Kidney Disease Epidemic in El Salvador: A Cross-Sectional Study." *MEDICC Review* 21, nos. 2–3: 29–37.

Osuna, Steven. 2017. "Obstinate Transnational Memories: How Oral Histories Shape Salvadoran-Mexican Subjectivities." In *U.S. Central Americans: Reconstructing Memories, Struggles, and Communities of Resistance*, edited by Karina O. Alvarado, Alicia Ivonne Estrada, and Ester E. Hernández, 77–97. Tucson: University of Arizona Press.

———. 2020. "Transnational Moral Panic: Neoliberalism and the Specter of MS-13." *Race and Class* 61, no. 4: 1–26.

Otero, Solimar. 2018. "Residual Transcriptions: Ruth Landes and the Archive of Conjure." *Transforming Anthropology* 26, no. 1: 3–17.

Ott, Katherine. 2015. "Prosthetics." In *Keywords for Disability Studies*, edited by Rachel Adams, Benjamin Reiss, and David Serlin, 140–143. New York: New York University Press.

Paarlberg, Michael. 2021. "Gang Membership in Central America: More Complex than Meets the Eye." Migration Policy Institute. https://www.migrationpolicy.org/article/complexities-gang-membership-central-america.

Pacheco, Melissa, Marielos Román, and Denni Portillo. "Elecciones El Salvador | Partidos buscan impugnar resultados municipales." *La Prensa Gráfica*, March 3, 2021.

Palacios, Claudia, and Andrés Dimas. "Los exguerrilleros que acusan al FMLN de crímenes de guerra." *El Faro*, December 18, 2021.

Pearce, Jenny. 1986. *Promised Land: Peasant Revolution in Chalatenango, El Salvador*. London: Latin America Bureau.

Pearce, Jenny, and Wolfgang Dietrich. 2019. "Many Violences, Many Peaces: Wolfgang Dietrich and Jenny Pearce in Conversation." *Peacebuilding* 7, no. 3: 268–82.

Pearce, Jenny, and Carlos Mario Perea. 2019. "Postwar and Nonwar Violences: Peace and Peacebuilding from Latin America." *Peacebuilding* 7, no. 3: 247–53.

Pederson, David. 2013. *American Value: Migrants, Money, and Meaning in El Salvador and the United States*. Chicago: University of Chicago Press.

Perea, Carlos Mario. 2019. "Extreme Violence without War and Its Social Reproduction Implications for Building Peace in Latin America." *Peacebuilding* 7, no. 3: 254–67.

Pérez, Yansi. 2019. *Más allá del duelo, otras formas de imaginar, sentir y pensar la memoria en Centroamérica*. San Salvador: UCA Editores.

Perla, Héctor, Jr. 2008. "Si Nicaragua Venció, El Salvador Vencerá: Central American Agency in the Creation of the U.S.–Central American Peace and Solidarity Movement. *Latin American Research Review* 43, no. 2: 136–58.

Peterson, Brandt G. 2007. "Remains Out of Place: Race, Trauma and Nationalism in El Salvador." *Anthropological Theory* 7, no. 1: 59-77.

Petryna, Adriana. 2002. *Life Exposed: Biological Citizens after Chernobyl*. Princeton, NJ: Princeton University Press.

Pickens, Therí Alyce. 2019. *Black Madness :: Mad Blackness*. Durham, NC: Duke University Press.

Pillen, Alex. 2016. "Language, Translation, Trauma." *Annual Review of Anthropology* 45: 95–111.

Pleitez Quiñonez, Ariana Ninel. 2018. "Plan Museológico Centro de Memoria Israel Márquez." Unpublished manuscript, San Salvador.

Popkin, Margaret. 2000. *Peace without Justice: Obstacles to Building the Rule of Law in El Salvador*. University Park: Pennsylvania State University Press.

Portes, Alejandro, and Rubén G. Rumbaut. 2014. *Immigrant America: A Portrait, Fourth Edition, Revised, Updated, and Expanded*. Berkeley: University of California Press.

Puar, Jasbir K. 2017. *The Right to Maim: Debility, Capacity, Disability*. Durham, NC: Duke University Press.

Quesada, James. 1998. "Suffering Child: An Embodiment of War and Its Aftermath in Post-Sandinista Nicaragua." *Medical Anthropology Quarterly* 12, no. 4: 51–73.

Raby, Dominique. 2019. "Calling through the Water Jar: Domestic Objects in Nahua Emotional Assemblages." *HAU: Journal of Ethnographic Theory* 9, no. 3: 529–44.

Ralph, Laurence. 2014. *Renegade Dreams: Living through Injury in Gangland Chicago*. Chicago: University of Chicago Press.

Ralph, Laurence. 2020. *The Torture Letters: Reckoning with Police Violence*. Chicago: University of Chicago Press.

Ramirez, Allison. 2017. "Never to Return: The New Disappeared of El Salvador." In *Deportation and Return in a Border-Restricted World: Experiences in Mexico, El Salvador, Guatemala, and Honduras*, edited by Bryan Roberts, Cecilia Menjívar, and Nestor Rodríguez, 169–84. Cham, CH: Springer.

Rapp, Rayna, and Faye Ginsburg. 2001. "Enabling Disability: Rewriting Kinship, Reimagining Citizenship." *Public Culture* 13: 533–56. https://doi.org/10.1215/08992363-13-3-533.

Rayner, Jeremy, and Valeria Morales Rivera. 2020. "The Counter-movement through the Lens of Generation: Emancipation, Protection, and Neoliberalization in Costa Rica, 2000–2018." *Journal of Latin American and Caribbean Anthropology* 25, no. 4: 569–89.

Redfield, Peter. 2013. *Life in Crisis: The Ethical Journey of Doctors without Borders*. Berkeley: University of California Press.

Renteria Meza, Nelson. 2018. "Strangers at Home, Salvadoran Deportees Welcomed at Call Centers." Reuters, January 12, 2018. https://www.reuters.com/journalists/nelson-renteria-meza.

Rey Tristán, Eduardo, and Xiomara Lazo. 2011. "¿Es la justicia el precio de la paz? Logros y limitaciones del proceso de paz salvadoreño." In *Conflicto, memoria y pasados traumáticos: El Salvador contemporáneo*, edited by Eduardo Rey Tristán and Pilar Cagiao Vila, 211–40. Santiago: Universidad de Santiago de Compostela.

Rivas, Cecilia M. 2014. *Salvadoran Imaginaries: Mediated Identities and Cultures of Consumption*. New Brunswick, NJ: Rutgers University Press.

Rivas, Ramón D. 2018. "La Artesanía: Patrimonio e identidad cultural. *Revista de Museología Koót* 9: 80–96.

Roberts, Bryan, Cecilia Menjívar, and Nestor Rodríguez. 2017. *Deportation and Return in a Border-Restricted World: Experiences in Mexico, El Salvador, Guatemala, and Honduras*. Cham, CH: Springer.

Roberts, Elizabeth F. S. 2021. "Making Better Numbers through Bioethnographic Collaboration." *American Anthropologist* 123, no. 2: 355–69.

Rodríguez, Ana Patricia. 2005. "'Departamento 15': Cultural Narratives of Salvadoran Transnational Migration." *Latino Studies* 3: 19–41.

———. 2017. "Salvadoran Immigrant Acts and Migration to San Francisco (circa 1960s and 1970s)." In *U.S. Central Americans: Reconstructing Memories, Struggles, and Communities of Resistance*, edited by Karina O. Alvarado, Alicia Ivonne Estrada, and Ester E. Hernández, 41–59. Tucson: University of Arizona Press.

Rodriguez, Leila, ed. 2021. *Culture as Judicial Evidence: Expert Testimony in Latin America*. Cincinnati: University of Cincinnati Press.

Rojas-Flores, Lisseth, Josephine Hwang Koo, and Jennifer Medina Vaughn. 2019. "Protecting U.S.-Citizen Children Whose Central American Parents Have Temporary Protected Status." *International Perspectives in Psychology: Research, Practice, Consultation* 8, no. 1: 14–19. https://doi.org/10.1037/ipp0000100.

Roseberry, William. 1988. "Political Economy." *Annual Review of Anthropology* 17: 161–85.

Ross, Norbert, and Antonia Ross Sanchez. 2018. "The Messy Little Thing Called Peace: Postwar Memories and Durable Disorder in El Salvador." *Journal of Global Faultlines*

5, nos. 1–2: 41–48. Accessed May 26, 2020. https://doi.org/10.13169/jglobfaul.5.1-2.0041.

Rostica, Julieta, Melisa Kovalskis, Lucrecia Molinari, and Matías Oberlin Molina. 2020. "La masacre de El Mozote en El Salvador: Una aproximación a la responsabilidad argentina." e-l@tina. *Revista electrónica de estudios latinoamericanos* 18, no. 71: 61–93.

Rothman, K. J., S. Greenland, and T. L. Lash. 2008. *Modern Epidemiology*. 3rd ed. Philadelphia: Lippincott Williams and Wilkins.

Ruiz, Pamela. 2020a. "Mara Salvatrucha (MS-13) and Barrio 18: Gangs, Terrorists, or Political Manipulation?" *Small Wars Journal*. https://smallwarsjournal.com/jrnl/art/mara-salvatrucha-ms-13-and-barrio-18-gangs-terrorists-or-political-manipulation.

———. 2020b. *Facing the Challenge of Extortion in Central America: Initiatives Implemented to Reduce Extortion*. Geneva: Global Initiative against Transnational Organized Crime.

Ruwitch, John. 2021 "Biden Moves to End Trump-Era Asylum Agreements with Central American Countries." NPR-WNYC, February 16, 2021. https://www.npr.org/2021/02/06/964907437/biden-moves-to-end-trump-era-asylum-agreements-with-central-american-countries.

Sala Negra de El Faro. 2013. *Crónicas Negras: Desde una región que no cuenta*. Madrid: Aguilar.

Samour, Héctor. 2013. "Jóvenes y cultura política en El Salvador." *ECA* 68, no. 735: 505–510.

Sanford, Victoria. 2003. *Buried Secrets: Truth and Human Rights in Guatemala*. New York: Palgrave Macmillan.

Sawyer, Stephen W. 2015. "Time after Time: Narratives of the Longue Durée in the Anthropocene." *Transatlantica* 1 (2015). https://doi.org/10.4000/transatlantica.7344.

Scarry, Elaine. 1985. *The Body in Pain: The Making and Unmaking of the World*. New York: Oxford University Press.

Scheper-Hughes, Nancy. 1992. *Death without Weeping: The Violence of Everyday Life in Brazil*. Berkeley: University of California Press.

Scheper-Hughes, Nancy, and Margaret Lock. 1987. "The Mindful Body: A Prolegomenon to Future Work in Medical Anthropology." *MAQ* 1 no. 1: 6–41.

Scheper-Hughes, Nancy, and Carolyn Sargent. 1998. *Small Wars: The Cultural Politics of Childhood*. Berkeley: University of California Press.

Schrading, Roger. 1991. *Exodus en América Latina: El movimiento de repoblación en El Salvador*. San José: Instituto Interamericano de Derechos Humanos.

Scornaienchi, Jean M. 2003. "Chronic Sorrow: One Mother's Experience with Two Children with Lissencephaly." *Journal of Pediatric Health Care* 17, no. 6: 290–94.

Seelke, Clare Ribando. 2009. *Gangs in Central America*. Washington, DC: Congressional Research Service.

Segovia, Alexander. 2009. *Transitional Justice and DDR: The Case of El Salvador*. New York: ICTJ.

Semple, Kirk. 2014. "Surge in Child Migrants Reaches New York, Overwhelming Advocates." *New York Times*, June 17, 2014. www.nytimes.com/2014/06/18/nyregion/immigration-child-migrant-surge-in-New-York-City.html.

Shakespeare, Tom. 2014. *Disability Rights and Wrongs Revisited*. London: Routledge.
Shankar, Shalini. 2019. *Beeline: What Spelling Bees Reveal about Generation Z's New Path to Success*. New York: Basic Books.
Shayne, Julie. 2004. *The Revolution Question: Feminisms in El Salvador, Chile, and Cuba*. New Brunswick, NJ: Rutgers University Press.
Sheridan, Mary Beth, and Anna-Catherine Brigida. 2020. "Photos Show El Salvador's Crackdown on Imprisoned Gang Members." *Washington Post*. April 28, 2020. https://www.washingtonpost.com/world/the_americas/el-salvador-prison-crackdown-nayib-bukele/2020/04/27/5d3cea4c-88c9-11ea-80df-d24b35a568ae_story.html.
Sierra Becerra, Diana Carolina. 2016. "Historical Memory at El Salvador's Museo de la Palabra y la Imagen." *Latin American Perspectives* 43, no. 6: 8–26.
———. 2017. "Insurgent Butterflies: Gender and Revolution in El Salvador, 1965–2015." PhD diss., University of Michigan.
Silber, Irina Carlota. 2007. "Local Capacity Building in 'Dysfunctional' Times: Internationals, Revolutionaries, and Activism in Postwar El Salvador." *Women's Studies Quarterly* 35, nos. 3–4: 163–83.
———. 2011. *Everyday Revolutionaries: Gender, Violence, and Disillusionment in Postwar El Salvador*. New Brunswick, NJ: Rutgers University Press.
———. 2014. "In the After: Anthropological Reflections on Postwar El Salvador." *Journal of Latin American and Caribbean* Anthropology 19, no. 1: 1–21.
———. 2018. "Entangled Aftermaths in El Salvador." In *Latin America Since the Left Turn*, edited by Tulia Falleti and Emilio A. Parrado, 326–52. Philadelphia: University of Pennsylvania Press.
———. 2019. "Está Bien Recordar: Stories of the 1.5 Insurgent Generation." Society for Cultural Anthropology, Fieldsights. https://culanth.org/fieldsights/est%C3%A1-bien-recordar-stories-of-the-1-5-insurgent-generation.
Sliwinski, Alicia. 2018. *A House of One's Own: The Moral Economy of Post-disaster Aid in El Salvador*. Montreal: McGill-Queen's University Press.
Smith, Carol A., J. Bayer, and M. Diskin. 1988. "Central America since 1979, Part II." *Annual Review of Anthropology* 17, no. 1: 331–64.
Smith, Carol A., and Jeff Boyer. 1987. Central America since 1979: Part 1." *Annual Review of Anthropology* 16: 197–221.
Smith, Christian. 1996. *Resisting Reagan: The U.S. Central American Peace Movement*. Chicago: University of Chicago Press.
Smith, Robert Courtney. 2006. *Mexican New York: Transnational Lives of New Immigrants*. Berkeley: University of California Press.
Smith-Nonini, Sandy. 2010. *Healing the Body Politic: El Salvador's Popular Struggle for Health Rights from Civil War to Neoliberal Peace*. New Brunswick: Rutgers University Press.
Speed, Shannon. 2007. *Rights in Rebellion: Indigenous Struggle and Human Rights in Chiapas*. Stanford, CA: Stanford University Press.
Sprenkels, Ralph, ed. 2001. *El día más esperado. Buscando a los niños desaparecidos de El Salvador*. San Salvador: Asociación Pro-Búsqueda de Niñas y Niños Desaparecidos y UCA Editores.

———. 2005. *The Price of Peace: The Human Rights Movement in Postwar El Salvador*. Amsterdam: CEDLA Publications.

———. 2011. "Roberto d'Aubuisson vs Schafik Handal: Militancy, Memory Work and Human Rights." *European Review of Latin American and Caribbean Studies* 91: 15–30.

———. 2012. "La guerra como controversia: Una reflexión sobre las secuelas políticas del informe de la Comisión de la Verdad para El Salvador." *Identidades* 2, no. 4: 68–92.

———. 2015. *Stories Never to Be Forgotten: Eyewitness Accounts from the Salvadoran Civil War*. Translated by Francisco Jiménez. Tempe, AZ: Bilingual Press.

———. 2017. "El Trabajo de la memoria en Centroamérica: Cinco propuestas heurísticas en torna a las guerras en El Salvador, Guatemala y Nicaragua." *Revista de Historia* 76, no. 1: 13–46.

———. 2018. *After Insurgency: Revolution and Electoral Politics in El Salvador*. Notre Dame, IN: University of Notre Dame Press.

———. 2019. "The FMLN's Electoral Implosion in El Salvador: A Fiasco Foretold?" *PoLAR*. April 15, 2019. https://polarjournal.org/2019/04/15/the-fmlns-electoral-implosion-in-el-salvador-a-fiasco-foretold/.

Sprenkels, Ralph, and Lidice Michelle Melara Minero. 2017. "Auge y declive de la persecución violenta en El Salvador: Patrones, variaciones y actores (1970–1991)." In *La Revolución Revisitada: Nuevas Perspectivas sobra la insurrección y la Guerra en El Salvador*, edited by Mauricio Ochoa Menjívar and Ralph Sprenkels, 79–148. San Salvador: UCA Editores.

Sprenkels, Ralph, and Nikkie Wiegink. 2020. "Beyond Reintegration: War Veteranship in Mozambique and El Salvador." *Development and Change*. https://doi.org/10.1111/dech.12576.

Stephen, Lynn. 2007. *Transborder Lives: Indigenous Oaxacans in Mexico, California, and Oregon*. Durham, NC: Duke University Press.

———. 2017. "Bearing Witness: Testimony in Latin American Anthropology and Related Fields." *Journal of Latin American and Caribbean Anthropology* 22, no. 1: 85–109.

Stephens, Sharon, ed. 1995. *Children and the Politics of Culture*. Princeton, NJ: Princeton University Press.

Stinchcomb, Dennis, and Eric Hershberg. 2014. *Unaccompanied Migrant Children from Central America: Context, Causes, and Responses*. Washington, DC: CLALS, American University.

Stocking, George W., ed. 1993. *Colonial Situations: Essays on the Contextualization of Ethnographic Knowledge*. Madison, WI: University of Wisconsin Press.

Stoler, Ann Laura. 2002. "Colonial Archives and the Arts of Governance." *Archival Science* 2: 87–109.

———. 2010. *Along the Archival Grain: Epistemic Anxieties and Colonial Common Sense*. Princeton, NJ: Princeton University Press.

Stoll, David. 1999. *Rigoberta Menchú and the Story of All Poor Guatemalans*. Boulder, CO: Westview Press.

Stuelke, Patricia. 2014. "The Reparative Politics of Central America Solidarity Movement Culture." *American Quarterly* 66, no. 3: 767–90.

Suárez-Orozco, Carola, and Marcelo M. Suárez-Orozco. 2001. *Children of Immigration.* Cambridge, MA: Harvard University Press.

Tate, Winifred. 2007. *Counting the Dead: The Culture and Politics of Human Rights Activism in Colombia.* Berkeley: University of California Press.

Taussig, Michael. 2012. "Excelente zona social." *Cultural Anthropology* 27, no. 3: 498–517.

Terrio, Susan J. 2015. Whose Child Am I?: Unaccompanied, Undocumented Children in U.S. Immigration Custody. Berkeley: University of California Press.

Theidon, Kimberly. 2012. *Intimate Enemies: Violence and Reconciliation in Peru.* Philadelphia: University of Pennsylvania Press.

Thomas, Deborah. A. 2007. *Modern Blackness: Nationalism, Globalization, and the Politics of Culture in Jamaica.* Durham, N.C.: Duke University Press.

———. 2011. *Exceptional Violence: Embodied Citizenship in Transnational Jamaica.* Durham, NC: Duke University Press.

———. 2013. "Caribbean Studies, Archive Building, and the Problem of Violence." *Small Axe* 41: 27–42.

———. 2019. *Political Life in the Wake of the Plantation: Sovereignty, Witnessing, Repair.* Durham, NC: Duke University Press.

Todd, Molly. 2010. *Beyond Displacement: Campesinos, Refugees, and Collective Action in the Salvadoran Civil War.* Madison: University of Wisconsin Press.

———. 2021. *Long Journey to Justice: El Salvador, the United States, and Struggles against Empire.* Madison: University of Wisconsin Press.

Tsing, Anna Lowenhaupt. 2005. *Friction: An Ethnography of Global Connection.* Princeton, NJ: Princeton University Press.

Tula, Maria Teresa. 1994. *Hear My Testimony: Maria Teresa Tula, Human Rights Activist of El Salvador.* Boston: South End Press.

Turner, Victor. 1978. Foreword to *Number Our Days*, by Barbara Myerhoff, xii–xvii. New York: Simon and Schuster.

Tutela Legal del Arzobispado de San Salvador. 2008. *El Mozote, Lucha por la verdad y la justicia: Masacre a la inocencia.* San Salvador: Tutela Legal del Arzobispado de San Salvador.

Tyler, Dennis. 2022. *Disabilities of the Color Line: Redressing Antiblackness from Slavery to the Present.* New York: New York University Press.

Ugalde, Antonio, Ernesto Selva-Sutter, Carolina Castillo, Carolina Paz, and Sergio Cañas. 2000. "The Health Costs of War: Can They Be Measured? Lessons from El Salvador." *BMJ* 321, no. 7254 (July 15): 169–72.

UNDP (United Nations Development Programme). 2005. *Informe sobre desarrollo humano de El Salvador 2005: Una mirada al nuevo nosotros; el impacto de las migraciones.* New York: UNDP.

United Nations. 1993. *From Madness to Hope: The 12-Year War in El Salvador: Report of the Commission on the Truth of El Salvador.* New York: United Nations.

Universidad Centroamericana. 2015. *Sueños deportados: Impacto social en las personas migrantes salvadoreñas deportadas y sus familias.* San Salvador: José Simeón Cañas.

USCIS. 2014. "Characteristics of Individuals Requesting and Approved for Deferred Action for Childhood Arrivals (DACA)." www.uscis.gov/sites/default/files/USCIS /Humanitarian/Deferred%20Action%20for%20Childhood%20Arrivals/USCIS -DACA-Characteristics-Data-2014-7-10.pdf.

Valencia, Ricardo J. 2018. "The Making of the White Middle-Class Radical: A Discourse Analysis of the Public Relations of the Committee in Solidarity with the People of El Salvador between 1980 and 1990." PhD diss., University of Oregon.

Valencia, Roberto. 2015. "La Tregua redefinió el mapa de asesinatos de El Salvador." *El Faro*, March 9, 2015. www.salanegra.elfaro.net/es/201503/cronicas/16490/La-Tregua -redefini%C3%B3-el-mapa-de-asesinatos-de-El-Salvador.htm.

———. 2016. Pequeñas batallas, grandes historias: Cinco Crónicas, cinco personajes, una búsqueda. February 1, 2016.

Valencia, Roberto, Óscar Martínez, and Daniel Valencia Caravantes. 2015. "La policía masacró en la finca San Blas." *El Faro*, July 22, 2015. www.salanegra.elfaro.net/es /201507/cronicas/17205/La-Polic%C3%ADa-masacró-en-la-finca-San-Blas.htm.

Van der Borgh, Chris. 2009. "Post-war Peace-Building: What Role for International Organizations?" In *Doing Good or Doing Better: Development Policies in a Globalizing World*, edited by Monique Kremer, Peter van Lieshout, and Robert Went, 303–20. Amsterdam: Amsterdam University Press.

Van der Borgh, G .J. C., and W. Savenije. 2015. "De-securitising and Re-securitising Gang Policies: The Funes Government and Gangs in El Salvador." *Journal of Latin American Studies* 47, no. 1: 149–76.

Vázquez, Norma, Cristina Ibáñez, and Clara Murguialday. 1996. *Mujeres Montaña: Vivencias de Guerrilleras y Colaboradoras del FMLN*. Madrid: Horas y HORAS la Editorial.

Velásquez Estrada, Ruth Elizabeth. 2015. "Grassroots Peacemaking: The Paradox of Reconciliation in El Salvador." *Social Justice* 41, no. 3: 69–86.

Verdery, Katherine 1999. *The Political Lives of Dead Bodies: Reburial and Postsocialist Change*. New York: Columbia University Press.

Viterna, Jocelyn. 2013. *Women in War: The Micro-processes of Mobilization in El Salvador*. Oxford, UK: Oxford University Press.

Vogt, Wendy A. 2018. *Lives in Transit: Violence and Intimacy on the Migrant Journey*. Berkeley: University of California Press.

Vrana, Heather. 2021. "The Precious Seed of Christian Virtue: Charity, Disability, and Belonging in Guatemala, 1871–1947." *Hispanic American Historical Review* 101, no. 2: 265–95.

Wade, Christine J. 2016. *Captured Peace: Elites and Peacebuilding in El Salvador*. Athens: Ohio University Press.

Warnecke-Berger, Hannes. 2020. "Remittances, the Rescaling of Social Conflicts, and the Stasis of Elite Rule in El Salvador." *Latin American Perspectives* 47, no. 3: 202–20. https://doi.org/10.1177/0094582X19898502.

Waterston, Alisse. 2014. *My Father's Wars: Migration, Memory, and the Violence of a Century*. New York: Routledge.

---. 2019. "Intimate Ethnography and the Anthropological Imagination: Dialectical Aspects of the Personal and Political in My Father's Wars." *American Ethnologist* 46, no. 1: 7–19.

Waterston, Alisse, and B. Rylko-Bauer. 2006. "Out of the Shadows of History and Memory: Personal Family Narratives in Ethnographies of Rediscovery." *American Ethnologist* 33, no. 3: 397–412. http://www.jstor.org/stable/3805330.

Watts, Jonathon. 2015. "One Murder Every Hour: How El Salvador Became the Homicide Capital of the World." *Guardian*, August 22, 2015. https://www.theguardian.com/world/2015/aug/22/el-salvador-worlds-most-homicidal-place.

Weld, Kirsten. 2014. *Paper Cadavers: The Archives of Dictatorship in Guatemala*. Durham, NC: Duke University Press.

Whitfield, Teresa. 1994. *Paying the Price: Ignacio Ellacuría and the Murdered Jesuits of El Salvador*. Philadelphia: Temple University Press.

Wiltberger, Joseph. 2014. "Beyond Remittances: Contesting El Salvador's Developmentalist Migration Politics." *Journal of Latin American and Caribbean Anthropology* 19, no. 1: 41–62

WOLA (Washington Office on Latin America). 2020. "Political Crisis in El Salvador Should Be Solved through Dialogue Not through Power Plays and Military Deployments." https://www.wola.org/2020/02/political-crisis-el-salvador-dialogue/. Accessed July 14, 2020.

Wolf, Sonja. 2017. *Mano Dura: The Politics of Gang Control in El Salvador*. Austin: University of Texas Press.

Wood, Elisabeth Jean. 2000. *Forging Democracy from Below: Insurgent Transitions in South Africa and El Salvador*. New York: Cambridge University Press.

---. 2003. *Insurgent Collective Action and Civil War in El Salvador*. Cambridge, UK: Cambridge University Press.

Woodward, Kathleen. 2009. *Statistical Panic: Cultural Politics and Poetics of the Emotions*. Durham, NC: Duke University Press.

Wool, Zoë H. 2015. *After War: The Weight of Life at Walter Reed*. Durham, NC: Duke University Press.

---. 2020. "Veteran Therapeutics: The Promise of Military Medicine and the Possibilities of Disability in the Post-9/11 United States." *MAQ* 34, no. 3: 305–23.

World Bank. 2020. *International Bank for Reconstruction and Development Project Appraisal Document on a Proposed Loan in the Amount of US $250 Million to the Republic of El Salvador for a Growing Up Healthy Together: Comprehensive Early Childhood Development in El Salvador Project*. Washington, DC: World Bank.

Yarris, Kristin E. 2017. *Care across Generations: Solidarity and Sacrifice in Transnational Families*. Stanford, CA: Stanford University Press.

Yashar, Deborah. 2013. "Institutions and Citizenship: Reflections on the Illicit." In *Shifting Frontiers of Citizenship: The Latin American Experience*, edited by Mario Sznajder, Luis Roniger, and Carolos A. Forment, 431–58. Leiden: Brill.

Young, Allan. 1997. *Harmony of Illusions: Inventing Post-traumatic Stress Disorder*. Princeton, NJ: Princeton University Press.

Zablah, Nelson Rauda. 2015. "Gobierno recicla ideas y estrena el plan El Salvador Seguro." *El Faro*. www.elfaro.net/es/201507/noticias/17195/Gobierno-recicla-ideas-y-estrena-el-plan-El-Salvador-Seguro.htm.

Zamora, Javier. 2017. *Unaccompanied*. Port Townsend, WA: Copper Canyon Press.

Zeitlyn, David. 2012. "Anthropology in and of the Archives: Possible Futures and Contingent Pasts. Archives as Anthropological Surrogates." *Annual Review of Anthropology* 41: 461–80.

Zetino Duarte, Mario, and Larissa Brioso. 2012. *Jóvenes urbanos. Cultura política y Democracia de posconflicto en Centroamérica*. San Salvador: FLACSO.

Zilberg, Elana. 2011. *Space of Detention: The Making of Transnational Gang Crisis between Los Angeles and San Salvador*. Durham, NC: Duke University Press.

———. 2016. "Disquieting Complicities: The Double Binds of Anthropology, Advocacy, and Activism." *Journal of Contemporary Ethnography* 45, no. 6: 1–25.

INDEX

Note: Page numbers in italic type indicate photographs.

Abarca, Gray Albert, 118
Abrego, Leisy, xvi
Abu-Lughod, Lila, xiv, 162
acompañamiento, 16
activist anthropology, 4, 10–11
afterlives: of revolution, xviii, 140, 155; of slavery, 176n27
after-stories: of 1.5 insurgent generation, 39, 135–65, 140–65; of postwar El Salvador, xv, xvii
Ahmed, Sara, 77
Alas, Adriana, 23–25, 70, 87, 113, 138, 156, 160
Amaya, Rufina, 12
Americans with Disabilities Act, 79
amnesty. *See* impunity
Amnesty International, 55
Anastario, Mike, 116, 131
Angel-Ajani, Asale, 14, 35
Annales School, 174n14
Anthropocene, 165, 217n74
anthropology: activist, 4, 10–11; confidentiality concerns in, 9–10, 18, 176n2, 177n12; context for ethnographic work, 21–25; critical transformations in, 10–11, 17; decolonization of, 4; fugitive, 17; material culture as object of study in, 104; methodological issues in, 8–18; moral responsibility of, 161–62; public uses of, 12–13, 179n54; relationships formed in practice of, xiv; salvage, 4; and white supremacy, xii
archive of the returned, xvii, 105, 118–27
ARENA. *See* National Republican Alliance/Alianza Republicana Nacionalista
army. *See* Salvadoran Armed Forces
Asociación PRO-VIDA, 138
Asociación Sumpul, 157, 159
Atlacatl Battalion, 12
Atlas de Violencia en El Salvador, 63–65
author, personal reflections of, 1, 10, 15–16, *15*, 78–80, 108, 114, 161–62, 176n3, 180n65

Ball, Patrick, 73
Barrio 18, 44
Bejarano, Carolina Alonso, 181n77
Bellino, Michelle, 177n21
Berlant, Lauren, 86
La Bestia (human cargo trains), 43
Biden, Joe, 45, 54
Bloque Popular Revolucionario (BPR), 32, 185n143
bodies, xv, 72–101; chronic, 76, 80, 81, 83, 86–90, 95–96; debility of, 85–90, 96–101; critical disability theory and, 76–81; as objects, 31, 73, 103, 106–7, 111–12; scholarship on, 76–77, 200n33; war and, 76–77, 81–82, 87–101, 202n66
Boehm, Deborah, 117–20, 122

249

Borofsky, Robert, 11
Bourgois, Philippe, 11, 70, 75, 81–82
BPR. *See* Bloque Popular Revolucionario
Braudel, Fernand, 174n14
Brooks, Ethel, 17, 80
Buckley, Liam, 126
Bukele, Nayib, 55, 59–61, 134, 182n109, 186n157, 187n13, 195n109, 210n2, 211n5, 212n16, 214n40
Bustillo, Juan Rafael, 159

Capitalocene, 165, 217n74
care: gender expectations contested by practice of, 145; for the injured, 90, 99, 111–12; intergenerational, 204n93; multispecies, 144–46, 164; "right to maim" contested by an ethic of, 89, 97, 99, 101, 130, 145. *See also* ethics of collective care
Caritas, 138
Castañeda, Heidi, 117
Catholic Church, 21, 159
CBP. *See* US Customs and Border Protection
Central Americans, 26, 43, 53, 148, 184n129
Central Intelligence Agency (CIA), 109, 111
Chacón Serrano, Fernando, 156
Chalatenango: background on, 21; bus in, *51*; families in, *6*, *40*; massacre (1980) in, xvii; migration from, 25, 52; postwar, 21–23; repopulation in, 21–22, *22*, 25, 64, 66, 100–101; as site of research, xii–xiii, *15*
Chávez, Joaquín, 35
Chichilco, María, 138
children/youth: border-crossings by, 43; development programs for, 36–38; health of, 36–37, 136–37; illnesses and injuries of, 84; of 1.5 insurgent generation, 35–41, *36*; in postwar contexts, 177n21; of postwar El Salvador, 23–24, 136–39, *137*; in repopulated communities, 35–38, *36*, *37*; as subjects of postwar discourse, 38, 159; violence against, 19, 38, *158*
chronic bodies, 76, 80, 81, 83, 86–90, 95–96
Clare, Eli, 86
code-switching, 88, 147, 174n15, 175n26, 176n5

coexistence, 68
Cold War, 19, 31, 35, 74, 81, 151
Colunga, Graciela, 138–39
Comaroff, Jean, 125
Comaroff, John, 125
Constitutional Chamber of the Supreme Court, 58
Coordinator of Communities in Development in Chalatenango, 159
CORDES, 11, 212n12
Córdova Macías, Ricardo, 62
Cosgrove, Serena, 16–17
Coutin, Susan Bibler, 16, 38, 118
COVID-19 pandemic, 55, 60, *61*, 159
CRIPDES, 159
critical disability studies. *See* disability studies
Cruz, José Miguel, 61, 62
curanderos (folk healers), 65, 66, 84, 100, 205n117

DACA. *See* Deferred Action for Childhood Arrivals
DDR. *See* disarmament, demobilization, and reintegration
debility (*debilidad*), xv, xvii, 4, 85–90, 95–101, 112, 145–46
decolonial turn, 10
Deferred Action for Childhood Arrivals (DACA), 43, 54
De Lauri, Antonio, 11
De León, Jason, 77, 105, 106, 129, 206n14, 210n79
deportations, 55–56, 105, 117–27, 192n73. *See also retornados*
Derrida, Jacques, 125
detention centers, 122–25
De Waal, Edmund, 122
DHS. *See* US Department of Homeland Security
diaspora, of 1.5 insurgent generation, xiv, xvi, xviii, 24, 41, 70, 103, 104, 116, 119, 128–29, 132–35, 141–55, 161–65
Dickson-Gómez, Julia, 100
dignified life (*vida digna*), 26–27, 35, 78, 135
Dirección General de Migración y Extranjería, 55

INDEX   251

disability studies, xvii, 76–81, 85–89, 93
disappearances, 18, 19, 38, 47–48
disarmament, demobilization, and reintegration (DDR), 19, 57, 115, 182n92. *See also* reintegration
disillusionment, 1, 20, 23, 134, 175n17
documents, of migrants, 118–25
Dyrness, Andrea, 144

education, 48–49
El-Haj, Thea Renda, 144
El Mozote Massacre, 12–13, 58, 151, 157, 210n2
El Salvador: gang violence in, 44, 59–60, 187n13; homicide rates in, 44, 60–64; migration from, 25–26, 52–54, 184n132; numerical representations of, 42–71; peace building in, 19–20, 140; population of, 35; post-postwar, 135, 138–39, 213n32; scholarship on, xiii, 19–20; *solidaridad* in, 16; violence in, 28–30, 47, 59–67, 73–74, 153; war in, 18–19, 181n86, 181n89. *See also* Salvadoran Armed Forces
ethical listening, 14, 31, 35
ethics of collective care, xvi, xvii, 27, 78, 85, 89, 91, 97, 105, 128, 130, 134, 145, 161
ethnography. *See* anthropology

Fader, Ayala, 7
FAES. *See* Salvadoran Armed Forces
Fanon, Frantz, 67
Farabundo Martí National Liberation Front (FMLN): branches of, xiii; in Chalatenango, 9; composition of, 178n23, 185n141; criticisms of, 115, 149, 160, 182n94; and end of war, 19; governance by, 52; human rights abuses attributed to, 19, 57, 156; 1.5 insurgent generation and, 113; origins of, 173n5; as political party, xv, 19, 21, 23, 39, 109, 111, 117, 134, 138–39, 140, 174n7, 178n23, 182n109, 213n34, 214n38; practical support for, 34; reintegration of combatants from, 57; wartime participation in, 20, 21; women in, 20, 90
Fassin, Didier, 43, 95–96

FECCAS, 32, 185n142
Fernandes, Sujatha, 44–45
fieldnotes, 8, 34, 39, 48, 67, 73, 84, 104
FMLN. *See* Farabundo Martí National Liberation Front
forgiveness, 46, 68, 134, 160–61
Foucault, Michel, 60, 125
FPL. *See* Fuerzas Populares de Liberación
Friedner, Michele, 77
Fuerzas Populares de Liberación (FPL; Popular Liberation Forces), xiii, 23, 32, 34, 90, 115, 130, 150, 153, 173n5, 185n141
fugitive anthropology, 17
Fundaungo, 62, 63
Funes, Mauricio, 23, 44, 58, 60, 188n13, 214n40

gang membership, 59–60
gang violence, 44, 59–60, 187n13
Garcia, Angela, 124, 126
García, José Guillermo, 159
Garni, Alisa, 63
gender: in daily life, 48, 69, 123, 149; disability and, 80, 82; in folktales, 2–3, 40, 117, 163; in postwar El Salvador, 1, 20, 22, 38; violence linked to, 59, 64, 92, 100, 164–65; in war, 2, 8, 90, 92, 110, 139, 164–65. *See also* masculinity; women
General Amnesty Law, 58
generations: arcs linking, 76, 89; impact of, in postwar El Salvador, xvi–xvii; scholarship on, xvi, 175n18; trauma passing through, 30, 35, 99–100
genocide, 46–48, 112
Ginsburg, Faye, 80–81, 85
Goldstein, Daniel, 67
Grande, Rutilio, 110
Green, Linda, 11
Guardado Torrez, Clara, 135, 138–39, 213n32
Guatemala, 46, 47, 120, 126
guerrillas: criticisms of, 153, 160; precursors of, 32; weapons of, 32–34; women as, 20, 90, 108. *See also* insurgency
Guinda de Mayo (1982), 74
guindas (flights from home), 21, 38–39, 90–92, 103, 182n106
Guzmán Urquilla, Jorge, 12, 58, 210n2

Hale, Charlie, 11
Haraway, Donna J., 7, 164–65, 217n74, 217n75
Hartman, Saidiya, xvii, 175n16, 176n27
Herrera, Orellana, 62
Heyman, Josiah, 118
Hirsch, Marianne, 100, 156
Holocaust Memorial Museum (US), 112
Honduras, 66, 136, 157, 160, 186n157. *See also* Mesa Grande refugee camp
Hoover Green, Amelia, 57, 63, 73, 193n95
hope, xvi, 1, 4, 8, 17, 26, 31, 76, 101, 140
Horton, Sarah, 118
HRW. *See* Human Rights Watch
humanity: disability in relation to, 79, 85, 89, 112; recognition and understanding of, 43, 81, 85, 93, 112
human rights abuses, 12–13, 19, 22, 38, 57–58, 91, 133
Human Rights Watch (HRW), 47, 53, 56
Hussain, Salman, 209n65

ICE. *See* US Immigration and Customs Enforcement
Illegal Immigration Reform and Immigration Control Act (IIRIRA), 56
illness narratives, 79–80
impunity, xvii, 12, 19, 23, 46, 52, 58, 113, 116, 133, 136, 140, 157, 160
Indigenous peoples, 29
infrastructure, 2, 22, 61–62, 104, 133, 140
insecurity, 59–65, 67
Instituto de Derechos Humanos of the Universidad Centroamericana José Simeón Cañas (IDHUCA), 59
Instituto Geográfico Nacional, 25
Instituto Salvadoreña para el Desarrollo de la Mujer, 63
insurgency: medical camps associated with, 75; origins of, 29–30; tasks (*tareas*) associated with, 31, 34, 70, 93, 94, 97, 115. *See also* guerrillas
Inter-American Commission on Human Rights (IACHR), 47, 48
International Organization for Migration (OIM), 56

intimate ethnography, 14–15
Iron Fist. *See* Mano Dura (Iron Fist) policies
ISIS, 44
Israel, 87

Jackson, John L., Jr., 7, 39, 46, 177n18
Jamaica, 126
James, Erica Caple, 96
Jenkins, Janis H., 96, 202n66
Jesuit Massacre case, 58, 194n98, 204n104
justice: amnesty and, 58; calls and struggle for, xv, 4, 12, 12–13, 14, 47–48, 83, 104, 135, 140, 152, 155–58; forgiveness and, 68, 160–61; Indigenous advocacy for, 29; insurgency as, 134; 1.5 insurgent generation and, 161; socioeconomic, 21–23, 52. *See also* impunity

Kafer, Alison, 81
Kanstroom, Daniel, 117
Kidron, Carol, 100
Kittay, Eva, 89

Landes, Ruth, 114
Lara Martínez, Benjamín Carlos, 157
Las Vueltas: migration from, 54; NGO activity in, 36; occupation of, 30; population of, 24–25; *retornados* in, 55
Law for Transitional Justice, Reparation, and National Reconciliation, 58
Lazo, Xiomara, 58
LeMoyne, James, 50
Levitt, Laura, 112–13
liberation theology, 21, 110
Liu, Roseann, 17
living proof, 17
Livingston, Julie, 86
longitudinal research, 10
longue durée: connotations of, 174n14; of former combatants, 70; framing of El Salvador in, xviii, 153; memory's role in, 156; objects and, 131; 1.5 insurgent generation and, 134; of postwar El Salvador, xiv, xvi, xvii, 23, 41, 52–53, 76, 83, 127, 134, 143–44
López Obrador, Andrés Manuel, 53

INDEX   253

madness, 93–94, 97
maiming. *See* right to maim
Mano Dura (Iron Fist) policies, 44, 59, 140
Mara Salvatrucha (MS-13), 44
Marroquín Parducci, Amparo, 26
Martín-Baró, Ignacio, 94–95, 204n104
Maryland, 127–31
masculinity: associated with the military, 34, 143, 153–55; care behaviors as challenging conceptions of, 145; debility and, 111–12. *See also* gender
La Matanza (massacre of Indigenous peoples), 29, 30
material culture. *See* objects
materiality of deportation, 105
McRuer, Robert, 77
Melara Minero, Lidice Michelle, 73–74
memory, 155–61
Mesa Grande refugee camp, xiv, 2, 21, 34, 90, 114, 150–51
methodology, 8–18
Mexico, 53–54
migration: from Chalatenango, 52; documents related to, 118–25; laws impacting Salvadoran, 184n132; life in detention centers, 122–25; numbers related to, 53–57; overview of, 25–27; political significance of, 26, 54; restrictions on, 53–54. See also *retornados*
Migration Policy Institute, 53
Millennium Development Goals, 136
Ministry for External Relations of El Salvador, 56
Misioneros de la memoria histórica, Chalatenango, 159
Molina, Arturo Armando, 32
Montano, Inocente Orlando, 194n98, 204n104
Montoya, Ainhoa, 20
Moodie, Ellen, 20, 67, 135, 138–39, 213n32
Myerhoff, Barbara, 180n64

Nagengast, Carole, 11
Narayan, Kirin, 78
narratives. *See* after-stories; stories

National Civilian Police (PNC), 47, 57, 60, 63, 140. *See also* police, Salvadoran
National Guard (El Salvador), 157
National Republican Alliance/Alianza Republicana Nacionalista (ARENA), 19, 20, 59, 134, 178n23, 182n109, 214n38
Nelson, Diane, 45–47
neoliberalism: individualism associated with, 64; and insecurity, 67; moral panics linked to, 60; and postwar El Salvador, 140; stories and discourses of, 44; violence associated with, 54, 64, 181n80
new-old stories, 9, 18, 94
New York Times (newspaper), 50, 75
NGOs. *See* nongovernmental organizations
Nguyen, Viet Thanh, 102
Nicaragua, 16, 84, 213n27
nongovernmental organizations (NGOs), 4, 17, 22, 36
Nordstrom, Carolyn, 11
Nuevas Ideas, 138, 182n109, 187n13, 213n34, 214n40
numbers, xv; critique of, 61–64, 188n28, 193n95; insecurity rendered by, 59–65; liberatory uses of, 49; on migration, 53–57; moral uses of, 47; narrative uses of, 24, 42, 44–46; political uses of, 42, 44–46, 48; in postwar El Salvador, 52; public narratives about, 43–44; US interpretation and use of, 43, 45; violence rendered by, 45, 59–67, 153; vulnerability rendered by, 45. See also *violencia encifrada*

Obama, Barack, 43, 54
objects, xv, 102–31; anthropological study of, 104; carried by couriers, 116; carried on *guindas*, 38–39, 103; of daily living, 104; the injured and wounded as, 31, 73, 103, 106–7, 111–12; of migrants to US, 105, 142; of 1.5 insurgent generation in US, 129–30; of *retornados*, 105, 117–27; survival-related, 98, 103; war-related, 98, 102–4, 106–14, 151
objects, as psychological metaphor, 102–31
O'Brien, Tim, 102–3, 105, 113, 130

1.5 insurgent generation: background on, 35–41; code-switching of, 176n5; defined, xiv, 174n12; diasporic, xiv, xvi, xviii, 24, 41, 70, 103, 104, 116, 119, 128–29, 132–35, 141–55, 161–65; diversity of, 40–41; and ethics of collective care, 89, 134, 145; historical context of, xvi, 7, 134–35, 138–39; hope represented by, 8, 76, 101, 140; and politics, 134–35, 138–39, 143, 149–55, 213n32; and postwar El Salvador, 23–24, 136–39; remittances from, 135, 143; in repopulated communities, 100–101, 117, 132–33; stories of war heard by, 138; traumas associated with war, 99–100; war memories of, 69–70, 110–12, 150–51, 155–56; youth of other countries compared to, 186n154
Organización Democrática Nacionalista (ORDEN; Democratic Nationalist Organization), 40, 157
Osuna, Steven, 60
Otero, Solimar, 114

Peña Arbaiza, Ricardo Augusto, 159
Petryna, Adriana, 70
Pew Research Center, 53
Plan Internacional, 36–37
PNC. *See* National Civilian Police
police, Salvadoran, 19, 21, 44, 47–48, 60. *See also* National Civilian Police
Pollo Campero, 51, 131, 143
Popular Liberation Forces (FPL). *See* Fuerzas Populares de Liberación
Portillo, Pocasangre, 62
Posada, Mendoza, 62
positionality, 9, 10, 11, 15–16, 88, 99, 108, 111, 153
Pro-Búsqueda, 38, 105, 106
Puar, Jasbir, 75, 86–89, 100
public opinion, 62–63

Quesada, James, 84
quitarle el agua al pez (drain the water from the fish), 19, 74

Ralph, Laurence, 44, 88–89
Rapp, Rayna, 80–81, 85
Rasnake, Roger, 16
Realidad (journal), 20, 157
reconciliation without the reconciled, 46, 58–59, 68
reintegration: discourses of, 21–22; of former combatants, 57; and impunity, 58; numbers related to, 46, 53–57; projects for, 21–22, 38; of *retornados*, 55–57, 105; of women, 20. *See also* disarmament, demobilization, and reintegration
remittances, 25–26, 53–54, 135, 143
retornados (migrants returned to El Salvador), xvii, 55–57, 105, 117–27. *See also* deportations
Revolución Revisitada (edited volume), 157
Reyes Mena, Mario Adalberto, 159
Rey Tristán, Eduardo, 58
Richtman, Richard, 95–96
right to maim, 75, 87, 89, 97, 99, 130, 145
Río Sumpul Massacre, xvii, 74, 136, 151–52, 157–60
Rivas, Ramón D., 210n80
Romero, Carlos Humberto, 32
Ruiz, Pamela, 61
Rumbaut, Rubén G., 174n12

Sala Negra of El Faro, 61
Salvadoran Armed Forces (FAES): guerrilla attacks on, 33; human rights abuses attributed to, 19, 30, 57–58, 91, 136, 152–53, 157; practical support for, 34; reform of, 19; reintegration of combatants from, 57
Sánchez Cerén, Salvador, 23, 59, 214n40
Scheper-Hughes, Nancy, 11
Schieffelin, Bambi, 4
Schonberg, Jeff, 70
Segovia, Alexander, 57
Seligson, Mitchell A., 62
Shange, Savannah, 17
shoes, 27, 90, 104, 114–15, 129, 130, 142
Smith, Carol, 11
solidaridad, 16–18, 33
Solidarity 3.0, 16–17
solidarity movement, 17, 181n80
Southern Poverty Law Center, 55
Spanish National Court, 58

spectacular violence, 71, 77, 81, 83, 89
Sprenkels, Ralph (Rafa), xiv, 6, 12–13, 21, 58, 70, 73–74, 87, 105, 106–7, 110, 139–40, 207n24
statistics. *See* numbers
Stephen, Lynn, 13–14
Stoler, Ann, 125–26, 209n64
stories: from before, xv, 2–8, 28–35; illness-related, 79–80; insecurity linked to, 67; methodological significance of, 174n7; new-old, 9, 18, 94; of postwar El Salvador, xv
Stuelke, Patricia, 17, 181n80
suicide bombers, 153–55
Sumpul Massacre Memorial Park, Las Aradas, 157–59
Super Mano Dura, 59
Supreme Court, 58, 63, 210n2
Sutton, Constance, 10

tareas (tasks of the insurgency), 31, 34, 70, 93, 94, 97, 115
Taussig, Michael, 67
Temporary Protected Status (TPS), 27, 54, 143, 184n132
Territorial Control Plan, 59
testimonios/witnessing, 3–4, 13–14, 17, 83, 107, 138, 177n8
Theidon, Kimberly, 100
thick description, 7
thin description, 7
Thomas, Deborah, 14, 35, 105, 126, 140, 209n73, 217n75
Tiempos Nuevos Teatros (TNT), 211n12
tierra arrasada, 18–19
TPS. *See* Temporary Protected Status
trauma: of bodies, 78, 80, 82; Central Americans linked to, 26; changing conceptions of, 95–96; embodied, 39–40; intergenerational, 30, 35, 99–100; linked to insurgency, 77, 82–83; psychosocial, 94; sequelae of, 93, 96; victimhood associated with, 96; of war, 150–51, 155
Trump, Donald, 45, 53–55, 66, 87, 143

Unidad de Salud, 24
United Nations, 19, 140

United Nations Committee on the Rights of Persons with Disabilities, 79
United Nations Convention on the Rights of People with Disabilities, 79
United Nations Convention on the Rights of the Child, 139
United Nations Truth Commission, 57–58, 73, 157; *From Madness to Hope*, 19
United States: contributions of, to El Mozote Massacre, 12; contributions of, to El Salvador counterinsurgency, 18–19, 33, 76; detention centers in, 122–25; immigration policies and practices of, 53–54; 1.5 insurgent generation in, xiv, xvi, xviii, 24, 132–35, 141–55, 161–65; Salvadorans in, 26, 53, 56, 128, 190n48; Salvadoran violence and, 45; and statistics, 42
Universidad Centroamericana José Simeón Cañas Maestría en Estadística Aplicada a la Investigación, 62
USAID, 149
US Citizenship and Immigration Services, 43
US Customs and Border Protection (CBP), 43, 53
US Department of Homeland Security (DHS), 55, 56, 126
US Department of State, 30
US Immigration and Customs Enforcement (ICE), 55–56
US National Security Archives, 30
UTC, 32, 185n142

Valencia, Roberto, 61
Velásquez Estrada, Ruth Elizabeth, 68, 70
victimhood: Central Americans linked to, 17; injury associated with, 83; postwar El Salvador and, 23, 83; trauma associated with, 96
vida digna. See dignified life
Vides Casanova, Eugenio, 159
violence: affective relationships to, 42–43; in detention centers, 124; in El Salvador, 28–30, 47, 59–67, 73–74, 153; of immigration policies, 118, 124, 206n14; numbers related to, 45, 59–67, 153; of

violence (*continued*)
    Salvadoran Armed Forces, 30, 57–58; spectacular, 71, 77, 81, 83, 89; stories about, 67. See also *violencia encifrada*
violencia encifrada (encrypted violence), 42–71; concept of, xvii, 42, 46, 175n26; and insecurity, 59–65; masking of inequalities in, 44–45; and migration, 53–57
Vogt, Wendy, 77

Wade, Christine, 20
Walter Reed medical center, 87
Waterston, Alisse, 14
Weingarten, Karen, 77
Weld, Kirsten, 126

Weyher, L. Frank, 63
white supremacy, xii
witnessing. See *testimonios*/witnessing
Witnessing 2.0, 14
women: in peace building, 20; in war, 20, 90, 108. *See also* gender
Wood, Elisabeth, 27
Wool, Zoë, 87
World Bank, 136, 149
World Health Organization, 60

Yarris, Kristin, 204n93

Zeitlyn, David, 125
Zilberg, Elana, 13, 179n54

CPSIA information can be obtained
at www.ICGtesting.com
Printed in the USA
JSHW022240290622
27466JS00005B/9